West Country MURDERS

West Country MURDERS

NICOLA SLY & JOHN VAN DER KISTE

The
History
Press

Devon Murders first published in 2006
Cornish Murders first published in 2007
Somerset Murders first published in 2008
Bristol Murders first published in 2008

This edition first published in 2009

The History Press
The Mill, Brimscombe Port
Stroud, Gloucestershire, GL5 2QG
www.thehistorypress.co.uk

ISBN 978 0 7524 5125 1

Typesetting and origination by The History Press
Printed in India by Nutech Print Services

CONTENTS

FOREWORD

When I was involved in filming the last series of *Murder Most Foul*, first shown on Channel 4 in 2007, it occurred to me that in over thirty-five years of service in the police force I have seen an unbelievable change in the way that my colleagues approach the investigation of murder. In just those few decades, the advancement of scientific knowledge as well as technology has brought about a complete revolution in proving guilt or otherwise, of eliminating suspects and reducing the risk of missing microscopic, yet vital, pieces of evidence. This is a far cry from the early years of my service in the 1970s, when the stereotypical image of the 'big-footed copper' destroying evidence as he blundered about a crime scene was perhaps more of a reality than we might like to admit.

What would our Victorian colleagues think – when many of the crimes in this volume were committed – of major investigation techniques of the twenty-first century? Is it perhaps any wonder that serious miscarriages of justice took place, that innocent men were sent to 'the drop', and that some offenders literally 'got away with murder' in those formative years of rudimentary investigation?

This book brings together many accounts of murders throughout the West Country, from yesteryear to comparatively modern times. The individual stories are retold in a way that makes it quite clear that the authors have spent countless hours of painstaking research, approaching each subject in a non-judgemental way and bringing the facts of the case to the reader in a clear, independent and concise manner.

Browsing through the varied and intriguing stories has literally been a trip down memory lane for me. As a fresh-faced young constable it was the indefatigable Dr Denis Hocking, the county pathologist of Cornwall mentioned throughout many of these accounts, who taught me how to prepare a body for his examination. My first post-mortem with him was late at night in a dim gas-lit stone mortuary at the rear of Cornwall's Launceston Town Hall, when he had come direct from an evening function, still dressed in bow tie and evening dress. I was to meet him countless times throughout the county at various 'morgues' until his retirement some years later.

I've trod the beat along the streets of Falmouth, passing by the deserted and boarded up tobacconist shop ('Murder on Christmas Eve, 1942') wondering at what horrors took place all those years before in that gloomy building. My time as Community Constable at Constantine and Mawnan Smith brought me into contact with those people of the village who well remembered the events of the murder of

Mr Rowe ('Murder of a Recluse, 1963') and made me realise that although years might pass, memories and pain last a lifetime. Even more recently during my service at Tavistock I rode my police bicycle along the same moorland lanes of Peter Tavy village that Constable Callard walked when he attended the double murder there ('Atrocity at Peter Tavy, 1892'), resulting in his early retirement due to the trauma he suffered during the investigation.

This book pulls no punches in bringing out the facts, but it does so in a compassionate and factual manner, without being ghoulish. If these following murderous stories, covering the length and breadth of the West Country, leave you better informed as to how dastardly events of the past have shaped the development of modern-day police investigation, then this volume is well-worth the effort it took to meticulously research it.

Simon Dell, MBE QCB
Devon & Cornwall Constabulary

INTRODUCTION & ACKNOWLEDGEMENTS

Over the last two or three centuries, a select few British murders – more often than not those committed by serial killers – have enthralled and horrified the nation. Others have been reported, made headlines and since then been little remembered except by the few, or by true crime historians.

The West Country may have few monsters of depravity on the scale of Jack the Ripper, the more recent Yorkshire Ripper, the Moors Murderers, or the Brides in the Bath Murderer, to name but a few, yet rural and urban Cornwall, Devon, Somerset and Bristol have all had their fair share of cases, which held attention beyond the immediate locality for a while. John 'Babbacombe' Lee, 'the man they could not hang' in 1885, has achieved semi-legendary status; the unsolved triple murder in the Maye family in 1936 provoked endless discussion for many years; and the guilt or innocence of Matthew Weekes, hanged in 1844 for the murder of Charlotte Dymond, continues to be a matter of debate to this day in the Bodmin area of Cornwall; while the brutal slaying of Sarah Watts in 1851, for which the prime suspects were tried but acquitted, cast a spell for some time.

These and many other cases of domestic differences between married partners or lovers which ended in tragedy, atrocities involving children, robberies which 'went wrong', and others, all feature in the chapters which follow.

We would particularly like to thank members of our families for their constant help, encouragement and support, namely Richard Sly, John Higginson, Kim and the late Kate Van der Kiste; the many friends who have ably assisted us, particularly Simon Dell MBE, Stuart Edwards, Dr Ian Mortimer, and Derek Fisher; and our editors at The History Press, Matilda Richards and Beth Amphlett.

Nicola Sly and John Van der Kiste, 2009

ALSO BY THE AUTHORS

ALSO BY NICOLA SLY

A Ghostly Almanac of Devon & Cornwall
Bristol Murders
Cornish Murders (with John Van der Kiste)
Dorset Murders
Hampshire Murders
Herefordshire Murders

Oxfordshire Murders
Murder by Poison
Shropshire Murders
Somerset Murders (with John Van der Kiste)
Wiltshire Murders
Worcestershire Murders

ALSO BY JOHN VAN DER KISTE

A Divided Kingdom
A Grim Almanac of Devon
Berkshire Murders
Childhood at Court 1819–1914
Cornish Murders (with Nicola Sly)
Cornwall's Own
Crowns in a Changing World
Dearest Affie (with Bee Jordaan)
Dearest Vicky, Darling Fritz
Devon Murders
Devonshire's Own
Edward VII's Children
Emperor Francis Joseph
Frederick III
George V's Children
George III's Children

Gilbert & Sullivan's Christmas
Kaiser Wilhelm II
King George II and Queen Caroline
Kings of the Hellenes
Northern Crowns
Once a Grand Duchess (with Coryne Hall)
Plymouth History & Guide
Princess Victoria Melita
Queen Victoria's Children
Somerset Murders (with Nicola Sly)
Sons, Servants and Statesmen
Surrey Murders
The Georgian Princesses
The Romanovs 1818–1959
William and Mary
Windsor and Habsburg

chapter one

Cornish MURDERS

1

'DO, WILLY, GO AND CONFESS'

Wadebridge, 1840

O n 8 February 1840, the merchant ship *Orient* was sailing en route from Manila to Cadiz. As it drew near St Helena its captain, Edmund Norway, was writing a letter to his brother Nevell, a well-known and highly-respected local timber and general trader, aged thirty-nine, who lived in Cornwall. Having finished his letter, Norway recorded in the ship's log that he retired to bed at about 10.45 p.m. His sleep that night was anything but peaceful, being disturbed by what he later described as a 'dreadful dream' in which he 'saw' his brother riding along the road from St Columb to Wadebridge. To his horror he dreamed that Nevell was accosted by two men, one of whom grabbed the bridle of the horse he was riding. A pistol was fired twice, but Captain Norway heard no sound. Then he saw one of the men strike his brother, causing him to fall from his horse. Nevell was severely beaten, dragged by the shoulders across the road and left for dead in a ditch.

When called to watch at 4 a.m., Captain Norway recounted his nightmare to his second officer, Henry Wren, remarking that in the dream a house which he knew to be on the right-hand side of the road had inexplicably moved to the left-hand side. Although Wren made light of the dream, joking about the superstitions of Cornishmen, Captain Norway was sufficiently disturbed by it to record the details in his ship's log.

Back in Cornwall, on 7 February, there had been a rare incidence of highway robbery. The victim, a miller named Derry, had enjoyed a prosperous day at Wadebridge market and had stopped at a public house on his way home to spend some of his profits.

As he enjoyed a few drinks, he failed to notice that he was being closely but surreptitiously watched and, on leaving the pub, he had ridden only a short way when three men jumped out of the hedge and knocked him off his horse. Somewhat befuddled by the effects of his celebratory drinks, Mr Derry was unable to offer much resistance as the men rifled through his pockets, making off with approximately £75.

On the following day Nevell Norway set off to ride home from Bodmin to Wadebridge. It was a moonlit night and, for the first part of his journey home, Nevell was accompanied by a farming acquaintance, Abraham Hambly. The latter was aware of the robbery of Mr Derry and, as a precaution, he had armed himself with two pistols, vowing to 'let daylight into the person of any man who might venture to attack him'. They parted company at Mount Charles gate, leaving Nevell to complete his travels alone. His road was isolated, but even at that late hour, quite well travelled.

He would have passed the house at Clapper, belonging to Mr Pollard. Just before Norway rode by, Pollard received a visitor, a preacher named Mr Harley. Seeing a man waiting outside the house, Harley had assumed that he was a manservant and had handed him his horse. When the mistake was discovered, Pollard and Harley went outside to investigate, finding the horse safely tethered to a fence and the mysterious stranger nowhere to be seen.

Later that night, John Hick and Christopher Bowen were riding the same route. On reaching Sladesbridge, just outside Wadebridge, they were hailed by a man shouting, 'Stop! The horse is gone on before.' Assuming that the man was tipsy, the two riders hurried on their way, but before long they spotted a loose horse in front of them, which galloped away as they approached it. A passer-by told them that he too had seen the horse and it bore a strong resemblance to Mr Norway's grey mare. Feeling uneasy, the two men went to Nevell Norway's house. Not wishing to alarm Nevell's wife, they instead approached his waggoner, Thomas Gregory, told him about the loose horse and asked if his master was at home. Gregory checked the stables and found that the horse had returned home riderless, bearing a heavily bloodstained saddle.

Hick and Bowen rode off in search of a surgeon, while Gregory and another servant, Edward Cavell, set out to retrace Norway's route home in search of the missing man. It did not take them long to find him. About two miles away, at North Hill, they noticed some scuff marks on the road, as if something had been dragged across it. Lifting their lantern, they could just make out a bulky shape lying in a ditch at the roadside. It was Nevell Norway, who lay seemingly lifeless on his back in the water, his feet pointing towards the road.

Hoisting the body onto the horse, they made haste back towards Wadebridge, meeting Hick and Bowen on their way. The two men had roused surgeon Mr Trehane Tickle from his bed, and it was he who examined the body at Norway's home, pronouncing him dead. He determined that the victim had received several blows to the head and face from a blunt instrument, causing severe injuries. It was noted that one wound on the chin was darkened, as if contaminated by gunpowder. There were severe cuts to the insides of his lips and he had a broken nose and a particularly deep wound on one eyebrow, beneath which the bone was fractured. The surgeon also found numerous skull fractures which, he determined, would probably have killed him instantly.

The site where Nevell Norway was murdered. (By kind permission of *West Briton*)

When the servant, Edward Cavell, searched his master's clothes, he found his wallet containing £25 in notes, watch and penknife, but noticed that an ivory writing tablet that Norway normally carried was missing, as were his purse and keys. Returning to the place where the body had been found Cavell and Gregory, accompanied by William Norway, a brother of the deceased, found evidence of a struggle having taken place. There were numerous bloodstains at the scene, along with two distinct sets of footprints from what looked like hob-nailed boots and the marks of a bare hand being drawn across the ground. They also found the broken hammer of a gun or pistol and, at a distance of 16ft from the first bloodstains, a button from Norway's coat, broken into three pieces. His hat lay in a nearby field. In the same field, they spotted a loose dog, which they described as dark bodied, white-faced and 'high on its legs'.

Over the next few days, the same dog was frequently seen at the murder site and, in the belief that its owner might be in some way connected with the murder, several attempts were made to catch it. The dog evaded capture for some time and, even when it was finally trapped, police were unable to establish who the owner was. It was rumoured by local gossips – falsely, as it happened – that the dog had led police to the bloodstained clothes of the murderer, buried in a field close by.

The death was reported to coroner Joseph Hamley the following morning, and he immediately travelled from Bodmin to hold an inquest at the Ship Inn, Wadebridge, that afternoon. Having listened to all the evidence, he requested that members of the public should leave the hearing and recommended that magistrates should investigate the matter further.

The magistrates did not have an easy task. Nevell had been a popular and well-respected businessman in the town, and on the day of his funeral every shop in the town closed for the day. Over 3,000 people took part in the funeral procession, including many of the town dignitaries. Several funds were set up, partly to assist Norway's widow and also to cover the expenses of investigating the crime. Some of this money was put forward as a reward for the apprehension of the murderer and an offer of £100, a small fortune in those days, brought forth a mass of information, almost more than the police could cope with. People were so keen to help with the murder enquiries (and perhaps to get their hands on the reward) that the daily meeting of magistrates in the Molesworth Arms public house quickly descended into chaos. The police were stretched to follow all the leads that came flooding in and, in sorting the wheat from the chaff, wasted a great deal of precious time investigating completely innocent people. They were soon forced to call in two police officers from London to assist in their enquiries.

One man who did provide a useful lead was shoemaker John Harris, who had travelled the same route as Nevell Norway and had noticed two men loitering at the place where the murder was later committed. His description of the two men, particularly of their being 'of short stature', led police to question James Lightfoot, a labourer and petty criminal from the small hamlet of Burlawn, just outside Wadebridge. When twenty-three-year-old James was arrested on suspicion of murder, the nervous reaction of his brother William, aged thirty-six, aroused police suspicions and he too was arrested and taken before the magistrates. Panic-stricken, William sang like a canary, believing that by betraying his brother, he could not only save himself but also claim the £100 reward.

The Lightfoot brothers were sons of the sexton of St Breock near Wadebridge, and had a reputation for being layabouts and ne'er-do-wells, opting for an easy life of crime over an honest day's work. Their criminal exploits included stealing poultry, poaching and housebreaking, in both Cornwall and Devon. Nevell Norway and his family had always treated the Lightfoots with kindness, offering them employment and even helping them financially in times of need. Yet, despite this generosity, neither brother seemed at all perturbed at being brought before the magistrates nor showed any sign of remorse. Both appeared more interested in searching the crowds for familiar faces than in the legal proceedings.

Several witnesses were called to give evidence. One, Richard Caddy, testified that he had been at William's house on the night of the murder and that William had arrived home late, his trousers soaked to the knees. To explain his wet clothes, William claimed he had fallen into a well.

Richard and Elizabeth Ayres, and Elizabeth's mother Betty Bray, were neighbours of James. They told of retiring to bed on the night of the murder, and then being woken in the early hours of the morning by a commotion from the house next door. James' wife was crying noisily while James beseeched her loudly to 'Lie still, damn thee, or folks will hear you.' Her response was that she would not lie still and could not care who heard her.

Richard Caddy had visited James' house on the morning after the murder. There he had seen a distinctive pistol, heavily decorated with brass work. He noticed that the lock and stock were missing but could not draw any further information from James, who simply mumbled about shooting a cat and damaging a screw.

It seemed that the cat story might have been concocted in advance by the two brothers to explain away any bloodstains. Labourer William Verdoe heard about the cat from William Lightfoot who, on the day after his brother James was arrested, turned up for work unusually early and explained that James was 'taken up'. Lightfoot told Verdoe that his brother had shot the animal on the previous Wednesday, bloodying the pistol. He blamed Betty Bray and her family for the trouble his brother was in,

James Lightfoot's cottage, St Breock.
(By kind permission of *West Briton*)

saying that if it had not been for them hearing James coming home so late nobody would have been any the wiser. Although a shot cat was subsequently found in James' garden, Constable William Bray was later able to prove that the pistol stock had been intact and attached to the murder weapon when the animal was despatched.

On 13 February PC Bray conducted a thorough search of James Lightfoot's cottage without finding anything of note. His companion, Constable Joseph Carveth, asked Lightfoot about the pistol and he too was told the story of the cat. Although reluctant to answer any questions about the pistol, the constables persisted and eventually James retrieved the barrel from a ceiling beam and handed it over. The barrel of the pistol contained powder, and, on closer examination, Bray found that it appeared to have been separated very recently from the stock.

A further search of James Lightfoot's house on the following day revealed a paper screw of gunpowder in the pocket of a waistcoat belonging to James and two concealed powder flasks, one empty and one containing powder. In an upstairs room, the police also found the barrel of another gun, while numerous slugs were discovered hidden at various locations around the house. Meanwhile a local farmer had discovered a bundle of papers and a bunch of keys in a furze bush, in a field near where the murder was committed. The keys were found to fit Nevell Norway's house and Norway's brother identified the papers as being accounts, some in his brother's handwriting, some written by his clerk.

Grace Verdoe, William's mother, had visited Burlawn and witnessed the ongoing search for the missing pistol lock. She appealed to William Lightfoot's better nature, saying, 'If you are free, Jemmy [James] is free; if he is guilty, you are guilty. Do, Willy, go and confess.' Her pleas fell on deaf ears. Even when she took him to one side and begged him to tell her about the pistol, he continued to pretend that he did not know what she was talking about. At this, Grace became exasperated. 'You know what you have done,' she told William. 'If you don't confess, I shall tell what you have told my son. If I were you, I would confess, and probably you may have the reward. But if it do go bad with you, perhaps your children will have it.' And with that, she went straight to the house of the local constable, telling his wife to pass on the message that William should also be 'taken up' for his part in the murder.

Both men were escorted to Bodmin Gaol and, on the journey from Wadebridge to Bodmin, each brother was keen to implicate the other. Their journey was broken by a stop at the murder site, where the brothers were persuaded to point out where they had concealed Nevell Norway's keys, personal papers and purse. When shoemaker Richard Harry removed a dresser in settlement of a debt owed to him by James Lightfoot, the missing ivory notebook was found beneath the dresser.

Both men made their confessions before the magistrates. William maintained that his brother had knocked Mr Norway from his horse and beaten him, having first shot at him twice with a pistol, which failed to fire. James's confession accused William of beating Norway with a stick, following the misfiring of the gun, although he admitted to striking the victim several times himself with the butt end of the pistol and assisting his brother in dragging the body to the roadside ditch. In due course they were committed to the assizes for trial.

Shortly before proceedings opened on 20 March 1840, a labourer gathering sticks near the murder site made a significant find. He pulled a stout stick from the hedgerow, which was about fifteen inches long and had a large oval knob on one end measuring about four by three inches. The other end had been whittled with a knife, roughened as if to prevent it being snatched from the hand of an attacker. Despite lying abandoned for some weeks, partially covered in mud and washed by the rain, it still appeared to bear significant traces of blood. The labourer promptly took the stick to magistrates in Wadebridge, where they took steps to try and establish a connection between the weapon and the Lightfoot brothers.

The trial in Bodmin was besieged by crowds of people all hoping to watch the proceedings, many having arrived at the court as early as 6 a.m. The javelin men, whose job it was to escort the judge, had to belabour the spectators with their javelins in order to clear a path. Charged with the wilful murder of Nevell Norway in the parish of Egloshayle by beating him over the head and inflicting mortal wounds, both men impassively pleaded 'Not Guilty'.

The prisoners were not legally represented in court, although they were allowed to question the witnesses themselves. They made the most of this opportunity by contradicting as much of the evidence against them as they possibly could. William Verdoe

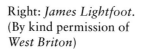

Left: *William Lightfoot.*
(By kind permission of
West Briton)

Right: *James Lightfoot.*
(By kind permission of
West Briton)

was accused of lying, as was another witness, William Roche, who testified that he was at Bodmin market on the afternoon of the murder and had observed William Lightfoot watching Nevell Norway as he took out his purse to make a payment. London policeman Charles Jackson introduced evidence he had obtained from James during the journey from Wadebridge to Bodmin, to the obvious displeasure of the judge who maintained that he had no right to question the prisoner when he had been committed to appear before magistrates.

The evidence presented at the trial was much the same as that which had been heard by the magistrates. Among the witnesses who testified was Thomas Dungey, a turnkey at Bodmin Gaol, where the brothers had been held in custody pending the trial. According to Dungey, William had been troubled by a guilty conscience on first arriving at the gaol and had wished to unburden himself. He had then confessed his part in the murder to Dungey, stating that it was he who had grabbed the bridle and that he had hit Norway with a stick after James' pistol had misfired. He still maintained that James had struck the fatal blow, he believed with the pistol.

Dungey had left William at that stage and gone to the cell where James was confined. Apparently James had greeted him with a smile, which angered Dungey who exclaimed, 'Good God! How can you smile knowing this dreadful thing hanging over your head?' The gaoler then proceeded to question James about his part in the murder. The judge, Mr Justice Coltman, interrupted to ask if the prisoner had been cautioned at this stage, to which Dungey replied that he had not. At this point, the judge put an end to Dungey's testimony against James, the evidence having been obtained in such an 'objectionable' way.

Once all the evidence had been presented to the court, the judge spoke to each prisoner in turn. First he turned to William, saying; 'If you have any account of this matter to give, you may tell your story or you may say whatever you wish about it.' All William had to say was; 'I never murdered Mr Norway.' Offered the same opportunity to speak, his brother James said only 'I never murdered the man.'

Next, both prisoners were asked if there were any witnesses that they wished to be called. James Lightfoot declined to call any, but William asked for four – two miners named Wills, John Rouncevell and Mary Carveth. William proposed that since all four had seen him leave his home on the day of the murder at about 3 p.m. and, since he lived about six miles from Bodmin, their testimony would cast doubt on the evidence of William Roche who had testified that he had seen Lightfoot observing Norway in Bodmin an hour later. The miners did not appear, but both Rouncevell and Carveth were called. Both seemed vague about the actual time when William Lightfoot had been seen leaving Bodmin. Rouncevell agreed that it was at 'about' 3 p.m., but could not be certain to within half an hour or so. Carveth also testified that William had left at about that hour, but had told the time by her clock, which she admitted was fast.

In summing up the evidence for the jury, Mr Justice Coltman was fair enough to remind them that a substantial reward had been offered for information, and that such an offer often tempted people to exaggerate or falsify evidence. He stressed that if there were any doubts in the jurors' minds, then the prisoners should be given the benefit of that doubt. Once again he questioned the admissibility of the evidence obtained by Jackson, saying that it was quite beyond the limits of duty of a constable to go into examinations and re-examinations of a remanded prisoner. He eventually ruled that Jackson's evidence was admissible, while cautioning him against obtaining a confession by such means in the future.

The judge pointed out that the statement obtained by Jackson could only affect James, since it was he who had confessed; it could not be considered as evidence against William. He also stated that he thought that it was improper for a gaoler to go from prisoner to prisoner to get evidence, so he had disallowed part of Dungey's testimony against James. Next the judge reiterated the evidence of Rouncevell and Mary Carveth for the benefit of the jury, stating that, if true, it made a strong case for suggesting that William could not have been seen in Bodmin at 4 p.m. on the afternoon of the murder.

Despite these wise words, the jury deliberated for only two minutes before finding both defendants guilty, and it was left to the judge to don his black cap and order that they each be hanged by the neck until dead. He urged the prisoners to prepare immediately to meet their God and to spend what little time remaining to them appeasing their offended Maker.

The Lightfoot brothers remained seemingly unconcerned at their fate. James asked to address the court in order explain how he had been drawn into the situation by his brother, whereas William was heard to ask for refreshments. Even after they had been taken to Bodmin Gaol, they still showed little concern for their situation and certainly no remorse, despite both having expressed regret for the murder in their earlier confessions to the magistrates. They acknowledged that the robbery of Mr Derry on the day before the murder of Mr Norway and the fact that the robbers had escaped detection had inspired them to commit a similar crime in order to obtain money. They also admitted to being heavy drinkers and to indulging in petty crime, with William putting his troubles down to 'bad company and keeping unholy the Lord's Day'. Meanwhile James confessed to having stolen the pistol from a Mrs Kendall of Mawgan, a statement that seemed at odds with the previous assertions of both brothers that they had never before committed highway robbery or robbed either a man or a house.

During their imprisonment in Bodmin, the brothers were in close contact with the prison chaplain to whom William promised a full confession. In the end none was forthcoming and William took the truth of Nevell Norway's murder with him to the grave. On the day before the brothers were hanged, the chaplain conducted a service in the prison chapel during which he asked the other prisoners to pray for their souls, pointing out that they could still enter heaven should they truly repent. Among the prisoners, only William and James showed no emotion at this service, although guards later heard William exhorting his brother from his cell to pray, and both men were observed kneeling in the early hours of the morning on which they were condemned to die.

The day of the execution saw Bodmin deluged by a constant stream of would-be spectators. Fearing a riot, authorities distributed notices entreating people to behave decently and maintain order. Meanwhile, the condemned men ate a hearty breakfast before leaving final messages for their wives and being led to the scaffold in chains. On their way to the gallows, they paused to shake hands with assembled dignitaries.

James was visibly afraid and trembling, but drew strength from his older brother who, as the rope was placed around his neck and the cap pulled over his eyes, again reminded James to pray. He then called for Parson Cole to come to his side, telling him 'I die happy' and asking to be remembered to his wife and family who, he hoped, he would meet again in heaven. Finally William beseeched his family to shun the paths of vice, not to break the Sabbath and to attend church regularly. When asked if he had anything to say, James too asked to be remembered to his wife and child and urged them to go to church.

These were the brothers' last words. The Lord's Prayer was recited and the chaplain made one last appeal to the Almighty to grant the sinners salvation. At this, the signal was given to the executioner to proceed. The bodies were displayed to the public for one hour before being cut down and buried without ceremony in the coal yard at the front of the prison.

It seems as though both men had seen highway robbery as an easy way of making money. After the attack on Mr Derry, they were, as William put it in his confession 'determined to enrich ourselves by similar means.' Whether they intended to go as far as actually killing someone is debatable. As William wrote, James visited his house on the day after the murder, saying; 'Dear me, Mr Norway's killed!' However, since they were known to the victim, it is probable that his death was the only way to ensure his silence.

Anecdotal evidence after the execution indicated that the brothers had already committed at least one other highway robbery. A labourer returning home from work was accosted by the brothers and relieved of his week's wages – the sum of 9s. The victim pleaded with his attackers not to take all of the money, as without it his wife and family would starve. Eventually the robbers agreed to give him back 2s, at which the labourer ran for home as fast as he possibly could. Soon he became aware that his attackers were following him. He quickly hid, hearing them pass by cursing and shouting, threatening to kill him if they could catch him. When the coast was clear, the labourer emerged from his hiding place and, on arriving home, was astonished to find that his attackers had mistakenly given him two sovereigns instead of 2s.

Perhaps the strangest aspect of the case is the uncannily accurate prediction of the murder by the victim's brother who, despite being thousands of miles away, 'saw' the whole scenario played out in a dream. The only difference between the content of the dream and what actually happened was the positioning of a house, which mysteriously moved from one side of the road to the other. It later emerged that since Edmund Norway's last visit to the scene, the layout of the road and been changed and the cottage he recalled so well *had* moved from the right to the left-hand side of the road.

Nevell Norway left behind a widow, Sarah, and six children unprovided for, but a subscription of £3,500 was made for their use, a noble testimony of the generous feeling of the public and the high estimation in which his amiable and spotless character was held. Sarah, who was also his first cousin, did not long survive her husband. Three years younger than him, she died at the age of thirty-six on 6 August

The grave of Nevell Norway, the 'Merchant of Wadebridge', in Egloshayle churchyard near Wadebridge.
(© Nicola Sly)

1840, the cause being recorded on her death certificate as 'hart [*sic*] disease'. Husband and wife are buried together in the churchyard at Egloshayle, about one mile from Wadebridge. Reflecting the esteem in which Norway was held in the area, the inscription on the headstone of their joint grave reads: 'Sacred to the memory of Nevell Norway, Merchant of Wadebridge, aged 39 years, murdered on 8 February 1840.'

The six children were all below the age of nine. The eldest, Arthur, was to become the grandfather of Nevil Shute Norway, who published several novels as Nevil Shute. In 1942 another novelist, John Rowland, published *The Death of Nevill Norway*, a work of faction which Shute made an unsuccessful attempt to have suppressed on the grounds of privacy.

[Note: In various contemporary accounts of the murder, the victim's forename is alternatively spelled Nevill.]

2

'SEE WHAT A WRETCHED END I HAVE COME TO'

Camelford, 1844

Rough Tor, which lies on the fringes of Bodmin Moor, can be a bleak and desolate place, often shrouded in thick mists and low cloud. Dominated by Brown Willy, the highest natural peak in Cornwall, it is a wilderness broken only by granite outcrops, grazed by sheep and a few hardy moorland ponies. A shallow stream provides a source of drinking water for the animal inhabitants and close to this stream can be seen a sturdy granite monolith, marking the site of the tragic murder in 1844 of a young servant girl, Charlotte Dymond.

Charlotte was born in the nearby coastal village of Boscastle. Although her real parentage has never been reliably established, she was rumoured to be the illegitimate daughter of the village schoolmistress. If this was true, it had the potential to cause a scandal of epic proportions in such a small, close-knit village. The untimely birth of a daughter to a woman of such high social standing in the community would explain why young Charlotte, her very presence causing her mother untold embarrassment, was placed in service at the earliest possible age. Her first position was as a maid at Penhale Farm near Davidstow, owned by a 61-year-old widow, Phillippa Peter, who ran the holding with the assistance of her 38-year-old son, John. Here Charlotte met farm labourer, Matthew Weekes.

Six years older than Charlotte, Matthew could hardly be described as a good catch. By all accounts he was short, with a heavily pockmarked face caused by a childhood bout of smallpox, a pronounced limp and several missing teeth which gave him a permanent expression somewhere between a smirk and leer. He compensated for his appearance by dressing much more flamboyantly than would be expected of a farm labourer of the period, favouring velvet jackets and fancy waistcoats. His interest in clothes was one that he shared with Charlotte who, despite her lowly status, took great pride in her appearance, often adorning herself with scarves, beads and other trinkets. Although sometimes described as shy, Charlotte liked to make herself as attractive as possible to the opposite sex and was not averse to some gentle flirting on occasions.

Even if Matthew was not the most handsome man in the neighbourhood, he was steady and thrifty with his wages, and when Charlotte left to take up employment at another farm nearby, they began formally walking out together. Soon, to Matthew's delight, Charlotte returned to work at Penhale Farm where their relationship flourished – until an old workmate of Matthew's, Thomas Prout, arrived on the scene. Both men soon started arguing and Thomas threatened to steal Charlotte's affections. Harsh words were exchanged, and the situation worsened when Charlotte was given notice to quit by her employer. Matthew must have felt as though his world was falling apart.

In the event Charlotte did not leave her employment, mainly because she had nowhere else to go. Yet while still living under the same roof as Matthew, she was seen in animated conversation with his bitter rival. Earlier that morning, Matthew had been in high spirits, teasing Charlotte with a letter which he held just out of her reach. Now the sight of his beloved Charlotte together with Thomas sent him into a state of jealous agitation.

Shortly after talking with Prout, Charlotte dressed herself in her best clothes and left Penhale. It was late afternoon on Sunday 14 April 1844 when she tried to sneak away for a secret tryst. Challenged by her employer, Mrs Peter, who was determined to find out where she was going so late in the day, Charlotte managed to evade the question before leaving, closely followed by Matthew, also dressed in his Sunday best and carrying an umbrella to protect them both from the rain.

Matthew was expected to be back in good time to do the evening milking. However it was 9.30 p.m. when he returned to the farm alone. Asked where Charlotte was, he mumbled that he did not know and soon found himself facing a barrage of questions from Mrs Peter as to Charlotte's whereabouts. Mrs Peter stayed up waiting for Charlotte long after Weekes had retired for the night but, by milking time the following morning, she still had not returned.

According to Matthew, he had only walked with Charlotte for a little way before they parted company. Alone, he had walked to nearby Hallworthy, intending to visit the Westlake family, but on his arrival, everyone except Sally Westlake had been out. Over the next few days, under intense questioning, he first suggested that Charlotte might have run off with Thomas Prout. Finally he told 'the truth' – Charlotte had taken up another position working for Mrs Peter's niece in Blisland. The letter offering her the position was the very one that he had been teasing her with on the morning of her disappearance. Concerned, Mrs Peter pointed out that Blisland was a 10-mile walk across the moors and, having set out so late in the afternoon, Charlotte could not possibly have reached her intended destination by nightfall. At this, Matthew argued that Charlotte could have stayed overnight with a neighbour, Cain Speare, who lived at Brown Willy, before resuming her journey in the morning.

Over the next few days, Matthew was the subject of much speculation by local people who suggested that he might have harmed Charlotte to prevent his rival from having her. Gossip and rumour abounded in the small community, until Mrs Peter felt obliged to tackle him once more on the subject of Charlotte's mysterious disappearance. Once again he managed to evade her questions by retiring to his bed, ignoring her parting remark: 'Matthew, I am quite frightened. If you have hurted [sic] the girl, you ought to be hung in chains.' When a Mr Bethson asked Matthew what he had done with the girl, the answer was, 'I don't know where she is gone, but if she is found murdered, they will take up her mother for it, for she said she would kill her if she came home again.' Though her mother's aversion to her daughter was well known, nobody thought for a moment that the former would be responsible for her murder.

A worried Mrs Peter waited until Matthew was out tending bullocks in the yard the following morning before asking her son John and another labourer, John Stevens, to check the facts as he had related them. Exactly one week after Charlotte had last been seen, the two men set off to Brown Willy and Blisland in pursuit of the truth. Seeing them leave, Matthew must have got wind of their errand. He went immediately to his bedroom and once again changed into his best clothes before leaving the farm, refusing to answer questions on where he was going, but promising to be back in time for supper that evening.

Meanwhile Mrs Peter's daughter, Mary Westlake, came to visit her mother and effectively broke Matthew's alibi. He had not visited the Westlake family as he had claimed. Now even more concerned for the safety of her maid, Mrs Peter and her daughter decided to search Matthew's belongings. To their horror, they found a handkerchief belonging to Charlotte in the pocket of the jacket he had worn on the day of her disappearance. They also found his heavily mud-stained trousers and a badly torn shirt that had been clumsily mended. A day or two earlier, Matthew had asked John Stevens, one of the other servants, for a needle and thread to sew a button to his shirt collar. John expressed surprise as the garment was a new one, but Matthew said it had been badly sewn. When Mrs Peter examined the shirt she found that it was not only new, but of good quality and particularly strong. She also found several spots of blood on the sleeve.

By nightfall, there was still no sign of Matthew. However John Peter and John Stevens returned with distressing news; there had been no offer of a job and Charlotte had not stayed at either Blisland or Brown Willy. Not until the following Tuesday morning, nine days after Charlotte had vanished, was a search party organised. Acting on information from two local farmers, both of whom claimed to have seen a young woman accompanied by a man with a distinctive limping gait, they concentrated their search on the fringes of the moor where, almost miraculously considering the length of time that had passed, they identified a woman's footprints in the damp ground. Opposite were a man's footprints, close enough to suggest there might have been a struggle.

These prints led searchers to a marshy area near Rough Tor Ford, where Charlotte's body was soon discovered lying partially submerged in the stream, her throat slashed from ear to ear. Surrounded by pools of diluted blood, Charlotte lay with one arm stretched above her shoulder, the other by her side. One knee was bent upwards, part of her bodice had been torn away and her dress was raised above her knees with one of her stockings pulled halfway down her leg. Her treasured coral beads were scattered around her head.

A surgeon, Mr Good, was summoned to examine the body, which he loaded onto a cart, returning it to Penhale Farm where it was placed in an outbuilding. After a more detailed examination of Charlotte's body, the surgeon concluded that she had died as the result of the horrific wound on her neck which, he surmised, had been caused by a rather blunt knife or similar cutting instrument. He could not rule out the possibility that the wound had been self-inflicted, but felt it unlikely and he further stated that Charlotte was not pregnant, nor could he find any evidence of sexual assault.

Rough Tor on the edge of Bodmin Moor, where Charlotte Dymond was killed in April 1844. (© Nicola Sly)

The stream on Rough Tor where Charlotte was killed. (© Nicola Sly)

Charlotte Dymond's grave,
St David's Church, Davidstow.
(© Nicola Sly)

Back on the moors, searchers were still combing the area for any trace of Charlotte's missing clothing. Her shawl, scarf, bonnet, shoes and the pattens that she had worn over her shoes to protect them from the mud were eventually found covered by moss, hidden in a bloodstained pit, almost half a mile from where her body was found. Her gloves and black silk handbag were still missing.

Several miles away, the prime suspect Matthew Weekes was visiting old friends at Coad's Green. His friends found him pensive, preoccupied and uncharacteristically reticent when it came to answering questions about his beloved Charlotte. When the young daughter of the house proudly boasted about owning a handbag, Matthew briefly produced a lace-trimmed black bag from his own pocket to show her.

Local police were already on Matthew's trail. Aware that he had relatives in Plymouth, Constable John Bennett hastened to the city and, quite by chance, bumped into Matthew on Plymouth Hoe, accompanied by his sister and her husband. He was immediately taken to Hallworthy Inn, Davidstow, where a search of his person located the missing gloves concealed in his jacket pockets. On this discovery he was charged with Charlotte's murder and summoned to appear before 'King John', the magistrate John King Lethbridge. He was then escorted in a cart to Camelford, then a gig to Bodmin, where he was committed to gaol to await his trial.

Numerous witnesses now came forward to testify that they had seen the couple on the moor that fateful Sunday afternoon. Although their accounts did not conclusively prove that the sightings had been of Matthew and Charlotte, the circumstantial evidence against Weekes was persuasive. Besides, he had effectively been condemned by gossip and innuendo, even before Charlotte's terrible fate was known.

Matthew was not allowed to give his own version of events in court, but maintained his composure in the face of a guilty verdict from the foreman of the jury. Only when the judge pronounced the death sentence did he react at all, slumping backwards in a faint, before being carried unconscious from the courtroom by two guards.

While awaiting his execution, Matthew seemed ashamed at having brought such disgrace to his family. In contrition he allegedly made a full confession, stating that he and Charlotte had initially walked together making idle conversation. Then he had

A memorial to Charlotte Dymond, erected on Rough Tor near the scene of her murder. (© Nicola Sly)

jealously accused his girlfriend of behaving disgracefully with another man and, to his horror, the woman he loved so much had turned her back on him, retorting that she would do as she pleased and had nothing more to say on the subject. At this he had seen red, pulling out his pocketknife and lunging at her. Even then, he maintained that he had come to his senses and put the knife away without harming her and that it was only when she repeated her remarks that he lashed out again, this time with fatal consequences. Panic-stricken by the sight of Charlotte's body toppling to the ground, blood gushing from her neck, he had quickly hidden her clothes and fled, discarding the bloodstained knife as he ran.

In Bodmin Gaol, the illiterate Matthew dictated two letters which he signed with his cross. In one, he asked his family to distribute his few personal belongings and urged his brothers to adopt a more Christian way of life. He addressed the second letter to his former employer, Mrs Peter, forgiving her for standing as a witness against him and thanking her for her kindness to him. He also thanked the judge and jury for giving him his just desserts and the chaplain for his endeavours to save his soul. And, in both letters, he made an impassioned plea to other young men and women not to place too much trust in the opposite sex, saying; 'See what a wretched end I have come to by loving too much'.

Weekes was executed at Bodmin Gaol before a crowd of almost 20,000 spectators on 12 August 1844. His body was suspended by the neck for the customary one hour and one minute, before being cut down and buried without ceremony in an unmarked grave in the prison grounds. Yet he was immortalised, forever tied to his true love by the wording inscribed on the granite monument, erected by public contribution, that still marks the site of her tragic demise:

This monument was erected by public subscription in memory of Charlotte Dymond who was murdered here by Matthew Weekes on Sunday April 14 1844.

The two lovers are also commemorated in a poem, *The Ballad of Charlotte Dymond*, by Charles Causley.

3
'I SUPPOSE IT WAS TEMPER'

St Erth, 1909

In the early years of the twentieth century there was often more opportunity for miners to work abroad than at home. One young man who discovered this for himself was William Hampton, of St Erth, who spent a year or so working in the United States. Yet the pull of home remained strong, and in November 1907, at the age of twenty-one, he returned to his home town. Early the following year he became engaged to Emily Barnes Trewarthen Tredrea, who lived in a cottage nearby in New Row, Old Vicarage Gate. She too came from a mining family. Her father John also spent long periods away from home as he had found work in the mines at Johannesburg, and she shared the cottage with her mother Grace, and her three younger siblings.

In the spring of 1908 Hampton moved into the Tredreas' cottage as a lodger. Towards the end of the year, he said that he was expecting to go to work in America again, but would not stay there long. By the time he returned, they would have enough money to marry and settle down together in a home of their own at or near St Erth.

Emily was a bright, cheerful girl of fifteen, and the neighbours said she always seemed to be singing. However the course of true love did not run smoothly in this case. Grace Tredrea had known William since he was a boy, and thought he would make her daughter an excellent husband, but after a while Emily had second thoughts. She was increasingly irritated by his uncouth manners and persistent swearing; at length she realised she no longer cared for him, to the extent of telling one of her friends in the village that she hated him, was afraid of him, and feared he might kill her. On Saturday 1 May 1909, she told him it was all over between them and she wanted to break off the engagement.

At first he did not react, and he probably assumed she would reconsider. It was equally probable that Grace Tredrea's presence in the house acted as some kind of restraint on his behaviour. This was not the case on Sunday night, when Grace had to go out at about 10 p.m. to look in on her elderly mother, who suffered from a bad leg and needed to be kept a regular eye on. Unaware of any problems between the young couple, she was happy to leave them in the house. Also at the house were William, her nine-year-old brother, her sister of five, and the fifteen-month-old baby. The latter started to cry as Mrs Tredrea was about to leave, so she was brought downstairs and Emily held her in her arms, trying to settle her. Sometime after she had put her little sister down another conversation ensued, and Emily told William Hampton that she had not changed her mind. She did not want to have anything more to do with him.

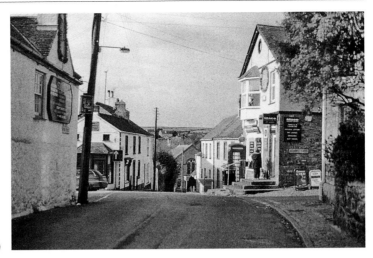

St Erth. (© Nicola Sly)

At this he lost his temper, grabbed her, threw her on the floor and pressed his hands tightly around her throat.

William had been upstairs in bed, asleep. He was woken by what he later described as 'a kind of rattling noise', and got out of bed, partly dressed, then went downstairs to see what was going on. He saw Hampton with his sister on the floor, his knee on her body, keeping her down, with his thumbs around her throat, choking her. His first instinct was to go and fetch their mother, and tried to leave the house. Hampton would not let him go; 'Step back, I am going out in a minute, and you can go out with me.' William asked what the matter was with his sister, and Hampton said she was very sick. The boy insisted that he wanted to go into the garden. Aware that it would make no difference to his ultimate fate, Hampton allowed him to go.

Before William left the house, he saw Hampton lift Emily up and try to make her stand in the corner of the room. As she was almost certainly dead by this time, there was no point, so he then placed her in a chair, her head falling limply to one side. William went as quickly as he could in the direction of his grandmother's house. He had only gone a few yards when he heard the door bang, and as he looked back he saw Hampton leaping over the hedge near the house and running off in the direction of Hayle.

Grace Tredrea soon came home, followed immediately by PC Ashford, who had been alerted to the problem. On arrival they found Emily's body still in the chair where Hampton had placed her. The baby was in another armchair, and it was assumed that Emily had put her there while she went to get a cup of tea and some biscuits. Between them, Ashford, Frank Trevaskis, the local postmaster and his brother carried the body upstairs and attempted artificial respiration, but it was too late. Ashford then started to search for Hampton. They checked the house, garden and outhouses, but there was no sign of him.

News travelled fast, and already several of the neighbours were aware that trouble had been brewing. Ashford enlisted the services of several young men with bicycles, who went to Hayle, Levant, and other villages in the district to tell the policemen what had occurred, and to ask them to join him at St Erth where their presence was needed. Another local resident, Cardell Williams, came and offered to give Emily artificial respiration again, though it was too late. Two policemen soon arrived, as did Dr Davis, who made a thorough examination of the body. He found very severe injuries to the throat; such had been the pressure of Hampton's hands that the skin was torn, and there was a small bruise on the left temple, which might have been caused by a blow sustained in a struggle.

By now the police had obtained a full description of Hampton. Sergeant Kent organised a search party, and there was no shortage of volunteers to help. They called at his father's cottage, searched in several outhouses, and even checked a deep pit near the church in case he had jumped in. However Hampton was aware that there would be no hiding place for him, and he surrendered to the inevitable. After running out of the house, he went across the fields to Foundry, Hayle, and then to Copperhouse. After some hesitation, at around midnight he met two constables near the police station.

'Have you heard the news?' he asked them, and then added, 'I might as well give myself up.' When they asked him what news he was referring to, he said, 'I think I have killed a maid at St Erth.' Roberts questioned him further, and asked Hampton how he did it. 'I choked her,' he told him. After a few more questions, Roberts said it was 'rather a funny story' (one assumes he meant funny in the odd sense), and suggested that perhaps the girl was not dead. Hampton was more positive; 'I think she is dead right enough, because I picked her up and she could not stand, and then I put her in a chair and her head fell over one side, meat came out of her mouth, and her lips were black.'

Why did he do such a thing, the policeman asked. 'I was going with her, and now she won't have anything to do with me. I suppose it was temper that caused me to do it.' Roberts took him into custody, and then went to St Erth to tell Sergeant Kent that the search could be called off. All his helpers were relieved, as many had sworn they would not go to bed that night unless they heard that the killer had been captured.

Pleading not guilty to a charge of 'wilful murder', Hampton went on trial at Bodmin on 24 June 1909 under Mr Justice Phillimore, with Mr Raymond Asquith and Mr Stafford Howard prosecuting, and Mr R.G. Seton defending.

The first witness to be called was Grace Tredrea. She said she had never known her daughter and the prisoner to quarrel, but knew her daughter objected to his swearing. On the Friday or Saturday before the crime, she heard Emily tell him, 'I don't think I shall go with you any more.' Even so, she had no idea of any impending tragedy, until young William came to look for her after Hampton had strangled Emily. Mother and son hurried home, meeting Constable Ashford on the way, and found the lifeless Emily in a wicker chair.

When questioned about her daughter's personality, Mrs Tredrea said that the girl was 'most industrious and respectable', and not nervous by nature, 'but sometimes fainted when she had nervous attacks'. She had never known the prisoner give the police any trouble before. William then followed his mother into the witness box and described the events of that fatal night as he had seen them. The policemen involved,

Bodmin Gaol. Built in 1777, the gaol witnessed fifty-five hangings, the last being that of William Hampton in July 1909. Closed in 1922, it now contains a museum and licensed restaurant open to the public. (© Kim Van der Kiste)

then Dr Davis, all followed him in giving their evidence. Also for the prosecution, Mr Asquith said there was no doubt that the prisoner killed the deceased by strangling her. The girl's brother had given his evidence with remarkable accuracy for a child of his age. There was nothing to suggest that the prisoner had been provoked, and he showed no remorse for his crime, making no efforts to revive the girl or get assistance after he had attacked her. His murder was the result of a grudge, a feeling of resentment, 'a premeditated crime' in which he was determined to wreak vengeance at the first opportunity, 'a cold-blooded crime, carried out with ferocity.'

For the defence, Mr Seton said there was no doubt that the person who caused the death of the girl was the prisoner, but it was a question of provocation, not of malice. The verdict should be one of manslaughter. If the intention was murder, as the prosecution averred, and the prisoner seriously meant to commit the worst possible crime, there had been ample means for him to use one of the knives lying on the kitchen table. In this case there was every reason why the verdict of the jury should be that of manslaughter.

In summing up the judge said that the jury were asked by Mr Seton to say it was not murder. 'Provocation was not a plea they could give much heed to.' The act had not been a momentary one, and all the evidence suggested that the prisoner had intended for some time to take the life of the deceased.

The jury were out for fifteen minutes before delivering a verdict of guilty, but with a recommendation to mercy. The judge told him that this would be 'forwarded to the proper quarter, but I advise you to prepare for your death.' Hampton stood calmly in the dock, showing no emotion, and did not reply when asked if he had anything to say as to why sentence of death should not be passed on him. When he was led out to the gallows on 20 July to be hanged by Henry and Thomas Pierrepoint, he became the last person ever to be executed at Bodmin Gaol.

4

'NEVER HAD POISON OF ANY KIND'

Tregonissey, 1921

Edward Ernest Black was born in Burnley in 1886. At the age of twenty-one the family moved to Tregonissey, where he, his father and two brothers were employed in the local china clay works, though father and brothers later returned to Lancashire. For a while he lived with Annie Nicholls, a native of Duloe who had lived in Tregonissey since childhood. Fifteen years his senior, with a small daughter, Marion, from a previous relationship, she was a teacher at Carclaze School for some years and then took over running the village general store adjoining their house at Lane End, Tregonissey. In 1914 Edward and Annie were married. He was rejected for military service on health grounds, possibly as the result of an industrial accident, and after he left the china clay works he took a post as an insurance agent for the Refuge Assurance Company. He had a fine bass voice as a singer and in his spare time he sang with the St Austell Church Choir. He was also a member of the local Red Cross detachment, and regularly attended football matches at the St Austell ground to assist with first aid.

To the local community, Edward Black was a fine upstanding citizen, always ready to play an active role in the area. Nevertheless some saw a very different side of him. As an insurance agent he was either very unlucky and unsuccessful, or else totally unscrupulous – probably the latter. Several of his customers paid good money for the delivery of policies which were later proved to be non-existent. By the time they realised, he had spent the proceeds, and on 2 November 1921 his employers dismissed him.

During the previous month, on 21 October, Annie had complained of feeling unwell. Nine days later she, her husband and daughter went for a walk together, during which she told them she had been feeling poorly that week. At breakfast on 31 October her husband poured tea out for the three of them from a teapot on the hearth. About an hour later Annie began vomiting severely and complaining of pains in her side. Edward called Dr Andrew, who did not consider the trouble serious and assumed it was probably ordinary gastritis. However Annie's condition may have given her husband an idea with regard to settling his debts. Eight days later he purchased two ounces of arsenic from the local branch of Timothy White's, the chemist, and signed the poisons register. During the next few days Annie became worse, and complained that the medicine burned like pepper in her throat every time it was administered by her husband. Dr Andrew began to have his suspicions.

On 8 November Black said he was going to cycle to St Austell to get some cigarettes for Annie's shop. He left her in the care of his stepdaughter Marion, now aged sixteen, and the neighbours, particularly Ann Best, one of Annie's closest friends, who had helped to nurse her.

Annie never saw him again. She had a relapse on 10 November, was violently sick and in severe pain. During the night she became weaker and died at 1 a.m. the next morning. Suspecting something more than natural causes, Dr Andrew refused to issue a certificate of death, but informed the police, and passed stomach samples to the pathologist Dr Bernard Spilsbury for analysis. An inquest was opened at St Austell three days later by the Coroner, Mr M. Edyvean, and adjourned pending arrival of the Home Office analyst's report on the contents of her stomach, which Police Inspector Trythall stated was expected within a week. (It was delayed and the inquest was not resumed until the next month). The only witness present was Miss Nicholls, who was asked by the coroner to confirm her identity, and that she, her mother and stepfather all lived at the same address. The jury were offered a chance to ask her any further questions but the foreman, ex-Police Inspector Hugo, assured Mr Edyvean that she was well-known to them all. This, said the coroner, was all the evidence he needed at this stage.

That same day, police questioning led to further information about Black's recent movements. After he had gone to St Austell, apparently for more cigarettes, he left his bicycle in the yard of a temperance house in the town, and caught the 6 p.m. train to Plymouth. One of his business associates confirmed seeing him at the station, and Black told him that he was going to Par, but would return later that evening. Black did not keep the appointment, and when questioned none of his friends had any idea where he had gone.

At this stage only a few people were aware that cases relating to his malpractice were about to come to court, and that he could probably not afford to reimburse the victims of his little frauds. His father had recently died, though his mother and brothers were still living in Burnley; he also had relatives at Cowdenbeath, Fife, and it was thought that after leaving Plymouth he might have gone north to either of these places.

Further extensive police enquiries revealed that a man answering his description had left St Austell wearing a grey suit with a grey trilby hat and dark tan lace-up boots, was later seen at Burnley in a dark suit and light cap, and had changed his brown boots for black ones. When the police tried to trace his movements, they had good reason to believe that he had been in Plymouth briefly on 9 November, and secured a sum of £50 from a local firm with whom he had regularly done business in the past. When he called upon them he told a plausible story about not having enough money with him to complete the purchase of some furniture he had come to Plymouth to buy, and if he wired home for the money it could not arrive before his train left Plymouth for St Austell. The people he spoke to had no reason not to trust him, and a very contented Black left the building with the money in his pocket. A fellow insurance agent in George Street reported having seen him on the next morning, after which it was assumed that he left Millbay Station on the 10.25 a.m. train, and arrived in Manchester at 7.30 p.m. in the evening. Part of the money he borrowed must have gone on new clothing, but it would take more than a change of apparel to remain beyond the long arm of the law.

On 15 November Mrs Black's funeral was held. The Revd T.S. Lea officiated, and several villagers accompanied the cortège from the house to the St Austell cemetery. The principal mourner was Marion, whom the press described as 'a pathetic figure (who) exhibited acute distress, particularly at the graveside', where she was supported by Mr Bertrand Parnell, superintendent of the Refuge Insurance Company. Few, if any, knew, that she had an extra cross to bear, as well as the sudden death of her mother. Not long before, she had learnt that she was not her mother's adopted daughter, something she had always assumed, but a child born out of wedlock.

A committee was spontaneously formed by the villagers, with Mr Parnell as one of the trustees, to help provide financially for Marion and enable her to continue the studies she had recently begun to follow in her mother's footsteps as a schoolteacher. After consideration she decided that she would leave her studies and continue working at the family shop. Shortly before her death Annie Black had made a will, leaving the furniture to her daughter, who decided she would retain the piano, music stool and a few other small mementoes, but wished to sell most of it by auction. She would keep the shop as a back-up establishment, and live with her neighbour, Mrs Kent, so they could let the rest of the house.

That same day the police took possession of a number of bottles, photographs and papers found at the Blacks' house. One item, which was only to be expected in view of his activities within the community, was a first aid book. However, this particular copy was folded down at the section dealing with arsenic poisoning. It would form a small but significant part of the evidence for the prosecution.

Also on 15 November a warrant was issued for the arrest of Black on two charges of obtaining money under false pretences, after both cases involving Black's malpractice were heard at St Austell County Court. In the first, Miss Norah Smith of Foxhole sued him for delivery of a policy in the Refuge Assurance Company, or another insurance company, on the life of John Rowse, to the value of £50. Alternatively she would claim £50 damages for non-delivery of the policy, as in February 1921 she had lent the defendant £15 on the security of a policy said to exist in the Refuge Company, and later gave him another £15, but never received the policy. Her solicitor said the company did not exist, and judgment was given for the plaintiff. In the second, Charles Smith, also of Foxhole, brought an action against Black for dissolution of the partnership said to exist between the parties in regard to certain Cunard shares and an account of the partnership dealings, assets, and liabilities. Again, it was clear that Black had obtained money by false pretences, and judgement was given for Smith.

On 19 November St Austell and Fowey played a charity cup football match on the former's home ground, and a first aider was required on the pitch several times. Whenever he appeared, there were shouts from the crowd of 'Where's Black?' The community could talk of little else that week, and the regular question 'Have they found him yet?' could only mean one thing.

While his whereabouts remained uncertain, the police took the precaution of contacting liners which had sailed the previous day. It was thought that he might have tried to leave Plymouth by liner, especially since he had visited the town a couple of times recently, without the knowledge of his wife or stepdaughter. He would have been unable to book a passage on such a vessel because of the inevitable passport problems he would face, but there was always the possibility that he might have left England as a member of a ship's crew. Those who knew him thought he was most unlikely to have committed suicide.

On Monday 21 November Joseph James Kelly, a Tregonissey butcher and one of Marion's guardians, received a letter from Black, with the address simply given as 'Burnley' and posted at Southport on the previous Friday or Saturday. It mentioned the names of several other people who had cooperated with the recipient in arranging Black's home affairs, and asked for the letter expressing his thanks to be shown them. Referring to the charges alleged against him, he protested that although he had made the greatest mistake of his life in leaving home under the circumstances, he was innocent and had nothing to do with his wife's death. It added that by the time this letter arrived, he would be 'hundreds of miles away' and that he would not be brought back to St Austell alive. Kelly promptly handed this letter to the police, who thought that if it had been posted at the weekend, Black must have been lying low in Lancashire all week. If he was still in England, his early arrest would be inevitable, but if he had gone to Ireland, his chances of escape were greater.

As Liverpool was the main English port in the area, and therefore the place from which he would be likely to effect an escape, efforts were concentrated on the area. Descriptions and photographs of him were published in the regional newspapers. He was 5ft 7in tall, readers were told, had black hair, was clean-shaven, with a heart tattooed on his left wrist and had a slight curvature of the spine which caused a lean to his left as he walked. It was not noticeable when he was standing erect or sitting upright, but only when stooping.

On the evening of 21 November a Mr Stevens, claiming to be a commercial traveller from Preston, booked in at Cashin's Temperance Hotel in Bell Street, Liverpool. Fortuitously, it was within a stone's throw of the Liverpool Central Police Station in Dale Street. When he presented himself at the reception desk the proprietress, described by the press as 'a youngish widow of smart appearance and great intelligence', whose name was deliberately not disclosed for obvious reasons, was unaware of the hue and cry going on.

As business was fairly quiet, she had a friendly conversation with him, just as she often had with other guests when there was time. He immediately struck her as being very genial and friendly. For about an hour, she later told the police, 'we talked on a variety of subjects. During the conversation he did not say much about himself, other than that he had been travelling about considerably, and among other places which he had visited he mentioned Hull and Southport,' about which he asked her a good deal.

At about 9 p.m. he went out for a drink, and as he walked downstairs and out into the street, she picked up an evening paper lying on the table. She could hardly believe it when the first thing to attract her attention was a photograph of a man astonishingly like the one to whom she had just been talking. There was only one discrepancy between the printed description and the reality; he had blue eyes and not brown, as the paper said. However the resemblance was so marked that she immediately went to report it at the police station.

Soon after her return Black came in, and sat down to talk again. This time, she noticed, he was eyeing her with suspicion. Her small son nearby had a piece of paper and pencil with him. He sat down and started doing a sketch of his mother, then turned to Black, saying, 'Now I will draw you.' Black smiled nervously, and as the boy looked into his face to capture his likeness, he became ever more restive. Eventually, as their eyes met, Black closed his, and he told them he was off to bed. Though he went straight upstairs he seemed unable to settle, and several times he came down again for no apparent reason. She could see he was apprehensive, and 'in dread of something.'

It was nearly midnight when two members of the Liverpool constabulary entered the hotel, and knocked on his door. A voice inside shouted, 'Who's there?' The officers demanded to be allowed in, but he refused. The officers forced the door, and found that Black had not merely locked it, but also wedged a chair under the handle. By the light of an electric torch they could see him sitting on the bed partly dressed, holding a penknife in his hand, and bleeding from a freshly inflicted wound in the throat. He sprang at them but they overpowered him and removed the knife, though only after he had succeeded in injuring himself even further and was bleeding copiously. As his condition appeared serious he was not taken straight to the police station, but an ambulance was summoned and he was taken to the Liverpool Northern Hospital, where his wounds were dressed. He had done his best to try and fulfil the prophecy (or boast) in his letter to Mr Kelly that he would not be brought back to St Austell alive.

When his hotel room was searched, it was found that he had only brought a small quantity of luggage with him, and his belongings included various articles which could have been used for effecting a disguise if needed. Only one of the photographs published by the press was said to be a good likeness, and rather oddly, it was this particular photo, which had been cut out of a newspaper and affixed to the wall of his room. Had he put it there in order to remind himself that he needed to improve on his disguise before travelling elsewhere? Though he had been described as clean-shaven, he now had a slight growth of moustache.

Once the story broke, it became apparent from police enquiries that he had visited Burnley and other towns in Lancashire. From Southport he had gone to Liverpool, where he had probably been for at least two or three days, wandering about quite freely, visiting various hotels and other establishments, looking in shop windows, behaving normally and evidently keen not to draw attention to his appearance. A porter at another Liverpool hotel, the Stork, had seen him there in the company of a woman in the smoking room, and noticed the tattoo on his wrist when he reached out to pick up a glass. The porter left the room to go and check the printed description, but when he returned Black and the woman had gone.

In hospital Black was placed under constant supervision by two members of the Liverpool police, working in turn, until he was better. He had lost much blood, and for some hours he was slipping in and out of consciousness. Within twenty-four hours he was well enough to sit up in bed and have a cigarette.

A few days later he was discharged, remanded in custody and taken to St Austell on 30 December. On arrival he presented a pitiful sight in his grey suit without collar or tie, and a black beard which he had grown in the last few weeks to hide the scar on the left of his throat. Still appearing far from well, he had a septic right leg and was too weak to walk into the guardroom at the police station without the aid of the two burly officers flanking him.

On the next day, at proceedings lasting about an hour and a quarter, he was charged at the town court with obtaining money by false pretences, two sums of £15 and £20 respectively, from another victim, George Moss, a stores manager for a manure and coal firm, for the purchase of non-existent insurance policies. Black still looked frail and ill as he was assisted into the dock by police. While part of the evidence was being read he looked as though he was on the verge of collapse, holding his throat, but he revived after a drink of water. Evidence was given that when he was asked for the policies, he assured Moss that they were at his office and that they were genuine. When charged he had nothing to say. He was committed for trial on this offence, and on a further charge of obtaining £30 from Norah Smith.

Nevertheless a much more serious matter than embezzlement had to be considered. On 21 January Black was committed for trial at Bodmin Assizes, charged with murdering his wife by the administration of arsenic. Dr Andrew said that no arsenic was present in the medicine he prescribed Mrs Black during her last illness. He denied that he had told her husband, as he had asserted, that the valves of her heart were gone, or that she was not likely to recover. After he had left home on his ostensible errand to St Austell, she seemed quite relieved that her husband had gone, and said she hoped she would never see him again. Her wish had been granted, but not in the way she might have wished.

James Webster, a senior Home Office analyst, said that he had found arsenic present in all the organs submitted to him. There was a total quantity of 3.73 milligrams of arsenic, or approximately 1/17th of a grain. His opinion was that there would not be less than ten milligrams, or about a sixth of a grain, in the whole body. In one full bottle of medicine, some ointment, and some tooth powder, he found a slight amount of arsenic, but the amount found in the medicine could not account for the quantity in the organs. The arsenic in the medicine was probably due to a slight impurity in the bismuth, and the amount found in the organs would be compatible with medicinal administration of arsenic over a considerable period.

Sir William Wilcox, physician at St Mary's Hospital and consulting medical officer at the Home Office, said that Mrs Black's symptoms had been entirely consistent with arsenic poisoning. He was sure that considerable doses of the substance were taken on 31 October, within twenty-four hours of the onset of her illness, and it was possible that poisonous drugs were given on the first few days of the illness, rather than towards the end.

After evidence was heard from Detective Sergeant McAllister of the Liverpool police, one of the officers who had arrested Black in the hotel room at Liverpool, Black asked if it was compulsory to make a statement, and was told that it was not. He was kept in custody at Exeter Gaol.

By the time the case came to trial at Bodmin Assizes early in February, public interest had reached a considerable level. That an apparently respectable member of the community could have been responsible for such crimes and sparked a manhunt well beyond the westcountry had generated a degree of curiosity not associated with any previous murder case in Cornwall for many years. Long before the judge was due to take his seat, there was a queue several hundred strong seeking admission to the Court. Only about half were allowed in, and the card 'Court full' was accordingly displayed on the Court gates. Those who could not get in at once lined up, hoping for access to resumed proceedings after the luncheon interval, but even so many of them were in for disappointment through lack of room.

The proceedings on 1 and 2 February 1922 were presided over by Mr Justice Rowlatt, the counsel for the prosecution were Mr Holman Gregory and Mr Harold Murphy, and for the defence Mr Lhind Pratt. By this time Black was in much better physical shape, according to the *Western Morning News*; 'gone was his previous dejected appearance, gone was the beard which had given him such an aged look, and gone also was much of his careworn demeanour.' Listening with evident interest to everything said by counsel and witnesses, he looked more his old self, with a black moustache, dressed in a neat grey suit with collar and tie. When charged, he replied 'Not Guilty' in a firm voice, and immediately objected to two members from the jury, a man and a woman from the St Austell district, both of whom were discharged and their places taken by two men.

The main witnesses for the prosecution were James Webster and Sir William Wilcox, who reiterated their statements made at the previous hearing. This time Webster stated that in his opinion the cause of death was arsenic poisoning; though Mrs Black had also suffered from kidney disease, 'that was not incompatible with her living for some years'.

Mr Pratt had little to offer in defence. When he asked Willcox that if Mrs Black had died from gastritis, in other words from natural causes, would the post-mortem examination have given the same negative result as it gave in this case? Wilcox agreed that it would, but said that gastritis would not have lasted as long.

Black continued to deny any wrongdoing. He told the court that he and his wife had lived happily together since their marriage, and that she had always been prone to gastric trouble. He denied that he had ever been to Timothy White's to purchase arsenic, either there or anywhere else; 'I have never had poison of any kind in my possession,' he stated categorically. Nevertheless he did admit to running away to Liverpool and attempting suicide because he was beset with financial difficulties, 'because I was placed in a rather peculiar position for the time financially', and charges were threatened against him. When asked why he had been sacked by the Refuge Insurance Company, he admitted that it was 'because I used their name illegally.'

When he was shown the poisons book, and told that the signature 'E.E. Black' was similar to his, he still denied it. Bertrand Parnell identified the signature, and the handwriting of the letter received by Mr Kelly, as being those of Black. The latter continued to deny that he ever told any of the neighbours that his wife was going to die, or that he had seen a Red Cross book in his house turned down at the section dealing with arsenic poisoning, for at least twelve months.

When his stepdaughter Marion began to gave evidence she was noticeably nervous at first. However, her confidence was restored as she proceeded to recapitulate on her former statements regarding the progress of her mother's illness. The judge asked her 'on what terms' were her parents. 'Very good', she replied, though when he asked her what quarrels there had been, she admitted there were 'several minor ones'. More damningly, she revealed that her stepfather had been forcing his attentions on her since she was fifteen years old, and continued to do so up to the time of her mother's illness. As she feared his outbursts of temper, she did not tell her mother.

Three of the female neighbours at Tregonissey who had helped to nurse Annie Black appeared in the witness box. Ann Best told the court that the dead woman had repeatedly complained of a burning sensation after taking the medicine from her husband, while Blanche Chesterfield and Mary Smith both said that Edward Black repeated a statement from Dr Andrew that the valves of his wife's heart had gone, and she was not expected to live very long.

Alfred Chubb, a clayworker and friend of Black, said that he was sitting up one night with him during his wife's illness, when the prisoner poured out a dose of medicine and took it upstairs. His wife said she could not take any more of the medicine, even if she was to die that moment. Mr Black replied that he would go downstairs and get a second dose. 'What did you understand by that?' asked the judge. 'I understood he was really forcing it on her,' was the answer. Immediately after she had taken the medicine she began to vomit. The prisoner took her another dose less than two hours later, but she objected again to having to take it, and continued to be sick nearly all night.

Joseph Kelly referred in detail to Black's letter, which he had received from Southport in November. It said it would be 'the last letter I shall ever write in this world,' that he was heartbroken and 'could not stand it any longer', and that he was 'going to Annie, God bless her!' Later it went on to say that he could not understand why Dr Andrew did not tell the others about the state of Annie's heart as he had told it to him:

Ask him to be a man and not a cad. What does he mean by suggesting arsenic? By God, Joe, you know me better than that, and I admit I made the biggest mistake of my life when I came away. What made me do it I can't say. But we all make mistakes, old friend, and I am going to pay a big price for mine.

In summing up, Mr Justice Rowlatt affirmed that the prosecution had proved that the deceased woman died of arsenic poisoning; that the prisoner had bought some just before she died; and that while she was ill, he was the main person in attendance on her, and was the one giving her medicine. Yet there was no evidence of motive, and the only one suggested was that Mr Black might have wanted to get rid of his wife, who was considerably the senior partner in age. It was true that his behaviour all through the illness was that of a devoted man faithfully attending his wife, but that would be consistent with the argument that he wanted to keep up the appearance that his wife was dying from gastritis.

After being out for forty minutes, the jury returned a verdict of guilty. As for the other charges of fraud in connection with the insurance policies, they were allowed to remain on the files of the court. Black was sentenced to death.

The trial had attracted such interest that over a thousand people were standing outside the Court to hear the news and watch the closed cab in which the prisoner was escorted to the railway station and taken to Mutley Prison, Plymouth, en route to Exeter Gaol. Bodmin Gaol was about to be closed by the Prison Commissioners, and was not admitting any new prisoners, much to the judge's irritation. He had to ask Mr Wood, governor of Mutley Prison, why it was necessary for the prisoner to have to return to Plymouth each night during the trial. It was 'perfectly monstrous', said Mr Justice Rowlatt, and as a result of his intervention, the Home Office agreed to open a cell at Bodmin for Black on a temporary basis.

Nevertheless it was to Exeter that he returned under sentence of death. He took the case to the Court of Criminal Appeal, who considered the evidence on 6 March, but Mr Justice Avory dismissed the appeal. Edward Black was hanged at Exeter by John Ellis and Seth Mills on 24 March 1922.

Some fifty years later, crime historian Colin Wilson suggested that Black was a 'killer who owed his conviction to loss of nerve'. Whether he was guilty or not, Wilson argued, he should have been acquitted. His wife died three days after he had left home for the last time, and she might have done so at her own hand 'in despair at his desertion'. Had it not been for his folly in denying the purchase of arsenic and then declaring that 'his' signature was a forgery, he might have escaped the gallows.

5
'BE A TRUMP, TAKE AND DO IT'

Titson, Marhamchurch, 1928

Richard Francis Roadley was an enigma. He lived in a squalid cottage in the small hamlet of Titson, near Marhamchurch, and was practically a recluse. The eighty-four-year-old bachelor was a woman-hater, and would not even allow one into his home. He was also deeply suspicious of strangers, and the only people with whom he willingly interacted were the local children. He was a retired farmer, although in name only. When farming he had not managed his land at all well and, although he purported to love horses, they had been allowed to run wild about his farm. He had sold up during the war, when landowners were forced to grow crops to support the war effort, retiring to a small cottage which soon fell into rack and ruin.

His only hobbies seemed to be reading, particularly engineering books, and attending local auctions where he regularly purchased all manner of junk on the

Marhamchurch village.

premise that it might just come in useful one day. The interior of his cottage reflected his preoccupation with acquiring seemingly useless objects, its rooms piled floor to ceiling with clutter, so much so that the stairs were used as a series of shelves on which his possessions were precariously stacked.

To all intents and purposes, he was a dirty, rather eccentric old man, who kept himself pretty much to himself and shunned contact with the world outside his decrepit home. However, all was not as it seemed. After the death of his brother in 1927, he had become Lord of the Manor at Scotter, near Gainsborough, Lincolnshire, and was in fact very wealthy. He was known to give generously to charities and was even rumoured to support financially a children's home in the Midlands. Though he shied away from contact with the villagers near his home, he accommodated many deserving requests for financial assistance and was also in the habit of buying sweets for the local children. When one family from the village were unable to send their children on a Sunday school picnic because they did not have sufficiently respectable clothes, Roadley treated the children to cakes to make up for their disappointment. On the occasions when he ventured into nearby Holsworthy to shop, he would regularly withdraw the sum of £50 from his bank account.

On Saturday 18 February 1928, he purchased some eggs from his neighbour, paying with a shilling, which he took from a purse that, the neighbour noticed, contained more silver coins. He was not seen again until Sunday when, at lunchtime, a little girl noticed that his blinds were still drawn closed. She mentioned this to Mr Hicks, Roadley's neighbour, and Hicks went to investigate.

Finding the front door of the cottage unlocked, Hicks pushed it open and heard the sound of heavy breathing. Tracing the source of the noise, he spotted Roadley's feet under a chair and when he raised the blinds to allow more light into the room, he found the old man lying on the floor, his head and shoulders tightly wrapped in a blanket. Removing the blanket revealed a large pool of blood and a wound to Roadley's forehead, oval in shape, measuring approximately 2×1½ inches. A doctor was immediately summoned and he confirmed that the injury had not been caused by a fall, but that the victim had been struck with a blunt object.

Roadley died from his injuries later that evening and the local police immediately called for the assistance of Scotland Yard in finding his attacker. Over the next few days, his cottage was subjected to a thorough search, a procedure no doubt hampered by the filthy and cluttered conditions. The police found several clues; from the soft mud outside the cottage door, they were able to obtain casts of footprints. Inside the house, the bedroom window had been obscured by bedding, presumably by the intruder to prevent lights being noticed from outside. They recovered several trunks from the cottage, the sides of which had been slit with a knife to gain access to their contents. There were also reports of a strange car, possibly a Morris, being observed in Titson shortly before the murder.

The police worked tirelessly, day and night, to secure an arrest, checking local lodging houses and workhouses and questioning anyone within a twenty-mile radius who was unable to account for their movements at the critical time. Over the next few days, two men were separately detained, one from Cardiff and the other from North Wales, and brought back to the police court at Stratton for questioning. Both were released without charge.

Then police stumbled across a clue that led them to William John Maynard, who was promptly called in for questioning. Maynard, a thirty-six-year-old rabbit trapper, lived in the nearby hamlet of Poundstock with his wife and son. He was taken to Stratton and, being unable to satisfactorily account for his whereabouts on the night of the murder, was detained at the police station while further enquiries were made. Meanwhile, officers conducted a thorough search of his home, outhouses and land, paying particular attention to the stream that ran along the bottom of a field in front of the house. Maynard's brother-in-law was forced to look on disconsolately as his recently planted potatoes and vegetables were dug up by the police and handed to him one by one.

Despite their thoroughness, the police located nothing of interest apart from an 18in adder in a hedge bottom, which was quickly killed. It was therefore decided to return Maynard to his smallholding to assist with the search. The rabbit trapper was brought home, but as he was leaving the police car heading for the fields, he dramatically collapsed and was immediately carried back to the car and driven back to Stratton. The journey was not without incident, since the police car suffered a burst tyre on the way.

Although he was examined by a doctor and pronounced fit, Maynard presented a pitiful sight. He spent his time in custody lying moaning on a rug on the floor, refusing to participate in the proceedings, even when he was charged with Roadley's murder. Seemingly incapable of answering any of the questions put to him, he was simply covered with rugs and left to his own devices. Brought before magistrates a few days later, he was still in a state of collapse, hence rather than transporting the prisoner to the courthouse, the magistrates went to the police station to conduct their hearing.

Dr Harold Holtby examined the prisoner a few minutes before the start of proceedings, and gave his opinion that the accused was able to appreciate and understand what was happening. Still, as the session began, Maynard continued to lie on a mattress on the floor, covered with a blanket, his eyes remaining tightly closed.

Hauled upright to hear the reading of the charges against him, he made no response and was gently returned to his mattress. Shortly afterwards, Maynard's father and wife visited the police station. The prisoner was told that they were there and asked if he wanted to see them – again, he gave no reply.

Having been remanded in custody, Maynard was taken to Exeter Prison by car that afternoon. Before the journey, he managed to compose himself somewhat; he got up, washed and drank a cup of tea, but refused food. He also requested a blanket to cover his head while walking to the car, which he was given.

By 7 March, when he was brought before the magistrates again, Maynard had adopted a very different attitude. He was calmer, replying promptly and in the affirmative to the only question he was asked, which was whether he understood the proceedings. Before being returned to Exeter, he was allowed to see his father, brother and brother-in-law. The case was adjourned until 15 March when he again appeared at Stratton Police Court. By now, the accused was much stronger and steadier, sitting quietly in the dock occasionally stroking his chin and smiling at remarks made by his counsel.

Counsel for the prosecution, Mr Sefton-Cohen, first outlined the circumstances of Richard Roadley's murder, explaining how his body had been discovered, then went on to discuss Maynard's first statement to the police. Asked to account for his whereabouts on the night of the murder, Maynard had stated that he had eaten his tea at about 5.30 p.m. then loaded his gun, with the intention of shooting a pigeon for his Sunday dinner. By dusk, he had still not managed to bag a pigeon, so had gone to his outhouse to overhaul his gin traps in preparation for his work on Monday. From the outhouse, he went back into his home at about 9 p.m. where he found his wife in the company of a visitor, Bert Yeo. However, in a written statement, made the same evening and signed by Maynard, he seemed doubtful as to whether Yeo was actually visiting or not. Maynard's wife told a contradicting story in which she said that her husband had not been home at all on the Saturday evening. Her statement was given while Maynard was actually present in the same room and standing around 4ft away.

According to Maynard, he and his wife retired to bed around ten minutes after he had come indoors from his outhouse. Their lodger, Harold Knight, had returned home later, although Maynard had not heard him come in. On the following morning, Maynard said that he had gone to visit his father, from whom he collected a batch of papers, before returning home at between 11.30 a.m. and noon. He had spent the rest of Sunday at home where he had listened to some gramophone records.

After making his statement, Maynard was detained while the police officers tried to verify his account of his movements. However, on the following day, while still in police custody, he asked to make another statement, which was taken by Chief Inspector Prothero.

In this subsequent statement, Maynard alleged that he had arranged to meet a man named Thomas Harris in order to accompany him to Titson to try and get some money. Harris, he said, had planned the robbery some time ago and Maynard had been included in the plan. Maynard had waited outside Roadley's cottage while

Harris had gone in, intending just to cover the old man with a blanket. A scuffle developed and Harris came out to tell Maynard that he had hit Richard Roadley. At this, Maynard had entered the house, finding Roadley lying on the floor of the front room. He had picked up a rug and thrown it over the old man's head before leaving the house again to keep watch.

Harris, said Maynard, had been in the house for almost three-quarters of an hour before he came out and the two walked home together across the fields. Harris had given Maynard two gold watches and a handful of silver coins, and had also returned the hammer with which Maynard had armed himself earlier that evening and which had inflicted the fatal wound on Roadley.

Early the following morning, Maynard had picked up his bloodstained boots and cap and the two gold watches. On the way to visit his father, he had thrown the boots into the stream, stuffed his cap in a rabbit hole and buried the two watches in a tin near the entrance to his father's home. He had kept the silver coins, amounting to around thirty shillings in his pockets. The hammer was later hidden in a neighbour's field.

Maynard stated that he had met Harris by chance during the following week when he had gone to Wainhouse Corner to buy groceries. Harris had told him that he had buried the money and hidden some silver. Harris' last words to him as they parted were, according to Maynard, 'For God's sake, don't split!'

Harris, a local chimney sweep aged fifty-six, did have a criminal record, having been convicted of stealing rabbits and fowls on several occasions. As a young man, he had also been charged with unlawful wounding, but later acquitted. Fortunately for him, he had been visiting a family called Hicks at their home in the nearby village of Jacobstow and had an unshakeable alibi for the time of the murder. When interviewed by the police, he maintained that it was Maynard who had planned the robbery and, more than once, tried to persuade him to act as his accomplice. Having known Richard Roadley all his life, Harris had declined.

Maynard, it was discovered, had asked Bert Yeo to provide him with a false alibi. Yeo and his wife and children had visited Mrs Maynard at home on the night of the murder, but had left at about twenty-five minutes to nine, not having seen Maynard. Some days later, Maynard had approached Bert as he was spreading manure in his employer's field, telling him that the police were asking questions and, if asked, he should say that Maynard had been at home at about 8 p.m., then gone out to get some 'baccy'. At first, Yeo had refused to tell a lie, worried that he might get himself into 'hot water', but Maynard had persisted, saying, 'Be a trump, take and do it – they will never find out.' Eventually, Yeo had reluctantly agreed and initially told the police the story that Maynard had concocted, but later retracted his statement.

John Marsh, a labourer employed by Maynard to trap rabbits, told the magistrates that, prior to the murder, he had not been paid his wages as his boss had claimed to be short of money. Immediately after the murder, Maynard had paid him in cash, drawing a handful of silver from his pocket and, a couple of days later, had handed him yet more money, which he asked him to pass on to another creditor.

Perhaps the most damning evidence of all was the fact that an apparently bloodstained cap, positively identified by Marsh as belonging to Maynard, had indeed been found stuffed in a rabbit hole, exactly where he admitted to placing it in his third statement. At this stage, the hearing was adjourned until 17 April to allow the police more time to complete their investigations.

When the hearing resumed, one of the first testimonies heard was that of Dr Roche Lynch. The senior official analyst for the Home Office had been asked by police to examine three hammers, one of which had been found in the outer hall of Roadley's cottage. In addition, he had also tested a sand stone, a pocketknife, a torch and several items of clothing belonging to the defendant. He was able to state that, of the three hammers examined, one bore traces of human blood and the second and third had 'suggestions' of blood, although in insufficient amounts to allow for reliable testing as to its origin. Human blood was also found on the torch, a jacket, a waistcoat and the cap.

Even though a witness had mentioned that Maynard had cut his hand badly on a rabbit trap shortly before the murder, Lynch discounted suggestions that the bloodstains may have resulted from the defendant cutting himself, since those on the jacket in particular were too widely spread. He also denied that the stains could possibly be rabbit's blood, having specifically carried out tests to eliminate that possibility. Besides, Dr Holtby, who had examined Maynard while he was in custody, had noticed no recent cuts on his hands that might have explained the amount of blood on his jacket and other effects.

Two bank managers also gave evidence before the magistrates. The manager of the bank at Bude testified that Maynard's account was in credit at the time of the murder, but his counterpart at a bank in Holsworthy had recently written to Maynard, concerned that his account was overdrawn by £238. Maynard's critical financial situation was thought to be sufficient motive for him to commit the robbery but, shortly after the murder, he had paid £40 cash into his Holsworthy bank account, an amount that had appeased his bank manager for the time being.

The hearing was resumed the following day, this time opening with evidence given by Inspector Pill. While Pill was being cross-examined, Maynard tried several times to interrupt him, asking if he might speak. Eventually, becoming more and more agitated, Maynard broke in, asking Pill to look him in the face and say he had told the truth.

Other police officers gave evidence throughout the day, and there were particularly searching questions asked about Maynard's medical state following his collapse when taken to assist in the search. The police asserted that a doctor had been called because they were anxious to do nothing that might have been deemed unfair to the prisoner. However, when the doctor had dismissed Maynard's condition as being 'bunkum and cowardice', they had charged him with the murder. The defence suggested that Maynard, a small man, had been bullied and harangued into giving a confession.

Finally, there appeared to be some confusion about the murder weapon. The hammer found at Roadley's cottage was the only one of three tested to show positive evidence of staining with human blood. Yet, due to the shape of Roadley's wounds, it was not thought that this was the hammer that inflicted his injuries. The hammer used in the murder was believed to be one to which Maynard had subsequently directed the police, found in a field opposite his home. This bore suggestions of blood staining but in insufficient quantities for reliable testing to determine whether or not it was human or animal blood. It had, however, been used for legitimate purposes for some time after the murder, before being hidden in long grass and police were of the opinion that this may have destroyed any significant traces of blood.

Once all the evidence had been presented, the magistrates consulted together before the chairman announced that, in their opinion, there was a *prima facie* case and that Maynard should stand trial for the murder of Richard Roadley. The accused was then returned to Exeter Prison where he was held in custody pending the start of his trial, to be held at Bodmin Assizes on 1 June.

When the trial opened, Maynard pleaded not guilty to the crime. Although he seemed calm in the dock, after a break for lunch, a message was sent up to the court that the defendant was 'indisposed'. He had suffered an acute attack of hysteria and the proceedings were delayed for a few hours to allow him to recover.

In the witness box, Maynard argued that he was always a little inconsistent in paying wages to Marsh, his employee. Sometimes he was late in paying him; sometimes he paid Marsh for his work in advance. The money that Marsh had been paid after the murder, including that which he had been asked to pass on to another debtor was Maynard's own money and not the proceeds of murder. 28s had come from the sale of seven hens at 4s each and another 27s 6d had been a payment for eggs, received on the day before the murder took place.

The defendant testified that he had cut his thumb in a rabbit trap and that the wound had bled copiously, accounting for the bloodstains on his clothing and on the hammer, which he agreed belonged to him. He admitted asking Yeo to provide a false alibi, saying that he was worried as he could not account for his movements at the crucial time.

With regard to the incriminating statement made to Prothero, Maynard testified that the two Scotland Yard policemen had 'called him all the blackguards they could lay their hands on.' He admitted signing his first written statement, but maintained that the police had held his hands and forced them to make an approximation of his own signature on the subsequent statement taken by Prothero. At this point Mr Goddard, Counsel for the Prosecution, asked incredulously, 'You say they were holding your hands and made you sign?' to which Maynard replied, 'I got to, or be half killed, my lord.' Much the same evidence was presented at trial as at the hearing, but this time the defence seemed better prepared to argue their case. They contended that the third statement, in which he admitted his guilt, had not been made by Maynard but had been compiled by the police, who had then forced Maynard to sign it.

They questioned the relevance of the testimony of Maynard's two bank managers on the subject of his financial affairs. While accepting that he was heavily overdrawn at one bank, they pointed out that he owned his home, outbuildings and also a considerable number of cows and poultry. The value of his property and stock far outweighed the sum of his overdraft and, it was argued, removed money as a credible motive for robbery and murder.

The defence counsel emphasised the prior criminal record of Thomas Harris, and the court was asked why they should believe a man with a history of crime over Maynard, who had no previous convictions. Finally, they maintained that Roadley's death had not been murder at all, but had occurred because of a tragic accident. The deceased, they claimed, could easily have sustained his fatal wound by falling and striking his head.

In summing up the proceedings for the jury Mr Justice Swift maintained that, in the murder of Richard Roadley, there was no question of manslaughter, provocation or self-defence. In short, the hand that held the hammer was responsible for the death of the old man. It took the jury just forty-five minutes to decide that it was Maynard's hand. Asked if he wished to say anything, the prisoner quietly stated 'I am not guilty, my lord', leaving the judge to don the traditional square of black silk before sentencing him to death by hanging.

Maynard appealed against his conviction on the grounds that it was based on what were referred to as 'inaccuracies' in the judge's summary regarding the identification by Marsh of Maynard's cap. The appeal was heard by the Court of Criminal Appeal comprising the Lord Chief Justice (Lord Hewart), Mr Justice Salter and Mr Justice Acton.

Mr Batt, counsel for the defendant, maintained that Marsh had never sworn to the identity of the cap, and that this was a very important point of misdirection by the judge. He also queried the admissibility of the evidence from the two bank managers. When the murder took place, Maynard's finances were in a better state than they had been for a long time and he was under no pressure from the manager of the Holsworthy bank to settle his overdraft. His bungalow was worth between £600 and £700, he owned three cows, fifty or sixty hens and several hundred rabbit traps and did not consider himself hard up. He therefore had no real motive for committing the robbery. Besides, stated Batt, investigation of the crime scene had revealed a wallet still laying in plain view at Roadley's cottage, in the very room where the old man was found. The wallet contained £11 10s in notes and, if the motive for the murder had indeed been money, it was curious that the prisoner had not taken it, if he had actually been in the cottage.

Finally Batt questioned the police handling of their suspect. He argued that Chief Inspector Prothero of Scotland Yard had persuaded Maynard to be interviewed at Stratton police station. Until that moment, there was not one shred of evidence to connect him to the murder. Maynard had attended the police station voluntarily – then, after twenty-four hours in custody, without sleep, he allegedly asked to make another statement. Prothero and a second Scotland Yard officer had been alone with Maynard when that statement was taken. According to Batt, local police officers had been deliberately excluded from the room. Even though Maynard could read and write, the statement, which eventually covered nearly three pages of foolscap paper, was not in the prisoner's handwriting, and it had clearly been edited. The whole statement, Batt contended, was a result of bullying and intimidation of the suspect by the police.

The Lord Chief Justice admitted that Mr Justice Swift had made an error in his original summing up of the case with regard to the evidence concerning ownership of the cap. However, he described the mistake as being 'of the most immaterial character when regard was paid to all the circumstances of the case'. Thus, Maynard's appeal was dismissed.

He was executed by Thomas Pierrepoint at Exeter Gaol on 27 July 1928. According to the *Post* on the following day, 'There was no incident out of the ordinary and, had it not been for the fact that police officials were posted at the various entrances to the prison, one would scarcely have realised that such a gruesome drama was being enacted inside'. Yet despite this assertion, the paper went on to comment on a remarkable feature of the execution – the 'great number of crows' that perched on the prison roof at the exact time at which Maynard paid the death penalty.

6
'THEY WILL BLAME ONE OF US'

Lewannick, 1930

In 1921 two sisters, Sarah Ann Hearn, known as Annie, and Lydia Everard, known as Minnie, moved from the Midlands to the small hamlet of Lewannick, near Launceston, to look after their ageing aunt. When she died in 1926, the aunt left everything to Annie, 'in appreciation of her devoted nursing'. However 'everything' was little more than her home, Trenhorne House, so although the women had a secure roof over their heads, they had no income.

For almost four years, the two sisters lived together in the house until Minnie fell ill. Once again, Annie's nursing skills were in demand, but by this time she had made firm friends with the married couple who lived less than 200yds away at Trenhorne Farm. Throughout Minnie's illness, William Thomas was a regular visitor, dropping off newspapers and bringing custards and junkets baked by his wife, Alice, to tempt the invalid. At one time, when the two sisters were in even more dire financial straits than usual, William even lent them £28, which was a substantial amount of money in the 1920s.

After years of suffering from gastric complaints Minnie died in 1930, leaving Annie, then in her forties, living alone. William and Alice Thomas remained friendly and supportive, often including Annie in outings and picnics. In October 1930, William's mother had been staying at the farm and needed to be driven back to her home near Bude on the north coast. Annie was invited along for the ride. She was delighted by the prospect and happily joined the Thomas's in their car, leaving Lewannick at 3 p.m. It was a very typical outing; after dropping off William's mother, the party parked their car in Bude. William went to get his hair cut, while both women walked around the shops. At 5 p.m. the three met in Littlejohn's tea rooms where William ordered tea, cakes and bread and butter. Annie had made her own contribution to the

The Strand, Bude, with the Globe Hotel on the right and Littlejohn's tea rooms (with white sun blinds) roughly in the centre of the picture, c. 1930. (Adrian and Jill Abbott)

meal, producing from her bag some tinned salmon sandwiches and chocolate cake, and these were shared between them.

After tea they parted company again, with William making his way alone to the Globe Hotel. There he complained of nausea, but after a shot of whisky he felt much better. His wife was not so fortunate. When all three met up again, she complained of having a sickly-sweet taste in her mouth and asked if there was a fruit shop nearby. William found one and bought her some bananas.

On the drive home Alice began to feel terribly ill. William had to break the journey several times for her to be sick at the roadside, and when he kept a pre-arranged business appointment near Launceston, he returned to the car to find her in the public toilets vomiting again. As soon as they arrived home, Alice was helped to her bed and the doctor sent for. When he examined her, Dr Saunders found she was suffering pain in the stomach, coupled with a racing pulse and cramp in the legs. Hearing that she had eaten tinned salmon that afternoon, he immediately suspected food poisoning. Fortunately Alice was on hand to help and, once again, volunteered her nursing skills. She stayed at the farm for several days, cooking for William and caring for his bedridden wife.

Alice was expected to recover from her bout of food poisoning without any complications, but instead her condition gradually worsened. Some days, she would seem better, only to relapse the following day. Soon she was complaining of a tingling sensation in her hands and feet and of having no control over her limbs. When the doctor noticed she had developed cold sores on her lips and chest, he suggested that she should go into hospital, but she resisted the idea. In desperation William sent for her mother, Tryphena Parsons, who promptly arrived to help Annie with the cooking and nursing.

Despite their best efforts, Alice continued to deteriorate. At the beginning of November she rallied sufficiently to eat some mutton, potatoes, vegetables and a sweet cooked by Annie, but after eating, complained of the lingering sweet taste in her mouth. In an effort to rid herself of this sickly taste, she asked for lemon juice, which was served to her by Annie, but soon afterwards she began vomiting again and suffering from nosebleeds. On 1 November she became delirious, and her doctor was so concerned by her condition that he summoned a specialist from Plymouth City Hospital for a second opinion. Dr William Lister diagnosed arsenical poisoning and Alice was rushed into hospital, where she died three days later, aged forty-three.

William, who had been at his wife's bedside, returned home to Trenhorne Farm. There, according to Annie, he all but accused her of murdering his wife, saying, 'They will blame one of us and the blame will fall heavier on you than on me.' William was later to deny saying this, claiming to have little recollection of any conversation. He did recall asking Annie for a written IOU for the £28 she still owed him.

At a post-mortem, it was found that Alice's organs contained a residue of 0.85 grains of arsenic, consistent with her having consumed around ten grains. Since a dose of between two and four grains is normally fatal, her death certificate was issued citing the cause of death as 'Arsenical poisoning due to homicide' and also stating 'but there is not sufficient evidence to show by whom or by what means the arsenic was administered'.

Annie had an uncomfortable time at Alice's funeral. She felt that the other mourners were looking at her with suspicion, particularly Alice's brother, Percy Parsons. The latter asked about the food that his sister had eaten on her trip to Bude and, when Annie mentioned that she had provided sandwiches, informed her that the matter 'would have to be looked into'. When the funeral party returned to the farm for refreshments, Annie soon made her excuses and left.

On 10 November, William received a letter from Annie, which read:

Dear Mr Thomas,
Goodbye. I am going out if I can. I cannot forget that awful man [Parsons] and the things he said. I am innocent, innocent [sic], but she is dead and it was my lunch she ate. I cannot stay. When I am dead, they will be sure I am guilty and you, at least, will be clear. May your dear wife's presence guard and comfort you still.
                                                                    Yours, A.H.

In a postscript, Annie complained that her life was nothing without Minnie. She asked that her love be given to Bessie (another sister) and begged them not to worry about her, writing; 'I am all right. My conscience is clear. I am not afraid of afterwards.' Finally, she gave instructions that her goods should be sold and her debt to Thomas paid from the proceeds.

William took the letter straight to the police who arrived at Trenhorne House, to find it locked and empty. They soon discovered that Annie had taken a taxi to Looe, and a few days later her coat and hat were found there on a cliff top. It looked as though she might have committed suicide by flinging herself over the cliff into the sea, but there was no trace of her body on the shore below, apart from a solitary shoe that was washed up on the beach.

Meanwhile, in Torquay a 'Mrs Ferguson' booked a room at a hotel, staying for one night and leaving early the following morning. She did not go far. Calling herself

Alice Thomas's grave,
St Martin's Church,
Lewannick. (© Nicola Sly)

'Mrs Faithful', she took lodgings in Torquay, later applying for a job as a live-in housekeeper to a local architect, Cecil Powell. Seduced by Mrs Faithful's excellent but fake references, Mr Powell hired her and, it seems, was highly satisfied with her work.

When Alice Thomas's inquest was opened on 24 November her husband was questioned about her death. William stated that, aside from the sheep dip and worming concoctions that any farmer might reasonably be expected to own, he possessed no poisons and certainly no arsenic. He also maintained that his wife had never objected to his friendship with Annie – and why should she, since he had never given her any reason to be jealous? Damningly, a member of staff at Shuker and Reed, a Launceston grocer and chemist shop, testified that he had sold an arsenic-based weedkiller to Annie Hearn in August 1928. The signature against a 1lb tin of Cooper's Powder in the shop's poisons book matched that of Mrs Hearn. Searches of poison registers in chemist's shops at nearby Stratton, Holsworthy, Liskeard and Camelford produced no sales of poison that could be directly tied to either Hearn, William Thomas or any members of the Parsons family, although Shuker and Reed's register did reveal a sale to a Mrs Uglow some eight years previously. Mrs Uglow was a sister to Mrs Thomas, and it was Mrs Thomas herself who had introduced Mrs Uglow as a purchaser at the chemist's shop. A thorough search of Trenhorne House, conducted on 20 November, had revealed no arsenic in any form.

On 26 November the inquest returned a verdict of murder by arsenical poisoning by person or persons unknown. This was enough for police to initiate a search for the missing Annie, issuing a wanted poster that described her as 5ft 3in tall, brown haired and grey eyed, with a sallow complexion. It mentioned that she walked briskly, holding her head slightly to the left, that she was well-spoken and had rather a reserved manner.

It was also sufficient cause for the police to exhume the bodies of Annie's sister Minnie and her Aunt Mary. Both bodies were found to contain arsenic, with Minnie's containing considerably more residue than that of Mary.

The possible poisonings in Cornwall were fast becoming national news and the *Daily Mail* offered a £500 reward for anyone finding the elusive Annie Hearn. Quite by chance, Mr Powell was a *Daily Mail* reader and he was also beginning to harbour suspicions about his housekeeper, 'Mrs Faithful'. He had noticed that a coat that she bought from a mail order firm had arrived addressed to a 'Mrs Dennis'. Moreover, his copies of the *Daily Mail* were being tampered with before he got to read them each morning, as someone was carefully removing all reports relating to the missing Annie Hearn.

Mr Powell alerted the police, and on 12 January 1931 Annie Hearn was detained on her way to an errand. At first she continued to protest that her name was Mrs Dennis but she eventually admitted her true identity when confronted by a police sergeant from Lewannick, Sergeant Trebilcock, who immediately recognised her. She appeared very cool and positively talkative. Superintendent William Pill took a statement from her, and almost immediately her words resulted in some confusion. Sergeant Trebilcock claimed that Annie said 'Mr Thomas used to come to our house every day with a paper. Of course, that was only a blind.' Pill and another officer present at the time did not hear her say this, and Annie later claimed that she had actually said; 'Mr Thomas used to bring a paper. He was very kind.' When describing the trip to Bude, she stated that on previous outings with William and Alice, they had always taken lunch with them. On the day she was invited to accompany them, she had cut some salmon sandwiches and chocolate cake, which she placed on the table at the café. Mrs Thomas had taken the first sandwich, Annie herself the second and Mr Thomas the third.

As for her argument with Alice's brother, Mr Parsons, at Alice's funeral, Annie said it had not really been a row. He had asked some searching questions about the sandwiches, leading her to believe that people suspected her of poisoning Alice. Thinking that either she or William was about to be charged with murder, Annie had fled, taking a taxi to Looe with the intention of killing herself on arrival. Her nerve failed her and she was unable to go through with her suicide.

Finally, Annie addressed the concerns about the roast mutton served to Alice shortly before her admission to hospital, stating that while she had cooked the meat, she had neither carved Alice's portion, nor helped with the gravy or other accompaniments to the meal.

Annie appeared on remand before Launceston magistrates no less than fourteen times. Initially charged only with the murder of Alice Thomas, on 24 February she was also charged with that of her sister, Lydia (Minnie) Everard. Minnie was described as an invalid, having previously suffered a nervous breakdown and with a long history of stomach troubles that had been variously diagnosed as chronic dyspepsia, bowel trouble, gastric ulcer, colitis and gastric catarrh. The most persistent of her symptoms was an inability to digest food. To aid digestion she was prescribed a mixture of bismuth, aromatics and pepsine, but by 19 April 1930, Minnie was complaining that the medicine was giving her pain. Her doctor Dr Gibson was surprised to hear this, but nevertheless gave her a check up, at which he noted that her heart sounded 'a little feeble'. He issued a new prescription for 'a soothing bowel mixture', but within a fortnight noted that his patient's condition had worsened and she was now vomiting.

Dr Gibson and his colleague Dr Galbraith continued to visit Minnie on a regular basis. By 4 July Dr Gibson observed that she had lost weight and was now complaining of rheumatic pains in her arms in addition to her usual digestion problems. At this time he checked Minnie for any signs of cancer, but his examinations did not reveal any malignancy. Two weeks later, Minnie was feeble and emaciated and seemed to the doctor to be only semi-conscious. She was so weak that she was unable to turn over in bed without assistance. The doctor believed that Minnie was slowly starving to death and made his concerns known to Annie. Her condition continued to worsen, until by 21 July she was barely able to speak and obviously in great pain. She died that night and Dr Gibson signed the death certificate, giving the cause of death as 'chronic gastric catarrh and colitis'. He described Annie Hearn as 'a good nurse and a devoted sister'.

Dr Roche Lynch, the Home Office analyst, testified for an entire day at Annie's hearing before the magistrates at Launceston. He explained that arsenic poisoning could be divided into three types – acute, sub-acute and chronic. Acute poisoning was normally but not always characterised by a swift death, usually within thirty-six hours of ingesting the arsenic, either through heart failure, poisoning of the heart muscle or by dehydration caused by persistent vomiting and diarrhoea. It could take two forms, either presenting with similar symptoms to gastro-enteritis or in narcotic form, which gave only transient nausea and vomiting before unconsciousness. Sub-acute poisoning could result from either one dose of arsenic or several doses given over a period of time. It began with symptoms of gastro-enteritis. The condition of the victim might appear to improve temporarily, before deteriorating into restlessness and neuritis, and culminating in unconsciousness and death. Chronic poisoning, on the other hand, gave rise to a variety of symptoms including digestive catarrh, disordered sensation and paralysis, with inflammation of the mouth, nasal passages and eyes. This would be accompanied by strange tingling sensations, almost as if the victim had ants crawling on their skin. Eventually the victim would experience a loss of power to the limbs with muscle pain and wasting. He was of the opinion that an initial dose of several grains of arsenic was administered to Mrs Thomas at around 5 p.m. on the day of the outing to Bude, and that her resulting symptoms were consistent with sub-acute arsenical poisoning.

As far as Minnie was concerned, Lynch felt that she had been administered regular small doses of arsenic over a longer period of time, possibly around seven months. He confirmed this by testing a length of her hair and showing that it contained arsenic throughout its length. Knowing the rate at which human hair grows, he was able to establish a time period over which Minnie had, in his opinion, been slowly poisoned. She was, according to Dr Lynch, a textbook case of chronic poisoning.

Once all the evidence had been heard, the magistrates retired to debate their decision. After only fourteen minutes' discussion, they returned to commit Annie Hearn to Bodmin Assizes for both offences.

The trial opened at Bodmin on 15 June 1931, with the defendant pleading not guilty to the murders of Alice Thomas and her sister, Lydia Everard. She was defended by Norman Birkett KC, assisted by Mr Dingle Foot, a future Liberal and then Labour MP. Cecil Powell paid for the expensive services of these gentlemen, generously donating the £500 reward he had received for being instrumental in Annie's capture.

The prosecution relied largely on the expert testimony of Dr Lynch. He testified that Alice Thomas had died from arsenic poisoning and that, by examining her organs post-mortem, he had been able to calculate that she had ingested a dose of ten grains. Minnie also had large quantities of arsenic in her body.

The counsel for the defence instantly refuted these findings, pointing out that the soil at Lewannick contained high levels of arsenic. Although the exhumation of Minnie's body had been carried out in a snowstorm, just a tiny amount of local soil could have contaminated the specimens taken and accounted for the high results of the tests. The doctor who conducted the autopsy at the graveside was called, and was forced to admit that he had taken no precautions against contamination, and also that Minnie's organs had been left in open jars next to her grave for over an hour.

Having planted the idea of contamination firmly into the minds of the jury, the defence team then set out to discredit Dr Lynch. Under questioning, he admitted that he had never seen or treated an actual case of arsenic poisoning, but only read about it. He conceded that the base level of arsenic in the soil at Lewannick was unusually high and that he had not taken this into account when calculating the levels of arsenic in Minnie's body. The prosecution maintained that Lynch's calculations were fundamentally flawed, since he had analysed a portion of muscle from the dead woman. He had then assumed that muscle represented about 40 per cent of the human body, multiplying the amount of arsenic accordingly. Yet when Minnie died, her muscles had been severely wasted following her prolonged illness and would have accounted for only around 15 per cent of her total body weight.

The court heard testimony from the Launceston chemist who had stated at Alice's inquest that he had sold arsenic-based weedkiller to the defendant. The defence team did not dispute this, merely pointing out that this particular brand of pesticide was bright blue in colour. It was demonstrated in court that, had it been used in the sandwiches, it would have turned the bread bright blue too.

The defence called just one witness to the stand, Annie Hearn herself. Her calm demeanour as she maintained her innocence impressed itself on the jury. She vehemently denied poisoning either Alice or Minnie, admitting only to panicking and fleeing when she feared that she might be a suspect. It had been her intention to commit suicide, but she had eventually been too afraid to go through with it and had tried to start a new life in Torquay.

Mr H. du Parcq KC was left to sum up the case for the prosecution, even though he was clearly unwell and eventually fainted in the courtroom. He pointed out to the jury that both women had died from arsenic poisoning, both after having eaten food prepared by Annie. However, on the day of her panic-stricken flight to Looe, she had allegedly worn two coats, one on top of the other. To du Parcq, this clearly negated Annie's claims that she had intended to commit suicide, proving instead that she had been bent on duping people into believing that she was dead, leaving her free to make a new life for herself. And why, asked du Parcq, should an innocent woman flee in the first place, if not to avoid justice? Annie, he maintained, was a liar. She had lied about her intention to kill herself and, by inventing new names for herself in Torquay, had also lied about her identity. It was thus probable that she was also making false claims about her innocence.

For the defence, Birkett concentrated his closing arguments on undermining the testimony of the prosecution's expert witness. Having planted doubts in the minds of the jurors by referring to the high levels of arsenic in the Lewannick soil, he proceeded to labour the point, even though his contamination theory was not strictly true. While the arsenic levels in the soil were exceptionally high, they were not present in soluble form, so they would have been unlikely to affect the test results, even if contamination had occurred. He then tried to discredit Dr Lynch, the Crown's analyst who, he pointed out 'never attended a single person suffering from arsenical poisoning, yet he spoke of the symptoms with the same confidence that he spoke of other matters.'

Finally, Birkett asked the jury to consider the supposedly poisoned sandwiches. If a packet of sandwiches was placed on a table for three people to share, how was the poisoner supposed to ensure that the intended victim, Mrs Hearn, took the right sandwich, particularly as the bread would be bright blue?

After both sides had summed up their evidence, it was left for the judge, Mr Justice Roche, to address the jury. He quickly ruled that there was insufficient evidence in the case of the murder of Lydia Everard and instructed the jury to acquit Annie Hearn of that charge. They should focus instead on the murder of Alice Thomas, asking first if her death was due to arsenical poisoning and, if they decided that it was, did the defendant administer that poison?

Annie's guilt or innocence was dependent on whether the jury believed that she had administered arsenic to Mrs Thomas in the sandwiches eaten on the outing to Bude. If indeed the sandwiches had been laced with arsenic, then only two people could possibly have been responsible – Annie Hearn or William Thomas. The judge pointed out that it was up to the prosecution to satisfy the jury that the poisoner was not William Thomas, rather than the responsibility of the defence to satisfy them that it was. The jury deliberated for less than an hour before acquitting Annie Hearn of Alice Thomas' murder and were then instructed by the judge to acquit her of Minnie's murder as well. Within minutes Annie was a free woman again, vowing to settle her affairs in Cornwall, then never to set foot in the county again. However her innocence was not as clear-cut in the minds of the jury as their verdict suggested. One juror was allegedly heard to say later in a public house that the jury had believed that Annie and William Thomas had acted together in murdering Alice. They had found Annie not guilty, even though they felt that she had committed the murders, because they had not wanted to see her 'swing' on her own.

As there was insufficient evidence to link William Thomas to the deaths, he was never charged with the murder of his wife. Nobody but Annie was ever charged, and the murder remains unsolved.

The case has become something of an enigma in the annals of true crime. Was there ever more than friendship between Annie and William and, if so, was Alice Thomas the only obstacle that stood in the couple's way? If their relationship was, as both claimed, merely friendship, then what motive did either William or Annie have for murdering either Alice or Minnie? And, was Minnie murdered at all, or was her early death simply the consequence of a long-standing battle with illness? Was William in any way to blame for his wife's death? Or did Annie Hearn literally get away with murder?

7

MURDER ON CHRISTMAS EVE

Falmouth, 1942

When Albert James Bateman was in his mid-fifties he retired from his profession as an accountant and took over a tobacconist's shop at Commercial Chambers, Arwenack Street, Falmouth. As the site was close to the harbour and docks, business was generally brisk. Every weekday he opened punctually at 9 a.m. and always stayed open throughout the lunch hour, until 2.30 p.m. so the dockyard workers would be able to call in during their break. After this he returned home, to Winnots, Fox's Lane, for lunch, returning to the shop at 3.30 p.m., sometimes accompanied by his wife as an assistant. He usually closed at around 5.30 p.m., leaving the premises about twenty minutes later so he would be home to hear the 6 p.m. news on the radio at home.

In 1942 he was aged sixty-one but he had always kept himself in good health, remaining fit through his regime of daily exercise.

On Christmas Eve trade was good, as was to be expected before the festive break. He was too busy to go home for lunch, so his wife took him some sandwiches. As he did not return home at his usual time in the early evening, she assumed at first that he had been deluged with customers and might have stayed open late in order to avoid disappointing anyone. However, when there was no sign of him by 7.30 p.m. she was concerned that something had gone wrong. She went to the shop and found it closed, locked and unlit. Her husband, she decided and hoped, must have gone home by another route, so she went back – only to find he had still not arrived. She collected a set of duplicate keys and walked back to the shop, but still there was no sign of light or any activity. Getting more worried by the minute, she ran down the street to get help, and soon found two policemen, Sergeant Bennetts and Constable (War Reserve) Drummond.

They entered the shop together about 8.30 p.m., and found it in total darkness. Although blackout time was around 5.45 p.m. – about the time he normally left to come home – the curtains had not been drawn. Sergeant Bennetts switched on his torch, and at once they saw the body of Albert Bateman lying in a pool of blood around his head, on the floor behind the counter. He was fully clothed, wearing his overcoat, and his face had been badly battered. It was assumed that he had been attacked as he was about to lock up and leave. Dr Dudley Harris was summoned to examine the body, and confirmed that he had been dead for around two hours.

Across an inner passage from the shop was a tailor and outfitter where Phyllis Cooper worked as an assistant. She said that it had been part of Mr Bateman's usual

Arwenack Street, Falmouth.
(© Kim Van der Kiste)

The body of Alfred Bateman behind his shop counter. (© Devon & Cornwall Constabulary)

routine to come out of the shop, pick up the doormat from outside his front door and take it to a cupboard under the stairs, then bang the door to and leave it locked. He would then return to the shop, put on his overcoat, change his cap for a trilby hat and set out for home. On the night he was killed, she heard all these things happen as usual, and assumed that he had gone home. Unfortunately, on this occasion he must have been confronted by an intruder as he was about to leave.

Superintendent Thomas Morcumb, head of the Falmouth Police Division, was sent for, and he contacted the pathologist Dr Hocking. After a preliminary examination of the body they took it to the Falmouth public mortuary for the post-mortem. This revealed evidence of asphyxiation, with several injuries to the face and head. There were bruises on the point of the chin, and over the larynx or Adam's apple. The left cheek was heavily bruised, and the upper jawbone underneath had been fractured. The lips were split, as was the skin over the left eyelid. The skull had been fractured at the back, and there was a large associated bruise in the scalp, and mottled bruising of the brain. The upper and lower dentures were smashed into several fragments, two lying on the floor of the shop near the head, the others embedded in blood clots at the back of the mouth. A considerable quantity of blood had run down the air passages into the lungs, and these passages were completely obstructed.

Death had been caused by suffocation due to the inhalation of blood from injuries to the mouth and face while lying unconscious as a result of blows to the head, causing concussion. Two or more heavy blows had been struck on the face, one on the chin, the other on the left cheek. The fracture of the skull and damage to the brain might have been caused by Mr Bateman falling backwards after having been struck in the face, or possibly by contact with the wall or shelving behind him, as a result of blows to the face. It was also possible that some of the injury had been caused by stamping on the face, after falling. The blows could not have been self-inflicted, nor caused by any fall in the premises. There was no sign of any disturbance, and no sign of any blood on any object on to which the deceased might have accidentally fallen. The injuries and therefore death were due to assault. Temperature recordings confirmed that death had taken place at around 6 p.m. that evening.

An examination of the premises was carried out. The shop had not been ransacked, for £14 in notes was found on Mr Bateman, and almost £16 in silver and copper coins in an attaché case on a shelf behind a plywood screen. On the counter, in the till and various other places about seven shillings was recovered. Mrs Bateman said that at least £25 was missing. The crime, therefore, had probably been committed in the course of robbery, and the assailant must have known something of the habits of his intended victim, waiting until he disappeared into the back premises of his shop to lock up. He then ran into the shop, took what money was in the till, but as he tried to leave he was confronted by the tobacconist on his return from shutting up before he could get away.

Most significantly, on the counter was a bloodstained handkerchief, which Mrs Bateman recognised as having belonged to her husband. When taken for examination, it was proved that the blood on it was from his group, and it would appear that he had taken it out to staunch blood running from his face as a result of the first blow. Beside it was a 0.55 Mark II Webley revolver. At the request of Dr Harris he picked it up and broke it. All the chambers and the barrel were empty, and no expended cartridges were found nearby. Mrs Bateman said she had never seen it before. It had not been fired shortly before its discovery, as there was no lingering smell of cordite or gunpowder. It had been left behind by the assailant, who had entered the shop with it, probably in order to frighten and hold up the shopkeeper for money. Not finding him there he had put the weapon down, helped himself to what was in the till, then attacked the hapless shopkeeper who had just surprised him, and fled in panic – leaving the gun behind. It was packed up and taken to Scotland Yard to be examined for fingerprints, but none could be identified apart from those who had handled it since its discovery in the shop.

The gun, stamped with the number 33748, proved to be a crucial exhibit. On the outbreak of war in 1939 Falmouth Docks had been taken over by the Admiralty. The armed forces had commandeered some civilian equipment, including a 130-ton yacht *Ceto*, which had been converted into a compass calibrating vessel and thus become HM yacht *Ceto*. She was armed rather sparsely with three Lewis guns, four rifles, and a Webley service revolver – No. 33748.

Superintendent Morcumb recalled that some ten months earlier, a docks employee had reported the revolver as missing. All the arms had been removed from the *Ceto* to ammunition stores at the docks, lifted by crane and loaded into a Royal Naval covered truck just before dinnertime on 27 February 1942. The storehouseman reported that when he returned to the store at about 12.30 p.m. he saw that the weapons had

The Webley revolver, left behind in Albert Bateman's shop after he had been killed. (© Devon & Cornwall Constabulary)

been deposited in one particular store. He checked them, and noticed that although the canvas bag in which he had placed the weapon was still there, the revolver was missing. Several people who had been involved in the moving of weapons were interviewed, but without any results.

However one of the other dock labourers, Gordon Horace Trenoweth, who had unloaded the crane, had a police record after being sentenced for larceny in his youth. Aged thirty-three, he was married with five children. His wife had been in a mental institution since January 1941. When he found out that she was working there, as opposed to being a helpless patient unable to do anything for herself let alone for other people, he decided that she must be earning her keep and therefore refused to contribute anything towards her maintenance. For this he was sent to prison and released in November that year, after which he had gone back to live with his parents at Mallin's Cottage, High Street, Falmouth. When the weapon was reported missing he had allowed the police to come and search his home, and they found nothing incriminating.

Even so, Morcumb had not forgotten the incident, and decided that it might be well worth their while to interview Trenoweth again. At 3.45 a.m. on Christmas Day, he and Inspector Martin went to Mallin's Cottage. They found Trenoweth in bed; alongside him was a suit of clothes and a pair of brown shoes. When they examined the suit they noticed what seemed to be bloodstains on the right sleeve, and specks of blood on the shoes. He was detained and taken to the police station for questioning, where he was asked to account for his movements the previous afternoon and evening. He said he had been out shopping in the afternoon, before taking the 7 p.m. bus to Truro. Two packets of Woodbine cigarettes were found on him. When offered a Players cigarette by his visitors, he said he preferred Woodbines. Asked where he had bought those found on him, he told them they came from Reginald Pearce's in the high street. When questioned later neither Pearce nor his daughter, who had been working behind the shop counter, could recall having seen Trenoweth recently.

Trenoweth was told that a man had been found with severe facial injuries, and made the statement which probably did as much as anything else to put him in the dock. 'I bought the cigarettes at Pearce's,' he insisted, 'I was not in that man's shop.' How did he know who 'that man' was? When asked to account for the cash in his possession, a little over £5, he said, 'I don't want to say anything about the money.' As for the blood on his clothes, he told them it must have come from a nosebleed.

When Dr Hocking arrived at the police station on Christmas morning he examined Trenoweth, and found no sign of any recent nosebleed. He carried out tests on the hands with chemical reagents to indicate the probable presence of blood, and traced some on the back of the right hand and at the side of the nail of his third finger.

At this stage, Morcumb told Hocking that Bateman had been found dead in his shop at Falmouth with facial injuries, and that the detained man had failed to account for the blood on his clothes, or for his whereabouts on the previous evening, or indeed for the money found on him. At about 10 p.m. on what must surely have been the least pleasant Christmas Day any of those involved had ever known, Morcumb charged Trenoweth with the wilful murder of Albert James Bateman. His jacket, waistcoat, trousers and a shirt were handed over to Hocking, as well as the Webley revolver. The pathologist noted that on the right cuff of the shirt was a mark which looked like a washed-out bloodstain. Later laboratory tests showed that it was indeed human blood. Similar stains were found on the suit on the right cuff of the jacket, seven circular drops, up to quarter of an inch in diameter, and a small drop on the middle button of the waistcoat.

The suit was of good quality, and the good state of the trouser pocket linings suggested that the garment had not been heavily worn. However, at the bottom of the left trouser pocket was a tear about two and a half inches long. The hole had been torn by the Webley revolver. Hocking suspected that the weapon, about a foot in length, would be extremely obvious if placed in a trouser pocket. The accused must have carried it around with him, concealed in the pocket, probably as he was walking around the shopping centre of Falmouth on the day before, planning to intimidate some shopkeeper into handing him the savings. This would also explain why no fingerprints were found on the gun, as they would have been rubbed off while Trenoweth was out walking.

An inquest was opened on 28 December by the Coroner, Mr Carlyon. Mrs Bateman gave evidence of identification of her husband, Dr Hocking described the injuries in detail, and Superintendent Morcumb gave an account of events. Trenoweth was remanded in custody for twenty-one days, and the Coroner adjourned the inquiry until the conclusion of criminal proceedings.

Later, Hocking and Inspector Martin went to Trenoweth's home to investigate the possibility that the revolver, missing from *Ceto* for nearly a year, may have been in his possession all that time. Mallin's Cottage, they discovered, faced the waterfront of the Fal estuary, and was approached down a narrow passageway where in sailing ship times men and youths were shanghaied for service at sea. The upper part of the house was a large sail and spar storing loft, and when entered seemed to be full of the unwanted junk of generations. They searched carefully among this material, and found a strip of multicoloured carpet. Brushings from the carpet examined through a microscope showed the presence of all the hairs, cotton and wood fibres, and miscellaneous objects such as black horsehair and portions of feather, which an examination of the revolver and trouser pockets had revealed.

All this was almost enough to condemn Trenoweth. One more piece of evidence proved his guilt beyond a shadow of a doubt. When he was first interviewed at his home, his clothing was searched, and when the money was checked, four £1 notes were found. One of these notes, numbered H 59D 650932, was torn on one corner and carefully repaired with a strip of white paper. The ever-organised Mr Bateman was known to be very careful about repairing torn banknotes, and had sometimes been seen in his shop doing so. Early on the day of the murder, a Mr Sowden had called in the shop and noticed him engaged thus. On 31 December, Sergeant Bennetts and Detective Constable Eden searched Mr Bateman's shop and sorted through all the waste paper they could find. Eventually they came across a crumpled bill head with a corner cut out, and when they matched it with the stolen note, they found the missing corner matched the repair exactly. The note, gum and cut bill head were sent to the Forensic Laboratory at Bristol, and the Director, Mr Parkes, confirmed that the gum on the note and bill head were identical in composition.

Trenoweth was charged with murder at Exeter Assizes on 11 February 1943, presided over by Mr Justice Tucker, and the trial lasted for five days. On the first day, after giving evidence, Mrs Bateman collapsed and had to be carried out of court. Dr Harris confirmed that Mr Bateman was dead when he examined the body. The tobacconist had been a patient of his, and was treated for occasional injuries to wrist and knee, but had otherwise been in good health.

The evidence with regard to the revolver and the pound note was overwhelming. The Woodbine cigarettes found on Trenoweth when he was arrested, and other packets of the same brand, were also sent to Mr Parkes at Bristol. He proved that the cigarettes in the prisoner's possession had been part of a delivery made to Mr Bateman, and to nobody else in Falmouth. In the end this was not used in court, as the other evidence was considered proof enough.

For the prosecution, led by Mr J.D. Caswell, the court had the evidence of Dorothy Allen whom he had met in Truro, later on Christmas Eve. She said that they had arranged to meet in Truro on Christmas Eve and he was late for the appointment; he had missed the 6.15 p.m. bus, but caught the next one at 7 p.m. When they went to the Market Tavern, Gordon was being quite lavish with his money that night for an unemployed man usually short of money. On this occasion he paid for drinks for her, two for her mother, and one each for two soldiers, in addition to his own. Before he left he said he was going to buy her a new pair of shoes, but she said she would rather have the money instead, so he gave her a £1 note. His spending at the bar was confirmed by the barman, Frederick Griffiths. The cash had almost certainly come from Bateman's shop.

Mr J. Scott Henderson, Counsel for the Defence, suggested that Trenoweth could have picked up the banknote from the shop in the course of other transactions during the day, but to no avail. The likelihood of his having done so was very remote.

On the last day of the trial, Trenoweth told the court that he spent much of Christmas Eve looking for work. As there was none to be had at the docks, he visited the Employment Exchange. He bought two packets of cigarettes at Pearce's shop, and had several drinks. Instead of going home for dinner he bought himself a pasty, then

A £1 note repaired by Albert Bateman and found in Gordon Trenoweth's pockets when he was searched on Christmas Day. (© Devon & Cornwall Constabulary)

in the afternoon 'patrolled around the shops'. At 5.30 p.m. he went to Messrs Harris's coalyard, looking for work, and spoke to Harry Osberg, the managing clerk. He arrived home for tea about 5.40 p.m., a fact readily confirmed by his father Gordon, saw his parents and children, and read the newspaper for half an hour. He asked them the time, was told it was 6.35 p.m., as his sister Mona, a cinema usherette, confirmed. Leaving to check on the time of the next bus to Truro, he then visited the pub before catching the 7 p.m. to Truro. He stayed at the Market Inn with Dorothy Allen for about two hours, caught the 9.30 p.m. bus back to Falmouth, returned home about 10.15 p.m. and was in bed by 11 p.m.

'What did you think the police came to your house about?' Henderson asked him.

'About the maintenance,' he answered.

'Was there any reason why they should get you out of bed in the middle of the night?'

'Not that I know of.'

The jury found Trenoweth guilty, 'but with a strong recommendation to mercy, as it is not considered the accused intended to kill.' He showed no emotion, and remained silent when Mr Justice Tucker asked if he had anything to say as to why he should not be sentenced to death. The judge said he would forward the recommendation to the proper quarter. Nevertheless the Court of Appeal saw no reason to intervene, and on 6 April 1943 Trenoweth went to the gallows, his executioners being Thomas Pierrepoint and Herbert Morris. He was the last man to be hanged at Exeter Gaol.

Writing his memoirs some years later, Dr Hocking said he was sure Trenoweth did not have murder in mind when he was caught with his hands in the till, believed the sentence was too severe for the crime, and thought him unlucky to have done so at a time when the law was administered 'with much more harshness'. The Court of Appeal took the not unnatural view that Mr and Mrs Bateman were the really unlucky ones, particularly at what should have been the season of peace and goodwill to all mankind.

8
'PLEASE, DON'T LET US THINK OF SATURDAY'

Lizard Point, 1943

The possibility of an early death at the hands of the enemy was all too realistic for British fighting forces during the Second World War. Hence, whenever they got the chance in those uncertain times, young people tended to live for the moment and seize any opportunity for pleasure. The troops stationed in Cornwall during the hostilities were no exception to the rule. Those who counted themselves particularly fortunate were the young men and women stationed at the RAF base near Lizard Point, since they were billeted in a commandeered luxury hotel. The Housel Bay Hotel, set high on the cliffs of the rugged Cornish coast, is said to be the most southerly hotel in Britain and the servicemen and women staying there enjoyed many a party on the beach below.

Corporal Joan Lewis, aged twenty-seven, a WAAF from Porthcawl, had been at Housel Bay for some time before the arrival of a new station commander, Flying Officer William Croft from Bath, who was five years older. The couple first met at a beach party and, thrown together by their work, their initial friendship soon deepened into a passionate affair.

Their relationship troubled Croft, a married man with two children. He was not just committing adultery, but also engaging in fraternisation between the ranks, a practice very much frowned upon by the armed forces. At length his guilty

Housel Bay Hotel,
The Lizard.

Housel Bay and Lizard lighthouse.

conscience prompted him to confide in Freda Catlin, the officer who was in charge of the WAAFs. Catlin advised him in no uncertain terms that the affair should stop immediately, since it was not conducive to either morale or discipline. Not only must the association cease, but one of the lovers must be reposted.

Croft's application for a transfer was refused, so arrangements were made for Joan Lewis to be moved to another station in Devon on Saturday 16 October 1943. Once her move had been organised, Croft found that he could hardly bear the prospect of being parted from her. In one of the many love letters to pass between the couple, Croft wrote: 'The thought of some other male sharing your company drives me to distraction. Please, don't let us think of Saturday, Joan darling. I cannot dare to think of it. Every time, I get a horrible aching pain.'

Joan was permitted a couple of days leave before her transfer, which she spent with Croft, before returning to duty on 14 October. On the following day, she seemed quite cheerful, if resigned, and the couple spent that night together in a summerhouse in the hotel garden. Towards dawn, the noise of two shots was heard coming from the summerhouse. Seconds later, Croft ran to the hotel where he approached the Duty Officer and told him that he had killed Joan. He later telephoned another officer and begged him to come to the summerhouse immediately. In the course of the call Croft was heard to say; 'I have killed Joan Lewis' and 'I have shot Joan.'

Flying Officer Norman Page and a sergeant rushed to the summerhouse. Climbing through the window, they discovered the body of Joan Lewis, which had apparently fallen from a sofa and lay in a pool of blood on the floor. On a table, near to the body, they saw a Webley service revolver, later found to contain two empty cartridges and four live rounds of ammunition. The firing pin had struck a third bullet, which had not fired.

Croft asked the officers to inform the police, explaining that, in desperation at being parted, he and Lewis had made a suicide pact. Joan had, he maintained, fired both shots. He had been supposed to shoot himself with the same revolver, but had not had the courage to go through with it.

Police Superintendent Thomas Morcumb arrived at the hotel at about 7 a.m., accompanied by Dr Hocking. There, in the summerhouse, they completed a preliminary examination of Lewis' body, concluding that she had been shot twice, once in the chest and once in the head.

Joan's body was removed to the RAF headquarters at nearby Predannack, where Hocking was able to conduct a full post-mortem. He found that Joan had first been shot in the chest, the shot probably aimed at her heart, but missing by some five or six inches. The bullet had struck a rib and then deviated upwards and backwards, exiting via the woman's armpit, damaging the left lung and also the musculature used in raising the arm. This shot had been fired while she was sitting on the sofa and a bloodstained hole was found in the sofa back, from which a flattened bullet was subsequently removed. The second shot had been the fatal one, entering the skull just above and behind the left eye and exiting behind the right ear.

Croft was charged with the murder of Joan Lewis at Helston Police Court on 16 November. Despite having been clearly heard admitting to shooting and killing Joan, Croft now stuck to his revised story of a suicide pact between them, saying 'At this stage all I wish to say is that I did not murder Joan Lewis. She shot herself twice. We had both agreed to commit suicide.' He said that the pair had woken in the summerhouse at about 4.30 a.m. on a rainy, windy morning, on which the moon was obscured by clouds. Having spent their time together talking, smoking and dozing, Croft now placed the gun on his lap and the pair agreed that whoever felt like making the first move would use the gun, leaving the survivor to follow. According to his confession, Croft fell asleep again, to be awakened by a loud bang.

He saw Joan clasping her chest, complaining of pain and begging him to go and get help, at which he climbed out of the window and ran towards the hotel. He had no sooner set off, than he heard the second shot. Rushing back to the summerhouse, he snatched up the revolver and put it to his own head, but was unable to fire.

The summer house at Housel Bay Hotel. (© Devon & Cornwall Constabulary)

Interior of the summer house. (© Devon & Cornwall Constabulary)

Mr E.G. Robey, prosecuting, said that a number of letters had passed between Croft and Lewis, and letters in the possession of the prosecution clearly indicated the state of mind of both before 16 October. 'They will show you he was a man obviously very jealous, very much in love with this girl and she with him; a man who was married and thought of his marriage as an obstacle which seemed to worry him much. They were both obviously dreading the separation.' He claimed that it was quite impossible for Lewis to have shot herself.

Croft went on trial for the murder of Joan Lewis at the Winchester Assizes on 14 December 1943, before Mr Justice Humphreys. Throughout the trial the defence maintained that Lewis had fired the shots, as part of a suicide pact. However, the prosecution insisted that this was impossible, calling Hocking as an expert witness. Hocking put himself through a number of contortions in the witness box to demonstrate to the jury the difficulties that Joan would have faced in firing both shots herself.

He conceded that Joan could possibly have fired the first shot, although he felt that this was unlikely. For a start, the gun was heavy and required a trigger pressure of almost seven pounds when cocked and eighteen pounds when uncocked to discharge it. The degree of burning on the front of Lewis' uniform tunic indicated that the gun had been about five inches away from the body when fired. Hocking maintained that, to fire the gun from this position. Joan would have been forced to pull the trigger with her thumb, an awkward and unlikely occurrence.

However Hocking was adamant that Lewis could not have fired the second, fatal shot to the head herself. The first shot had so damaged the muscles on the front of her chest that it would have been impossible for her to raise the heavy gun, hold it a distance of twelve to eighteen inches from her head and pull the trigger with her thumb. The final placement of the gun was also a consideration. Hocking felt that the awkward position in which the gun was held for the first shot, would have caused it to fly uncontrollably from Lewis' hand, had she been the one to pull the trigger. It seemed beyond belief that, bleeding heavily and in severe pain, she had then scrabbled about in the dark summerhouse to find the weapon, before cocking it and firing the second shot.

In summing up the case for the jury, the judge outlined the finer points of the law on suicide. It was, he explained, self-murder and, if Lewis had indeed committed suicide, as the prosecution maintained, then she was guilty of murder. At the same time, if Croft had in any way aided and abetted the suicide, he was as guilty of murder as if he had shot her himself.

The jury debated for less than twenty minutes before finding William Croft guilty of the murder of Joan Lewis and he was sentenced to hang. Almost immediately, the case was sent to the Court of Criminal Appeal on the grounds of misdirection by the judge.

It was argued that the judge had neglected to mention the possibility that Lewis' death may have been accidental. The prosecution had suggested that, having fired the first shot, Joan's hand or elbow might have violently struck the table near to the sofa, causing the gun to fire again, resulting in the fatal shot to the head. In addition, if the second shot had, as Croft contended, been fired by Joan while he was on his way

*An artist's impression of the ghost of Joan
Lewis.* (© Devon & Cornwall Constabulary)

to summon help, then he could hardly have been accused of counselling, procuring, advising or abetting suicide, since he was not present when the fatality occurred.

In taking the loaded revolver to the summerhouse, Croft had clearly provided the means for Joan Lewis to commit suicide, if indeed his story of a mutual pact were true. And, in leaving the summerhouse to seek help, he had undoubtedly left a severely wounded woman alone with a loaded revolver, rather than trying to offer first aid or removing the revolver from the scene to prevent further injury. And, if Joan had actually asked him to seek help, did that not indicate a wish to live, so negating any suicide pact?

After much legal wrangling, including a hearing at the Court of Criminal Appeal on 21 January 1944, Croft's appeal was dismissed. His sentence was however reduced from the death penalty to life imprisonment and, in the event, he was released from prison only a few years later.

The case of Croft and Lewis still holds many mysteries and Hocking, in *Bodies and Crimes* (1992), outlines further evidence, which was not presented to the jury in the original trial. It was mentioned that the pistol contained a further four live bullets, in addition to the two that had been discharged in the course of the fatal shooting. Hocking points out that five of the six cartridges in the weapon were 0.455 inches in diameter – the sixth, was a smaller cartridge, measuring 0.450 inches, intended for use in a Smith and Wesson revolver, which was also common military issue at the time. It was this smaller cartridge that showed evidence of being struck twice by the firing pin, but because of its size, it had slipped slightly in the cylinder. Thus, the impact of the firing pin was lessened, with the result that the gun did not fire.

Hocking cites this as evidence of confirmation of a suicide pact between Croft and Lewis, in that Croft may have tried unsuccessfully to kill himself, before leaving Joan to seek help. However it does not alter the fact that it was Croft who pulled the trigger, if not twice, then at least for the fatal head shot. In Hocking's opinion, the tragic death of Joan Lewis was indeed the result of a suicide pact that went wrong.

And, it appears that this opinion may even have been confirmed from beyond the grave! Several seemingly reliable witnesses, with no prior knowledge of the tragedy, have reported seeing a young woman sitting on a bench in the gardens of the Housel Bay Hotel. The woman, whose physical description tallies closely with that of Joan Lewis, wears a WAAF uniform and is always reported as either looking sad, or weeping. One witness, who was a spiritual medium, even managed to engage the young woman in 'conversation'. The medium was told that the young WAAF was waiting for her lover – who was also her murderer – to join her, as he had promised in a suicide pact, in 1943.

In recent years, there have been no further reported sightings of the ethereal woman on the bench. Is it possible that, so many years after her murder, she has finally been joined by her lover and is now able to rest in peace?

9

'I HAVE HAD A TERRIBLE ROW WITH THE OLD MAN'

St Austell, 1952

On 7 August 1923 Charles Giffard married Elizabeth Goodwin at the Church of St Mary's, Rockbeare, near Exeter. His family came from Englefield Green, Surrey, and while she was Irish by birth, previously her parents had moved to the Westcountry. They made their home in Cornwall, and to all outward appearances were a happy, well-to-do family. Charles, or 'Charlie' to his friends, had served with the Royal Flying Corps towards the end of the First World War, and became Commandant of the Special Constabulary in the St Austell Division during the Second World War. He was the senior partner in a firm of solicitors, was later made Clerk to the Social Justices with particular responsibility for advising on sentences, and was also an undersheriff of Cornwall. During his leisure time he was often to be found in the club or his local, the White Hart, St Austell. He had a favourite registration number, ERL 1, which he transferred from one car to the next. Elizabeth, the elder by three years, was Vice-Chairman of the St Austell Conservative Association and President of the Conservative Women's Association, and played bridge two or three times a week with her friends.

Porthpean, near
St Austell.

At first they settled in the parish of St Mewan. A few years later they had their own house built on the cliff top at Porthpean, overlooking St Austell Bay, and about two miles from the town. Carrickowl, an imposing residence, tended to overawe visitors, with its fishing rods and golf clubs in the hall, a large breakfast room with dishes and hot plates on the sideboard.

Elizabeth was much liked in the community, but the same could not be said of her husband who was known as a hard, unsympathetic man, overbearing and brusque, never one to suffer fools gladly. Their elder son Miles found it hard to live up to the exacting standards of two such pillars of the community, especially in view of his history of instability, bordering on mental illness.

Miles was born in 1926, and his brother Robin about three years later. Both used to play together around the cliffs and in the woodland nearby. Miles often had nightmares as a child. When he was about two he had a nanny who beat him and often locked him in a dark cupboard for punishment. When this was discovered she was dismissed for cruelty, but the psychological damage to the boy had already been done. During his adolescence he was often punished for lying and stealing his mother's jewellery, though she always stood up for him. At the age of thirteen he was sent to Rugby public school where he was hopelessly dirty and untidy, still an incorrigible liar, wet the bed, and screwed up his sheets with his hands, then bit holes in them, an inch or two in diameter. After four terms the masters found him impossible. There were consultations between Mr and Mrs Giffard and the headmaster and he was removed from the school. It was the worst possible time for the family as his father was then in the throes of a nervous breakdown, probably as a result of his taking on too many cases for absent colleagues during the war years and driving himself too hard.

At the age of fourteen Miles was sent home and an appointment was made for him to see a Devon psychiatrist, Dr Roy Neville Craig. The doctor found Miles abnormally apathetic, dull and stupid. He had a psychopathic personality, was unresponsive to love and punishment and therefore impossible to control, so lacking in normal emotions that it was impossible to make him laugh or upset him. Adolescence had not lessened his tendency to lie or have nightmares, and there was now an alarming new development – panic attacks (or 'paroxysms of fear for no apparent reason') as well. Diagnosing his problems as a rare form of schizophrenia, implying that he had in effect lost touch with reality, the doctor treated him for two years, but was reluctant to give him any more than the most basic treatment, because of the risk that he might activate deep and violent disturbances in his mind. Nevertheless he warned Charles and Elizabeth of the possibility that their son could suffer a mental breakdown in the future.

If another school was found for Miles where he could make a fresh start, Dr Craig hoped there was a chance that he might be able to develop more or less normally as long as he was treated with care. Craig used his influence to get him into Blundell's, a public school at Tiverton, far nearer to the Giffards' home than Rugby. He entered at the start of summer term 1941 and stayed until the end of autumn term 1943. At first arrangements were made for him to receive treatment three times a fortnight at school, but this meant he would miss games, the only thing at which he was any good. It must be assumed that they managed to treat him at different times instead, for denying Miles the chance to play cricket or other sports would have been the worst punishment anybody could devise. Even so, his behaviour at Blundell's still gave cause for concern. One day he flew into a violent rage, stuck a knife into his leg, and then seemed surprised that it hurt and was bleeding. Nevertheless, though his academic achievements were negligible, he became a good sportsman. He played squash and excelled at cricket, playing for the school First XI in his final summer term. According to the school magazine, *The Blundellian*, in his last summer term, he evidently had good and bad cricket days:

> For one who gave such promise at the beginning, the season was a series of disasters relieved only by some good innings in house matches. The belief that he is full of runs still persists in spite of his failures and we think this belief justifiable. His fielding improved noticeably.

The main buildings, Blundell's School, Tiverton. (From The Blundellian, 1932)

At one time Miles considered becoming a professional cricketer. His exacting, hard-to-please father dismissed the idea as absurd, and wanted him to become a solicitor. He sometimes spoke of his cricketing aspirations to Joan Baxter, landlady of his local, the Carlyon Arms at Sandy Bottom. She was a regular confidante of his, and he always struck her, she said, as 'a decent boy'. More than most others in the neighbourhood, she knew how much he loathed his father, with good reason. Chilly relations between both men became more distant still. To make matters worse, Robin was apparently an ideal son and never caused his parents any trouble at all. Elizabeth felt sorry for her unsatisfactory elder child, but maybe she found it difficult to conceal her preference for the second sibling.

Between 1943 and 1947 Miles did four years' National Service in the Royal Navy. On the lower deck this previously unstable and unhappy young adult suddenly came into his own. Though short he was strong and athletic, and the scapegoat, the useless child who could never live up to expectations, became a confident young man and an excellent sailor, well-mannered and liked by everyone. Far from resenting or railing against the ordered and disciplined conditions of service life, he adapted well. Being away from home, and particularly from his father, clearly did him a world of good. If he had chosen to remain in the Navy, tragedy might have been averted.

Unhappily for all concerned, afterwards Miles went back home. His time in the Navy had given him a greater degree of self-confidence. Until then he had probably assumed that his father was always right, and that if he was angry with him, he deserved it. Now perhaps he could see that his father was an authoritarian headstrong bully who would never admit he could be wrong. It was a view which many of Charles Giffard's peers shared.

Back at home Miles had a succession of poorly-paid jobs (including a boring, unhappy spell in the family's solicitors' office), none of which he kept for long, and took to drinking more than was good for him. One day Charles lost patience with him, ordered him to leave the house and never darken his doors again. Miles accordingly left, but returned when the premises were empty and robbed them. Elizabeth persuaded her husband to forgive their prodigal son and let him back, and Charles agreed to give him one more chance. Miles came back and promised to give the office another try – until in November 1951 he inherited a legacy of £750 and went to live in Bournemouth.

Within four months he had spent the money, taken a few more dead-end jobs to support himself, including selling ice cream and working in an estate agent's office in Ringwood, then 'scrounged around' before returning home in June 1952 for want of any alternative. Two months later he went to London where he rented a furnished room at Walpole Street, Chelsea, soon exhausted the £15 monthly allowance from his father, then bounced cheques and borrowed money from friends.

During this time he met a girl of nineteen, Gabrielle Vallance, and her mother, who lived in Tite Street, Chelsea. They both took an instant liking to him, and he was totally smitten by Gabrielle. Intent on impressing her, he took her to shows and smart dining establishments around the West End, continuing to live well beyond his means. One day she took him gently to task about his untidy appearance, and as he could not afford any more clothes, he told her that his parents would send him some from Cornwall. As there was little prospect of his father going out of his way to help, he decided he would have to make a quick visit back.

He hitchhiked back to Cornwall, spending the night of Saturday 1 November in a rat-infested barn in Somerset, returning to Carrickowl the next day. He was optimistic that his father would produce some more money. But Charles Giffard did not approve of Gabrielle, and told Miles he wanted him to end the relationship. Maybe he thought Gabrielle was bad for his son; maybe he resented the fact that someone was about to have more influence on the young man than his parents, and he, Charles Giffard, successful solicitor and pillar of the establishment, did not intend to lose control. At the age of twenty-six, he went on, it was time Miles settled down, got out of the habit of spending more than he could afford, stayed in Cornwall, gave up all these fanciful ideas of playing sport for a career, and came to work in the family solicitors' office like his father.

Miles was horrified by the thought of losing Gabrielle, whom he had known for only six weeks yet hoped would be the love of his life. A sixteen-year-old schoolboy who lived nearby had been getting a little too friendly with her, and he dreaded leaving the way clear for his junior rival. At around this time he proposed to her, and she agreed to marry him, as long as he found a steady job first, preferably in London, so that he would be independent of his parents. If his father was going to stand between them, there was only one drastic solution.

On Monday 3 November he wrote to Gabrielle, telling her that what he was afraid would happen had come to pass:

> I have had a terrible row with the old man, made worse by the fact that, as usual, he is right. Anyway, the upshot of the whole thing is that he has forbidden me to return to London at any rate for the time being. He says he will cut me off without the proverbial penny, so there does not seem to be any alternative until I can get a job. I shall not be able to take you to Twickenham. Who will? I am terribly fed up and miserable as I was especially looking forward to seeing you tomorrow, and now God and the old man know when I shall. Short of doing him in, I see no future in the world at all. He has stopped my allowance, anyway, is giving me a pint of beer and 20 cigs a day, and has said, 'No Pubs'. No doubt your mother would approve. Give her my love and tell her that when she sees me I shall be a reformed character (nominally anyway).

Two days later he told her that he hoped to get to London that weekend after all, if he could talk his father round. How much he tried, if at all, and how Charles Giffard reacted, can only be guessed at. What is known for certain is that on the evening of 6 November Mrs Giffard went to her regular charity bridge drive in St Austell. She might have had car trouble, for on the morning of 7 November she took her husband's vehicle to attend a local Conservative branch meeting in Plymouth, while husband and son went to St Austell together in hers. Whether they went for any purpose other than getting the car fixed, or what conversation passed between them, is not recorded. They returned home for lunch, and Mr Giffard went back to his office that afternoon.

Left on his own in the house, Miles spent the next few hours curled up with a book about a jealous soldier who had murdered his girlfriend. At some stage during the afternoon or early evening he took four aspirins and knocked back half a bottle of whisky. This may have been before or after 5.30 p.m. when he rang Gabrielle, saying he intended to drive to London that night to do some business for his father. Two hours after this phone call his parents returned to the house in quick succession, in separate cars. His father was the first to arrive, and his mother followed a few minutes later, after taking a friend home.

Taking an iron pipe from the garden, Miles walked up to his father as he was getting out of the car and hit him. One blow missed and tore the lining of the door, but the others struck Charles on his hand, which he had thrown up to protect his face. Several more on the right side of the head knocked him unconscious. Mrs Giffard had gone indoors; she almost certainly had no idea what was going on, otherwise she would surely have tried to restrain her son. Miles then followed her in and struck her from behind until she was unconscious as well. He had probably not intended to kill his mother, who had always staunchly defended him as best she could from his father's tyrannical behaviour, but he could not avoid the risk of detection. If he had killed his father (who was still alive at the time), she would not have found assault with a heavy weapon as easy to forgive as persistent lying and theft. In a panic, he decided that she would also have to die.

Next he telephoned Gabrielle again to confirm that he would definitely come to London. Returning to the garage to fetch his father's car, he found Charles was coming round, and a few more blows with the bar killed him. Miles then went back to the kitchen, found his mother also recovering consciousness, and attacked her again. This time he did not succeed in despatching her, and he was concerned at the amount of blood around the house. After loading his still-breathing mother into a wheelbarrow, he took her to the edge of the cliff and pushed her over, then did the same with his father's corpse. It took him an hour to clean the house.

Barbara Orchard, the nineteen-year-old live-in housemaid at Carrickowl, had had a half-day and was expected back at any moment, so he did not want to leave any tell-tale signs. He finished his grisly tasks in time to throw a few things into his mother's car, including a change of clothes, his mother's jewellery which he had already stolen once before, and some sleeping pills which he later said he intended to take in order to commit suicide, then drove off shortly after 10 p.m. Miss Orchard had spent the afternoon with her fiancé, John Vaughan, who was bringing her back at the same time. She noticed Miles accidentally reversing into the house – the Triumph was notoriously difficult to manoeuvre, even if the driver was not intent on making a swift getaway – before driving off at high speed. In the weeks to come, did she ever realise that had she arrived a few minutes earlier, she might have met a similar violent death?

Miles changed his clothes en route, and threw some of the bloodstained garments into the river at Fenny Bridges. At the same time he disposed of the iron pipe, 2½ft long and 3lb in weight. Picking up two hitch-hikers near Ilchester, he took them to Chelsea. They noticed that he seemed a little tense and was chain-smoking throughout the drive, but seemed 'a very good sort of chap'.

He reached Tite Street at about 6 a.m. the following day, and slept in the car for a couple of hours before knocking on the door. In view of the physical efforts involved in pushing a heavily-laden wheelbarrow twice some distance over rough ground late on a dark night, and the whisky he had consumed, combined with the complexity of a road journey from St Austell to London in the pre-motorway age, the overnight drive was no mean feat. He left the ignition key and some bloodstained shoes and clothing inside the vehicle, then spent about an hour with Gabrielle and Mrs Vallance, telling them that he had left his car at a garage and was staying with relatives at St John's Wood. He had a business appointment for 10 a.m., and would return for lunch. On leaving them he went to Piccadilly Circus and sold his mother's jewellery (not for the first time) for £50. Next he phoned Gabrielle to say he would not be able to make it back for lunch, but would meet her at 2 p.m. She came with her mother and all three went to see the Charlie Chaplin film *Limelight*, after which Mrs Vallance went home, leaving the young couple to their own devices.

Until then Miles had been unusually quiet, but a few drinks loosened his tongue. While they were drinking in the Star, Chesham Mews, he asked Gabrielle to marry him. She said yes, as long as he got a proper job first. Soon after this, he told her that he had done something frightful. 'What, pinched your father's car?' she asked. He replied that he had murdered his father and mother and would not be able to see her again. She realised he was upset about something, but she did not believe him, thinking he was trying to impress her and may also have been a little drunk. Perhaps she did not want to think that her boyfriend was capable of such a dreadful deed. They then went to another public house in the East End, the Prospect of Whitby beside the Thames at Wapping, for further refreshment. By the time he had summoned a taxi, they were both fairly tipsy. He was booked into the Regent Palace Hotel in the name of Gregory, and he gave her his room number, asking her to ring him early the next morning.

Meanwhile back in Cornwall, on returning to Carrickowl the previous (Friday) evening, Miss Orchard had not initially suspected anything wrong. Tired at the end of a long day, she had half-expected Mr and Mrs Giffard to be home, but as they sometimes stayed out late, their absence in itself gave no cause for alarm. At first she saw no reason to do a cursory check of the house indoors before going to bed. However, she noticed that the hall light was on, and then also found the garage light on. Entering the house, she noticed an outdoor coat and picnic basket which Mrs Giffard had taken with her to Plymouth that morning were lying on a kitchen chair, and her handbag and shoes were in the hall. She then noticed some coconut matting covering part of the floor had been removed, a rubber mat was damp, and there were smears on the floor, indicating that it had just been washed and probably in a hurry. Looking more closely, she saw what looked like bloodstains on the floor and cooker, and that a scrubbing brush, which was usually left outside the kitchen door, was still in the scullery sink.

Increasingly concerned that nobody was home, she rang two local hospitals to ask if they knew anything. As they did not, she sat down and considered the problem, then went to bed but not surprisingly had a sleepless night. After a few hours she could stand it no longer, so she got up and went to her fiancé's house at about 5 a.m. She told him of her discoveries and fears for the worst, in view of her employers being missing, that she had heard the larger car being driven away, and she was sure it must have been taken by the son of the house. That he was on the worst of terms with his father was no secret. Vaughan spoke to his gardener, Harry Launcelot Rowe, who promptly contacted the police, and then drove to Carrickowl to see for himself.

The message was passed on to Detective Superintendent Ken Julian of the Cornwall CID at his Bodmin headquarters. He and his Scene of Crimes Officer, PC Max Mutton, set out for the house, joined on their way by Dr Hocking, who was a family friend of the Giffards, Police Sergeant Lovering, and several other police officers. When they reached Carrickowl to join Rowe, tell-tale signs were evident. The earth floor of the garage and the interior and exterior of Mrs Giffard's car were covered with bloodstains; the other vehicle was missing. Another large stain outside the garage led to more of the same, together with a tuft of hair later identified as from the scalp of Mr Giffard, and marks on the garden path leading towards the gate suggesting that a heavily-laden wheelbarrow had been pushed that way. Further stains near the gate indicated that the barrow must have overturned at that point. A handkerchief heavily stained with blood was found just outside the gate, on top of the hedge. It had obviously been used by the person pushing the barrow to wipe his hands. Part of the wall at the rear of the house had been damaged and a car door handle lay nearby, bearing witness to Miles' hurried departure.

The trail of more of the same led them along a public footpath, beside the cliff top, and through a tangle of thorn bushes. At one point they found various articles including a wallet, a hat, a bunch of keys and a bundle of letters, most of which could be traced to the missing solicitor, a collection of loose coins, and a woman's hat, all stained with blood. The tracks took them across an area of ploughed land to the cliff edge. Below, on Duporth beach, they could see the sprawled body of a man lying on his back, with a wheelbarrow beside him. The top of his skull had been so badly damaged by the fall that his brains had splattered out over a rock.

At first they could see no sign of Mrs Giffard, and they suspected that her husband's killer might have taken her hostage. Then they saw more wheelbarrow tracks along the cliff path, and at one point, on the edge of a sheer drop, further bloodstains. Walking along the beach, they found her body about 200yds away from that of her husband, jammed face downwards between two rocks. When Dr Hocking examined her later, he decided that she had been knocked unconscious in the kitchen but was still alive when she was thrown over the cliff, and that she must have died when her head struck the rocks. She had two large bruises in her scalp, which had been split, with extensive injuries which had been caused about the time of her death, when her body was flung over the cliff and by sliding down the rough edge. The tide was within a few feet of the foot of the cliff, and under normal conditions a body thrown from the top would have been washed out to sea before long. It was unfortunate for Miles Giffard that the weather had been unusually mild at the time.

None of the men doubted for a moment who they were looking for in connection with the crimes. A general alert was sent out to all police stations, and within hours the missing Triumph, with its distinctive number plate ERL 1, was tracked down in Tite Street. Shortly after 11 p.m. on the Saturday night a taxi drew up outside the front door of No. 40, and a girl – Gabrielle Vallance – climbed out. As the taxi moved away police cars hedged it in, and plain clothes officers wrenched open the door. They had done so with some trepidation, as a search of Carrickowl revealed no sign of his father's revolver, and they thought Miles might have taken it with him. Their anxieties were unfounded, as a rather drunken and confused Miles called out, 'Help, police!' before being informed that they *were* the police and that he was under arrest.

On Sunday 9 November, at Cannon Row police station, Superintendent Julian cautioned Miles and told him that he was making enquiries regarding the discovery of his parents' bodies on the beach. He broke down, saying, 'I know what you are referring to. I wish to admit everything to you with as little trouble as possible.' He said he did not want Gabrielle brought into the matter, and after being cautioned, told them, 'I had a brainstorm', as if to imply that the killings were not premeditated. He was then formally charged with the murder of his father, aged fifty-three, and his mother, aged fifty-six.

The next day he was taken back to Cornwall. Wearing a fawn check suit and tartan tie, looking tired and his hair dishevelled, he was charged a second time, in the magistrates' court where his father had been Clerk to the Justices for twenty-three years, and was remanded in custody for a further period. The only words he spoke throughout the short hearing were the question, 'May I apply for legal aid?' His uncle, General Sir George Giffard, stepped in and offered to assist him in his defence, and Mr W.G. Scown of St Austell, a well-known advocate in the county who had known Miles for several years, agreed to act on his behalf. The Bodmin District Coroner, Mr E.W. Gill, opened an inquest on the deceased couple and adjourned it indefinitely after hearing evidence of identification given by another of Charles's brothers, Campbell Walter Giffard, a stockbroker, of Melina Place, London.

Miles told the police about the iron pipe which he had thrown into the river at Fenny Bridges. As it had been lying in running water for several days by the time they found it and there were no hairs or blood left on it, but inside there was a residue of mud which matched that on pipes in the garden at Carrickowl and, more significantly, on the car which Charles Giffard had been getting out of when he was attacked.

Though the community around St Austell was shocked by the Giffards' murders, not everybody regretted that Charles had gone, much as they might deplore the manner of his death. One man rang a member of the legal profession to tell him that the solicitor was dead, to which the second man's reaction was 'About time too.' Even some members of the police force thought likewise. When PC Mutton told the Assistant Chief Constable, Reggie Rowland, that Mr Giffard Senior had been murdered, the reply was a succinct 'Serves the bugger right.'

The footpath leading to Porthpean, along which Miles Giffard pushed the wheelbarrow containing his parents' bodies. (© Devon & Cornwall Constabulary)

Charles Giffard's car, photographed by the police shortly after the murders. (© Devon & Cornwall Constabulary)

The body of Charles Giffard on Duporth beach. (© Devon & Cornwall Constabulary)

A memorial service was held in the local parish church where they had worshipped for so many years, with two of Charles Giffard's brothers leading the mourners. Robin Giffard, who was in Kenya working on his uncle's farm, was informed of the grim news by telegram but could not return in time.

On 12 December Miles appeared on remand in custody at the court again and was committed for trial at Bodmin Assizes in February 1953. Dr Hocking, the Cornwall county pathologist, had examined the bodies on the beach and said that in both cases injuries had been caused before and after death. Mr Giffard was dead when he was thrown over the cliff. His face had been struck four times and split raggedly open, with another blow on the right collar bone, one or more on the top of his head causing severe bruising, and he had two black eyes. There was further bruising on the back of the right hand extending some six inches up the arm, and marked swelling but no laceration, suggesting that there had been heavy blows on the arm as well as a result of him holding it up to ward off blows aimed at his head.

Both of Mrs Giffard's wrists were broken, probably as a result of her falling on her hands while still conscious, and her lower left arm was broken. There was a deep jagged cut above the eye and both eyes were black, her skull was shattered and the base fractured. Nearly all those injuries must have been caused before death and the only ones sustained afterwards were some of the tears and splits in the scalp and extensive fractures of the skull. She had been beaten around the head at least twice. After this evidence had been presented to the court, the charge was again read to Miles Giffard by the Clerk, and the Chairman formally committed him for trial. His counsel declared that he would plead not guilty to murder, would not call any evidence at that stage, and that one of the defences at the trial would be that he was insane at the time of the killings.

The trial opened on 4 February and lasted for three days. Though Miles' mental state of mind was open to question, the same could not be said about his intention to commit murder. Gabrielle Vallance was one of the first witnesses to be called. She produced the damning letter from him, read out to the court by Mr Scott Henderson, QC for the prosecution, saying that Miles Giffard saw no future, 'short of doing him in'. The killing of his father was not the impulsive action of a hot-tempered young man who had lashed out in a fit of temper, but a clearly premeditated deed. Whether he was intent on the cold-blooded murder of his mother as well was another matter. Dr Craig, who had since left Devon and moved to County Kerry, gave evidence as to his mental condition. George Alexander Keay, Miles's former housemaster at Rugby, and Peter Saunders, a contemporary of Giffard at Blundell's and now studying architecture in London, both testified as to his strange behaviour at school, saying 'he was not at all like other boys'.

On the second day Dr Craig was asked about a letter he had written about Miles in August 1941 to Dr John Hamilton Hood of Truro, the family's General Practitioner. He had warned the latter that 'The door which was closed is slowly opening towards the outside world. We have got to go on if we are to save him from breaking down mentally as he reaches adolescence.' Giffard, Craig maintained, had never fully recovered. Only the disciplined and controlled nature of his life in the Navy enabled

Gabrielle Vallance outside Bodmin Assizes Court, February 1953. (Ellis Collection, Cornish Studies Library, Redruth)

him to survive as long as he did. Less sympathetic by nature than Dr Craig, Dr Hood had had more than enough of his young patient. He had never known Charles Giffard to suffer mental disturbances, but he thought the son was 'an idle little waster'. Somewhat startled by this hostile view, Dr Craig hastily said that in his profession he could not possibly subscribe to that word, 'waster'. The two men would not agree. Dr Hood had known the family for over twenty years and he said there was nothing wrong with Miles' mental state. The young man, he insisted, was idle, selfish and cared for nothing but his dreams of a sporting career.

A Harley Street psychiatrist, Dr Arthur Picton Rossiter Lewis, said in evidence that he had seen Giffard in prison three times. It was his professional opinion that when Giffard killed his parents he was suffering from a defect of reason due to disease of the mind, but at the time he knew what he was doing to some extent. He did not know that what he was doing was wrong either in the moral sense or in the sense of being against the law, as the disease from which he suffered was a particular form of schizophrenia. The low sugar content of his blood showed he had a defect in his blood of the normal amount of sugar. A person was dependent on his sugar content for efficient working of the brain, and brain cells might not function properly because of the sugar drop. Miles Giffard, said Dr Lewis, was a case in point. Some of the symptoms of his disease would be confusion, irritability, sudden impulsive outbursts, impaired judgment and an inability to distinguish between right and wrong.

When Mr Justice Oliver asked whether these symptoms were commensurate with those of schizophrenia, the psychiatrist affirmed that they were identical. The other doctor who had given evidence, said the judge, had no doubt the prisoner's behaviour was caused by schizophrenia, and did Dr Lewis have any doubt that it was caused by low blood sugar? 'I do not exclude schizophrenia,' was the reply, 'but I think there was a clear explanation for the schizophrenic outburst.'

For the prosecution, Mr Henderson asked whether the psychiatrist was prepared to say that Giffard was suffering from schizophrenia from what he knew of the events of 7 November and what he had seen of the patient? 'No, I should not be able to say that unless I had the earlier history.'

Dr John Matheson, the principal medical officer of Brixton Prison, told the court that an encephalographic examination had been carried out on Giffard during his time in custody, to indicate whether his brain was functioning normally or not. No abnormality was indicated. When questioned about the tests at Wormwood Scrubs into the sugar content of Giffard's blood, Dr Matheson said that Giffard had been deprived of food for twenty-one hours to see whether his sugar content would fall below the danger level.

'But what is the use of getting him below the safety line by starving him?' asked the judge. 'He was not starving on 7 November, was he?' Dr Matheson stated that he was not starving, 'but this is what the authorities lay down as being the way to make this test.' From all that he knew about the events on the night of the killings, he said he failed to find any evidence that Giffard might have been suffering from spontaneous hypoglycaemia. It would be most unlikely for an attack of that kind to occur that evening in view of his hearty lunch that day, and as during the afternoon he had drunk half a bottle of whisky.

The judge had one more question. Referring to the fact that Giffard had moved two very heavy bodies over several hundred yards of very rough ground, had then set to work cleaning up the house, and then driven well over 200 miles to central London – 'you do not think a hypoglycaemic patient could have done that?' 'I am certain he could not,' replied Dr Matheson. From what he knew of Giffard's history before the killings, everything suggested that he did not suffer from mental disease. He would not expect a schizophrenic to drink or to make friends easily, and he did not think Giffard was suffering from schizophrenia that night.

On 6 February, the third and last day of the trial, Matheson was questioned further by John Maude, QC counsel for the defence, about the prisoner's mental condition. He said that 'night terrors' as a child might be significant, but children tended to react out of all proportion to such trivial things, and mental cases were difficult to diagnose. While Giffard might have had hallucinations as a child, and while some of the things he did were peculiar, these could not be taken as proof of mental disease. Giffard had tried to avoid full responsibility for killing his parents, with a statement, 'God knows for what reason I hit them over the head with a piece of iron pipe. I hit him once then he slumped to the ground unconscious. Mother had gone into the house. I went into the house after her. I found her in the kitchen. I hit her from behind. Everything went peculiar. I got into a panic.'

Maude's final questions were very much to the point. Did it not look irrational for the prisoner to murder his mother and father 'in order to go up to see that girl?' When taking into consideration that 'he had been a liar, drinking, stealing from his parents, and so on, there is no doubt that to have killed his parents to go and see this girl is extraordinary?' Matheson agreed that it was, but one of the reasons that he did not think Giffard was going through a 'schizophrenic episode' when he killed his parents was the fact that everything appeared to have been carefully planned. Did he think the plan involved murder, asked Maude. 'It is very hard to say.

Mr Justice Oliver with policemen and various officials outside Bodmin Court at the time of Miles Giffard's trial. (Ellis Collection, Cornish Studies Library, Redruth)

The only indication is his remark in the letter to the girl – "short of doing him in, I see no future in the world at all."' Such a remark, Matheson went on, could possibly be intended in a jocular way, though the jury must have felt instinctively that in view of events, Giffard was definitely not joking.

Throughout the proceedings, Miles Giffard remained impassive. The only time he showed any sign of emotion was when his mother's death was described, with reference to her being unconscious but still alive when thrown over the cliff.

In summing up, Mr Justice Oliver stated that 'the man who butchered that old man and old lady, if he is not protected by being insane in law, is a murderer.' It was up to the jury to decide whether Giffard knew what he was doing at the time, as the defence did not pretend he did not; and whether at the time he did those acts, did he know he was breaking the law. It was up to the defence to make it at least more likely than not that at the time he did the act he was accused of, he was suffering from some defect of reason, due to some disease of the mind that made it impossible for him to know that what he did was unlawful. He had disturbed his girlfriend in her London house early in the morning, but instead of spending the morning with her, went off with his mother's jewels which he had stolen over her dead body and sold them for £50. Was that the act of a madman, or of somebody who was utterly wicked? As for the blood-sugar tests in prison, he pointed out that the findings applied to a man who had been starved for 26 hours. Could they be compared with those of a man who had just enjoyed a heavy lunch, followed by half a bottle of whisky?

At this stage of the summing-up Mr C.E. Venning, the undersheriff of Cornwall, sitting on the judge's bench, collapsed with a loud cry and had to be carried from the court. Resuming, the judge said there could be no acquittal. The prisoner was either mad or bad, guilty or guilty but insane. If he deliberately disposed of his parents' bodies over the cliffs and hoped the sea would wash them away, or if he pushed them over, expecting that the injuries he had inflicted on them would be completely submerged in the wreck that would normally take place involving bodies falling on to rocks 120ft below, in the jury's view did that indicate that he knew he had done wrong when he did that?

The jury retired at 3.32 p.m. and took thirty-five minutes to return a guilty verdict. The judge pronounced sentence of death and later that afternoon Miles was driven to Horfield Prison, Bristol, pending an appeal.

Miles' uncle General Sir George Giffard, who had been Commander-in-Chief in West Africa during the war and had been living in Winchester at the time of the trial, financed his defence and appeal. On 22 February Messrs Stephens & Scown, the St Austell solicitors acting on the prisoner's behalf, stated that a member of the jury which had tried him had written to the Home Secretary that he was convinced Giffard was insane when he killed his parents. The juror added that because of a misunderstanding, Mr Justice Oliver had not been informed. Mr Scown said a letter had been sent to the Home Secretary eleven days earlier informing him thus. A reply was subsequently received from the Home Office saying that the juror in question had already written directly to the Home Secretary, who had considered all aspects of the case before arriving at his decision not to grant a reprieve. When asked about a suggestion that the verdict of the jury would appear not to have been unanimous, the spokesman replied, 'That point goes to the secrecy of the jury room, and we cannot comment upon it.'

Other submissions were made to the Home Secretary from members of the public and from the headmaster at Blundell's among others, all bearing witness to his disturbed state of mind. The appeal was dismissed and on 24 February Miles Giffard was hanged at Horfield.

A few days later General Giffard wrote a letter to *The Times*, published on 7 March. It drew attention to his nephew's long history of abnormality and mental illness from the age of four, the fact that a specialist examined him when he was aged fifteen, and that his parents were warned of the possibility of mental breakdown in the future. After he left the Royal Navy he began once again to show symptoms of mental illness; but his father was ill at the time, no treatment was administered and it culminated in the grim events of November 1952. 'It is impossible for any ordinary human being to know how the mind of another is working,' he concluded, 'and for a jury to be expected to decide on February 6 how the mind of a man suffering from mental illness was working on the night of November 7 seems to the ordinary layman absurd. To decide such cases by rules which in the light of present-day knowledge are admitted to be in need of revision seems to me to be manifestly unjust.'

Nevertheless most of the jury, and many of those in the local community, were not convinced by the arguments as to Miles Giffard's lack of sanity. Charles Giffard had not been a likeable man or an admirable father, but the evidence that his son had put in writing that he planned to 'do the old man in' a few days beforehand, and had then set about killing his mother with equal violence, forfeited the young man of most if not all of any sympathy which might have been felt for him.

10
DEATH OF A RECLUSE

Constantine, 1963

William Garfield Rowe was born in 1899, the son of parents who lived and farmed near Porthleven. They were staunch pacifists, and in 1917 he was conscripted into the army. Reluctantly leaving Venta Vedna, the family home, he returned within less than a week, vowing he would never have anything to do with the war. His parents and brothers applauded him as a deserter with the courage to uphold his convictions, welcomed him home briefly, gave him £50 and sent him away before the authorities could find him. Relations and neighbours were told that he had returned to his unit, though in fact he had gone into hiding. Before long he was traced by the Military Police, arrested and taken to a detention centre, but escaped and returned home.

In order to avoid being arrested a second time, he remained a total recluse, only venturing out of the house under cover of darkness to help work in the fields. His father and brothers were often seen by neighbours cutting and bundling corn, picking and loading vegetables – but William himself remained virtually invisible to the outside world. Anybody who dared to ask was told that he had never returned home from active service, like so many other young men of his generation. Those who wondered why the family were so punctilious about locking and bolting the doors of their home every time they went out put it down to the eccentricity of a close-knit family who had suffered bereavement. Nobody apparently noticed that his name was absent from the local war memorial.

When the Second World War broke out in 1939, the family became apprehensive again lest any civil servants checking up on them would find out the truth. As a result nobody ever registered him for the purposes of obtaining an identity or ration card, or clothing coupons. The family's farm proved largely self-sufficient in providing the food they needed.

When William's father died in 1949, the family moved to Nanjarrow, an isolated farmhouse near Constantine. Standing at the end of about half a mile of a very rough cart track and one and a half miles from the nearest main road, this five-bedroomed property was ideal for continuing to conceal the identity of the man who to all outside appearances no longer existed. Yet nobody took any chances while they were moving house, and as the procession of carts went from Venta Vedna to Nanjarrow, one contained a pile of sacks, carefully concealing William Rowe.

In 1954 his brother Stanley, who like William had never married, but stayed at home and taken over responsibility for running the farm since their father's death,

Nanjarrow Farm. (© Devon
& Cornwall Constabulary)

died. The other brother, Joel, had married and lived with his family nearby. William
and his mother split the work on a shift basis, she working by day and he by night,
until she died two years later.

Fortunately for him, at the start of Queen Elizabeth II's reign an amnesty had been
declared for all who had deserted during both wars. At last, now in his mid-fifties,
William could abandon his reclusive lifestyle if he so chose. Though he no longer had
to remain indoors during the hours of daylight, needless to say, adjusting to such a
change in his life was not easy. The farmhouse was a reasonable size, but he lived in
one downstairs room, all the others being stacked from floor to ceiling with furniture
and general family possessions accumulated over the years. He continued to look
after his cattle and pigs, with the difference that he could now go to market and also
to the shops. Any local excitement that may have been caused by his reappearance did
not last long. Yet years of living a hermit-like existence had made him very shy and
reserved, and he was content to keep his own company. Visitors to the farm were not
welcomed, especially not his brother Joel, with whom he was never on good terms.
When cattle dealers called, he would always carry on any conversation in a farmyard
or outbuilding, rather than invite them into the house.

However, less savoury elements in the neighbourhood decided that any recluse was
bound to be wealthy. While Rowe was out shopping one day in 1960 an intruder
broke in, stealing at least £200 in cash and some of his late mother's trinkets.

Far worse was to happen three years later. On 14 August 1963, at about
9.15 p.m., he was noticed by a neighbour completing his farmyard jobs for the day,
then locking and bolting his doors as usual. Next morning PC James received an
urgent call from a neighbour to say a dead body had been seen on the premises at
Nanjarrow. James, several other officers and Dr Hocking called to investigate and
found William Rowe covered in blood, lying huddled face downwards with one arm
outstretched in a corner of the farmyard. Bloodstains led to the farmhouse door, with
a pool of blood by the doorstep and splashes on the door framework. There were

The dining room at Nanjarrow Farm.
(© Devon & Cornwall Constabulary)

drag marks in the mud between the door and the body, and mud had been heaped up under the man's face. Temperature recordings suggested that the time of death had been late on 14 August, between 10 p.m. and midnight. The house had been ransacked, with cupboards thrown open, furniture overturned and clothing strewn around at random.

A post-mortem examination revealed numerous injuries, some stab wounds inflicted with a dagger or similar weapon, and other blows from a blunt instrument. There were five stab wounds in the chest, one of which had penetrated the heart, two the upper surface of the liver. Another wound ran horizontally in the upper part of the neck on the right side, penetrating as far back as the spine, severing the main blood vessels on the side of the neck, and another, more superficial cut on the front of the neck. The head had been battered by several blows, with six ragged splits in the scalp. Both eyes were blackened. There were also scrapes, abrasions and cuts on the front of the face, and a ragged cut two inches long along the line of the lower jaw, the bone of which was shattered. These injuries had probably been caused by the body falling forwards on to the hard courtyard and then being dragged into the corner where it was found. The skull was shattered, with portions of bone depressed inwards, and the brain was bruised and lacerated.

Rowe had tried to defend himself from the attacks. The top of the third finger on his left hand was severed through the last joint. There were four heavy blows on the right arm, in a position to suggest that he had raised his arm to shield his head. Where the blows had fallen, the skin was split and a large bruise over the whole of the back of the left hand was further indication of his efforts to protect himself. Death was due to a combined attack made simultaneously by two assailants, one with a knife or dagger, the other with a blunt instrument.

Murder headquarters were set up in a nearby school, with a team including Cornwall Constabulary detectives Superintendent Tommy Walke, Superintendent Richard Dunn, Detective Inspector Bob Eden and Detective Sergeant Norman Arscott.

Chief Constable Richard Matthews telephoned Scotland Yard for assistance and by that evening Detective Superintendent Maurice Osborn and Detective Sergeant Andrew McPhee had come from London to assist.

Meanwhile five people were living at Kenwyn Hill caravan site, on the outskirts of Truro. The site, with about seventy vans, was owned by Charles Penhaligon, a well-respected businessman in the area and inspector in the local constabulary. Among those who lived here were newly married couples awaiting a council house, some who had just obtained work in Truro and were house-hunting, and various casual labourers who tended not to stay long but were liable to give the place a bad name. Living in one such caravan were three girls, all aged nineteen, and two male labourers. Russell Pascoe, a married man of twenty-three from Constantine who had recently left his wife, made a living by doing odd jobs in the area, while Dennis John Whitty, one year younger and engaged, was employed at Truro gas works. On 14 August Pascoe had asked one of the girls, Norma Booker, for some nylon stockings as they wanted to 'do a job'. Notwithstanding any suspicions she may have had about their motives, Booker handed a pair over. Pascoe was not a man to whom one said no lightly.

That evening the men set off on Pascoe's motorcycle without saying anything more. They took a starting pistol, iron bar and knife with them. When they returned to the caravan in the small hours of 15 August, according to the girls, Whitty was grinning, while Pascoe looked ill at ease and was seen wiping blood from Whitty's face. Whitty said there had been an incident involving a farmer, while Pascoe muttered, 'We didn't get nothin'.' The girls were told not to breathe a word about their absence and the men went to their usual jobs that morning.

Later that day, Pascoe's girlfriend bought a local evening paper and showed Whitty the story giving details of the discovery of Rowe's body. 'You went to Constantine,' she told him. 'Did you do this?' Whitty admitted that he had. At this point Pascoe came into the caravan kitchen and said that if the girls opened their mouths they would end up the same way as the farmer. One of the men said there had been trouble and Mr Rowe had been killed because he recognised them.

The girls themselves were no saints. They had not uttered a word of protest when Pascoe and Whitty had said they were going to 'do a job', though they knew what was meant. There may have been an element of self-preservation in this, but they had been willing partners in crime before. Two of them had accompanied the men on shop and housebreaking forays, and at least once one of the girls had carried an iron bar herself, ready to hit a night porter should one be in the way when they went to burgle a public house.

As part of the police investigation, roadblocks had been set up around the area. On 16 August Detective Sergeant Arscott saw Pascoe riding his motorcycle in Constantine. The police had had their suspicions about him for some time, so Arscott stopped him and asked him to go to the murder headquarters for routine questioning. Pascoe duly did so, and told Detective Superintendent Osborn that he had read about the murder in the paper. When asked about his movements at the time, he said he had been at the caravan with Whitty and the three girls that night. When asked if he knew Mr Rowe of Nanjarrow Farm, Pascoe replied that he had known him for some time and worked for him 'three or four years ago.' That would have been about the time that the farm was robbed in Rowe's absence.

Pascoe and Whitty were known to be acquainted with each other and the police decided to call the latter for questioning as well. On 17 August Pascoe was taken into the charge room at Falmouth police station, and Osborn told him that he had 'good reason to believe that you and Dennis Whitty killed Mr Rowe.' After being given the usual caution, Pascoe gave a statement in which he said he only knocked Rowe over the head with a bar. 'I told Dennis that was enough, but he went mad with the knife. I will tell you the truth. Last Wednesday night with my mate, Dennis Whitty, I went to Mr Rowe's farm. We went on my motorbike. We were going to see if he had any money. We knocked on the door about eleven o'clock. The old man answered the door. Dennis was standing in front of the door. He said he was a helicopter pilot and had crashed. I hit the old man at the back of the head with a small iron bar. I meant to knock him out, that's all. He [Whitty] took the iron bar and went for him. I had to walk away, honest I did. I went inside and found £4 under a piano. Denis took a watch and two big boxes of matches and some keys from the old man's pockets. We shared £4 – £2 each. I have spent mine.'

Pascoe continued to deny to Osborn that he had killed Rowe. Whitty, he said, 'went mad', and he was afraid to stop him 'or he would stick me. I had to walk away. I couldn't stop him. He said he finished him when he stuck the knife in his throat. I only knocked him over the head with a bar. I just knocked him out. When I did, I told Dennis that was enough, but he went mad with the knife. Then he took the bar from me and kept thumping him on the head.'

Both assailants seemed determined to blame the other for Rowe's violent death. When the police told Whitty that he and Pascoe were both responsible, he was adamant that 'Pascoe made me stick him.' When charged and cautioned, he seemed to accept the inevitability of their fate. 'We are both over twenty-one, so I suppose we can hang?' The police told him that it was not for them to decide, but if convicted of the offence with which they were charged, they could face execution.

Whitty then realised that there was no point in trying to evade the consequences of their actions any longer. 'I want to tell you about it. I was going to give myself up if I hadn't been brought in.' Under caution, he made a written statement confirming that it had been at the suggestion of Pascoe that they went to Nanjarrow for money. 'I didn't want to go, but he made me. I knocked and the old man came to the door with a lantern. I told him I'd had trouble with a helicopter and asked the old man to show me the phone.' At the time he had been wearing dark jeans and a dark double-breasted blazer with silver buttons which in poor light could have been taken for naval uniform.

Continuing his statement, Whitty said that Pascoe, who had been hiding against the wall, then hit Rowe on the head with an iron bar. The old man fell down and Pascoe kept hitting him, at the same time telling Whitty to 'stick him'. 'I didn't want to and I started crying. He told me he would use the bar on me if I didn't do it, so I stuck him in the chest three or four times and once in the throat, I think.' Pascoe then made him drag the body to a corner of the yard and take some keys from the pocket, they went in the house and took two packets of matches and an old watch. He had no idea what Pascoe did with the keys, but he threw the knife away and dropped the bar in the dam.

In his statement, Pascoe said that on their way back to the caravan they threw the bar and the knife in the Argel Dam reservoir. The police later recovered both weapons. One was an iron jemmy, about 14ins long, weighing 2lb and 5oz. The other was a sheath knife, 6ins long, sharpened on both sides, tapering to a point.

Pascoe and Whitty were jointly charged at Penryn Magistrates' Court on 19 August, remanded in custody, and appeared at court again on 26 September for the preliminary hearing of the Crown's case against them. The extent of Rowe's injuries as revealed by the prosecution horrified everyone present in court. John Woods, Director of Public Prosecutions, said that the obvious motive for this murder was theft, 'and this was murder in the furtherance of theft. Never has the well-worn phrase 'savage and brutal attack' been more typified than by this case.' In the space of about thirty seconds, he went on, the victim had sustained injuries including six or seven ragged cuts in his scalp, a shattered skull, a fractured jaw, and five chest wounds including one five inches deep inflicted by a stiletto-type knife which had penetrated the heart. Part of one finger of the right hand had been completely severed, an indication of how hard he had struggled to defend himself against his attackers.

The murder, Woods concluded, was premeditated to the extent that both men had agreed they were going out in the furtherance of theft. They had every intention of hitting anybody they encountered, as typified by the helicopter story; it was a cold-blooded and ruthless murder committed in the furtherance of gain and greed.

The trial of Pascoe and Whitty opened at Bodmin Assizes on 29 October 1963. A jury of nine men and three women heard Norman Skelhorn, QC counsel for Whitty's defence, enter a plea of 'not guilty', and James Comyn make a similar plea on behalf of Pascoe. According to Dr Hocking, Whitty may have been short of stature and the younger of the two, but he was 'almost a little weasel of a man' and it soon became apparent that he was the dominant partner in crime, whereas Pascoe was 'a simple lad, easily led'.

On the first day, Osborn brought forward new evidence when he revealed that the police suspected a sum amounting to thousands of pounds remained hidden in the fields and cowsheds at Nanjarrow, although a thorough two-day search by the police had initially brought very little of it to light. About £20 in silver had been found concealed in jam jars, a milk churn and among old clothes. Further investigations on the premises revealed a tattered two-page document in Rowe's handwriting, which proved to be the key to a buried sum of £3,000 in £5 notes. The paper had been written in Spanish, with the aid of a copy of *Teach Yourself Spanish*, and contained several clues which led the police to the discovery of large sums of money hidden all over the farm. Only then did they realise that Rowe had spent much of his daylight hours, while concealed in the house, studying in order to better himself.

Comyn described the case as 'one of the most horrible and gruesome murders ever known in this county or in this country'. He appealed to the jury not to let horror blind them to the need for care in reaching a verdict, and warned them against being carried away by feelings of wrath or indignation. The nature of the evidence, he said, should be considered with extra caution. Pascoe, he went on, had 'a discreditable story to tell, but there was never one single instance when he was trapped. It is my submission that he told his story well and told it truthfully.'

On behalf of Whitty, Skelhorn suggested that either he was acting under the influence, fear and pressure of the suggestion of the more forceful Pascoe; or that his psychiatric background was such as to make him guilty of the lesser charge of manslaughter on the grounds of diminished responsibility. It was Pascoe's idea, he submitted, that they should carry out the robbery on Rowe's farm, especially as Pascoe had admitted to the theft at Nanjarrow a few years earlier. Skelhorn reminded the jury of Whitty's claim that when he had told Pascoe he did not want to be involved, Pascoe had threatened him; 'You will have to come. If you don't, I will scar you for life.'

Whitty's mental state was clearly an issue. Skelhorn said that he suffered from hysteria and a tendency to have blackouts. Pascoe's claims that Whitty 'went mad with the knife,' he declared, were consistent with the action of a man not totally in control of himself. Giving evidence on his own behalf, Whitty spoke of 'strange and unnatural things' that he claimed had happened to him, among them watching doors opening themselves for no good reason and pictures changing overnight. He said he believed in ghosts, and early one day at 4 a.m. he saw a figure with wings in the sky as he was walking down to the beach.

One witness called for the defence was David Penhaligon, the nineteen-year-old son of the owner of Kenwyn Hill caravan site. He told the court that on one occasion, while at the family bungalow, he had been asked for help by some passers-by who had found a man they thought had been knocked down by a car. At once Penhaligon recognised the man as Dennis Whitty. He seemed to be unconscious, with bruises and scratches on his face, so they called an ambulance and took him to hospital. Some days later Whitty called at the bungalow and thanked Penhaligon for his help, explaining that he had not been knocked down, but had just had an epileptic fit. This added to Whitty's defence that he became uncontrollably violent when attacked by epilepsy, and that he had had such a fit while robbing Rowe.

Although Penhaligon's parents had both been staunch Conservatives, his experiences as a witness inspired him to join the Liberal Party, as he was profoundly shocked that the court 'showed no understanding of what it was like to live on the fringes of society'. Living alongside some of the poorest people in the Truro area, he had seen the day-to-day difficulties faced by less fortunate members of the community, problems that could not be solved by what he called the typical middle-class response of 'they should pull themselves together'. In December 1974, a few weeks after his election as Liberal Member of Parliament for Truro, in a Commons debate he voted against restoration of the death penalty. Nevertheless, after another similar debate one year later he supported a motion calling for further investigation into whether or not it should be reintroduced for acts of terrorism that caused death.

Shortly before his untimely death in a car accident in December 1986, Penhaligon recalled the trial in a radio programme. He said that his evidence in the court at

Left: *Dennis John Whitty.*
(© Cornish Photonews Ltd)

Right: *Russell Pascoe.*
(© Cornish Photonews Ltd)

Bodmin was followed by that of three psychiatrists, who were asked whether Whitty had acted under the influence of hysteria. The first one took an hour to say he did not know; the second took three quarters of an hour to say 'he could have done'. The third took four minutes to tell the court, 'Garn, he's having you on' – and he was the only one to be believed. The member for Truro wondered whether if he had given the same evidence as David Penhaligon, forty-two-year-old MP and chartered engineer, as opposed to David Penhaligon, nineteen-year-old fitter-and-turner apprentice, his testimony would have made more of an impression.

On the final day of the trial, 2 November, the judge, Mr Justice Thesiger, told the jury that he would ask them to say whether or not it was their opinion that Whitty was acting under fear of grievous bodily harm, or even death, from the ruthless Pascoe. Regarding Skelhorn's second defence, that of diminished responsibility, the judge asserted that mental responsibility depended on a man's ability to know what he was doing and that he would be punished if he was caught. The jury had to decide whether there was any abnormality in Whitty's mind and if there was evidence of hysterical behaviour. He thought it significant that the prisoner's 'hysterical attacks' were manifested in blackouts and moments of unconsciousness. The result of his attacks of mental abnormality, he said, were the fits of unconsciousness. There was no evidence that he had suffered a fit or blackout on the night of the murder.

In his final speech for the prosecution, Norman Brodrick QC asked the jury to accept that Whitty used a knife to stab Mr Rowe while Pascoe struck him with an iron bar. Skelhorn submitted that Whitty did what he was forced to do under threats from Pascoe, that he suffered from mental hysteria and could claim diminished responsibility. He asked for an acquittal on the murder charge and a verdict of manslaughter. Comyn likewise urged the jury not to find his client Pascoe guilty of murder. The jury took four and a half hours before they returned to record verdicts of guilty against both prisoners. Mr Justice Thesiger said he 'entirely agreed' with them; 'I think they were the only possible verdicts in this case.'

After sentence of death had been pronounced, the condemned men were driven away from the Assize Court. Three weeks later their appeals were heard and rejected by the Court of Appeal. Their executions were set for 17 December; Pascoe at Horfield Prison, Bristol, and Whitty at Winchester.

In Falmouth a petition was started, not so much for the reprieve of both men as for the abolition of capital punishment, but less than 600 people signed. One of the disappointed organisers commented that the response seemed to be in favour of the hangman; 'this appeared to be out of an emotion born of revenge and not from a desire for punishment.' Those who had been arguing and campaigning throughout the country for the abolition of the death penalty had undoubtedly underestimated the sheer revulsion felt by most people in the community at such a barbaric crime. The two young men who were prepared to rob a defenceless elderly man and commit such a callous murder in the process plainly deserved what was coming to them.

On 13 December Rowe's provisional will was published, which gave the value of his property, goods and chattels as £8,082. It was assumed that most of this related to Nanjarrow, but an element of it included the cash recovered. Meanwhile Rowe's brother had taken over the running of Nanjarrow, and in order to discourage sightseers he surrounded the property with barbed wire barricades and 'Keep Out' notices.

Pascoe celebrated his twenty-fourth birthday in Horfield. On the evening of 16 December, he was visited in his cell by the Bishop of Bristol, Dr Tomkins. At Pascoe's request the Bishop baptized and confirmed him, and offered him Holy Communion. That same evening Bridget Hamilton, Whitty's nineteen-year-old fiancée, was allowed into the prison at Winchester to say farewell to him. Earlier that day she had stood weeping on the steps of the Home Office in London as members of the 'Committee of 100', a group which had set up to organise mass sit-ins and blockades, attempted to stage a peaceful demonstration there. They also handed in a petition, signed by over 2,000, asking the Home Secretary, Henry Brooke, to advise the Queen to exercise her prerogative of mercy. Later they tried to see him at the House of Commons, but without success. All-night vigils by anti-capital punishment demonstrators were held outside Brooke's home in his London constituency of Hampstead, as well as outside both prisons. Among the protesters at Horfield was Tony Benn, Labour Member of Parliament for Bristol South-East.

On the morning of 17 December both men were hanged. Within the next few months there would be only one more murder case on mainland Britain, again a robbery in which the victim was killed in cold blood by two perpetrators, which would lead to the gallows. One year after Pascoe and Whitty paid with their lives, campaigners for the abolition of the death penalty for murder had their way with the first reading of the Murder (Abolition of the Death Penalty) Bill, and Royal Assent was given to the Act in November 1965, suspending capital punishment for murder for five years. In December 1969 a further parliamentary vote reaffirmed the decision that it should be permanently abolished.

chapter two

Devon MURDERS

11
MURDER IN CHURCH

South Brent, 1436

The majority of facts surrounding any violent death in the fifteenth century are bound not to survive, but that does not detract from the gravity of one of Devon's most notorious murder cases, one which a contemporary, Bishop Lacey of Exeter, called 'a crime without parallel in our time and in these parts'. One evening in June 1436 the Revd John Hay, who had been Vicar of St Petroc's Church, South Brent, for eight years, was officiating at a service and had just said Vespers at the Festival of Corpus Christi, when there was a commotion in the building. One of his parishioners, Thomas Wake, entered the building, seized Hay and dragged him from the altar through a small doorway in the side of the church. There, with the help of a few partners in crime, he put the unfortunate man to death, either by beating him or stabbing him with a sword.

The nature of Wake's motive is anybody's guess. Rumour has it that although Hay was a man of the cloth, he may have been something of a womaniser, and was suspected of having an affair with Wake's wife. The latter was apprehended, and duly hanged, drawn and quartered for his sacrilegious misdemeanour. Whether any of his accomplices suffered the same fate is not recorded.

It has been claimed that South Brent shares the sorry distinction with Canterbury Cathedral of being one of only two places of worship where such a barbaric deed has occurred, the instance at Canterbury being the notorious murder of Archbishop Thomas Becket in December 1170. However, a similar incident was recorded at St Winwaloe Church, Poundstock, Cornwall in 1356, when the Revd William

The doorway of St Petroc's Church, South Brent, through which the Revd John Hay was dragged to his death. The doorway was later walled up. (© Kim Van der Kiste)

Penfound was hacked to death on the chancel steps during a service there. Thankfully, such occurrences were rare, even in medieval times.

On 11 September 1436, Bishop Lacey reconsecrated the church and churchyard. He also sought to draw a line under the murder by dedicating three altars.

The door through which the murderers dragged Hay is thought to have been a small opening in the north wall of the chancel, an outline of which can be seen on the outside of the building. It was bricked up when new chapels were added at a later date. Sadly, John Hay was not allowed to rest in peace. Fragments of his tomb, with recumbent effigy, were discovered in the church in 1870 – a mutilated head is now all that remains of the figure.

12
DEATH AFTER THE FAIR

Moretonhampstead, 1835

Jonathan May of Sowton Barton, Dunsford, was a well-to-do farmer in his late forties. Although a bachelor, he was believed to be courting a lady from Tiverton. Maybe he planned to settle down a little later in life than his contemporaries, not just for the benefits of family life but also to have children who would inherit the farm after him. In the community he was widely respected, though he had a reputation as a harsh employer with high standards. At least one of his men discovered this to his cost.

In 1834 George Avery, a well-built young man who supplemented his wages by taking part in occasional wrestling matches, was sent by the farmer to collect some logs from an outlying woodpile and deliver them to his house. May then set off for Exeter, but for some reason he turned back – only to find Avery unloading wood

The White Hart,
Moretonhampstead.
(© Dr Ian Mortimer)

from the wagon not at the farm, but instead at the tied cottage in which May had allowed him to live. He was promptly sacked and May said he would give him no references in future; moreover, he would ensure that everyone knew of his dishonesty, so he would be unlikely to find work. Avery vowed he would get even and then left the area, determined to make his living as a wrestler.

Thursday 16 July 1835 was the day of the annual fair at Moretonhampstead. The town had a flourishing wool trade, and the fair attracted people from near and far. May was there, hoping to get a good price for his livestock. The fair had a variety of stalls for home-made goods and sideshows, including wrestlers, fortune-tellers and other entertainers. It was one of the most important local events of the year, and a magnet for low-lifes from the neighbourhood and other parts of the country, who tended to travel from one fair to another. Among the less desirable elements present were Avery, his girlfriend Elizabeth Harris and possibly a couple of friends they had just made, whom they knew as Oliver and Turpin.

May sold about £80 worth of animals, then visited Thomas White, a tanner who lived on the corner of the square, to collect payment for oak bark used for tanning. His next stop was George Norrish, a shoemaker to whom he owed money for boots and repairs. Afterwards he returned to the White Hart, where he had left his horse. Full of good ale at the end of a good day, he was tempted to hold forth a little less than wisely about his profits, and displayed his money to prove his point that he was 'a moderately warm man' – in other words, a success and not ashamed of it.

It was probably some time after witnessing this display of wealth by his former employer that Avery returned to his lodgings, telling his companions he was tired. As he came in through the door, he asked them what the time was and they replied that it was 8 p.m. Going upstairs to bed, he rested briefly, then came back down and asked them the time again. One of the household remarked that it was odd he should be doing this repeatedly, especially as there was a clock on the wall in front of him.

Meanwhile, merrymaking continued in Moretonhampstead, with bands playing, crowds dancing in the streets, and much cider, ale and spirits flowing. At about

The Rectory, Moretonhampstead.
(© Dr Ian Mortimer)

10 p.m. May left on horseback to return to his farm. On his way he rode slowly through the tollgate and spoke to James Nosworthy, the toll-keeper, bidding him goodnight.

At about midnight Nicholas Taverner and his wife Grace, and her brother John Tallamy and his wife, set out to go home to Harcot. They were taking a shortcut home down Shute Lane, a track near Jacob's Well, a natural spring where a horses' drinking trough was to be found. At the top of the lane they found a horse wandering around beside the hedge. Nicholas took it back to the town, and only then did he realise that it belonged to Jonathan May. Suspecting an accident or something worse, he headed back along the main Exeter road where he found May lying unconscious on his back in a pool of blood, his pockets turned out and his waistcoat undone. He shouted 'Murder!' and his wife, who had stayed there waiting for her husband to return, came running over. She stayed with May while Nicholas made his way as quickly as possible to Moretonhampstead for help. He went to Dr Alfred Puddicombe's house in Cross Street, now The Old Rectory, then got a horse and cart to take the injured man back to the White Hart, where May had recently been celebrating in such good spirits. His wounds were so severe that he never regained consciousness, despite the care and attention of his surgeon, Dr John Ponsford, and he died at 9 p.m. the following day. May's assailant assumed that death would be attributed to a fall from his horse.

A receipt for 30s for some boots and shoes that had been given to May on the evening of his death by George Norrish was missing from his coat. It was found in his pocket-book in a field at Hennock, a few miles away, some months later. Two £5 notes were still in a pocket on the inside of his waistcoat, although his watch could not be found. At the scene of the crime a local thatcher, Henry Luscombe, found a broken blood-covered stick 3 feet long, cut from an ash tree, and this was assumed to be the murder weapon. Another part of the stick was found in a nearby ditch by William Bracknell, a stonemason, along with a piece of blood-soaked material from a shirt frill. Blood was also spattered on the leaves of a hedge, and it seemed that May had managed to crawl on his hands and knees about 50 feet from where he first fell after being attacked.

A post-mortem was carried out by Dr Ponsford and his Moretonhampstead colleague, Dr Alfred Puddicombe. As there was very little gravel in any of the wounds, they ruled out any possibility that May had fallen and been dragged along the road by his horse. The wounds must have been caused either by kicks or by blows from a stick, though Ponsford conceded that a wound on the temple might have been caused by a kick from a horse. A coroner's inquest returned a verdict of wilful murder on 21 July, and May was buried in the churchyard at Dunsford. His gravestone bore the inscription, 'Erected to the memory of Jonathan May of Sowton Barton in this parish who was murdered as he was returning from Moreton fair about ten o'clock on the evening of 16th July A.D. 1835. Aged 48 years.'

A local solicitor, Moses Woolland Harvey, had seen the site of the struggle and the bloodstains in the hedge and on the road. He had also noticed the tracks of two men across the adjacent barley field, leading towards Crammer's Brook, where May's pocket-book was later found by labourers William Crocker and William Caseley. In the absence of any effective police operation in the area, he took up the case in an effort to apprehend the culprits – he assumed that at least two people must be responsible for the murder. Harvey and May's brothers, Walter and John, jointly offered a reward of £100 for any information leading to conviction of the guilty party. A free pardon was offered to anyone who confessed to being an accomplice, on condition that they had not been directly involved in the murder. Harvey was regarded by less law-abiding elements as a dangerous man and a tiresome busybody who would not rest until he had somebody in the dock, and he took to carrying a pistol for his protection. One day it went off in his pocket, wounding him in the thigh.

Suspicion immediately fell on Avery, whose dismissal by the farmer and subsequent threats against him were no secret. He and his girlfriend Elizabeth Harris, who had been travelling around the country with him for the previous few months, were taken into custody at Exeter, but released when Avery managed to prove that he was in his lodgings on the night May was killed.

George Avery had been arrested on a charge of murder some months before, but he was discharged owing to a lack of evidence and the corroboration of his witnesses. He was later detained on a separate charge of assaulting a Dunsford labourer at Alphington in the spring of 1835, sentenced to death, but reprieved and sentenced to transportation instead. Within a few days he became the ringleader in a plan to escape from the gaol.

In the summer of 1836 Thomas Oliver was in Dorchester Gaol, awaiting trial on a charge of robbery with violence. While exercising with other inmates in the yard, he boasted that the biggest job he had ever done was when he and 'Turpin' had knocked a Devonshire farmer on the head and robbed him. This reached the ears of the prison chaplain, who knew of the May murder, and he wrote to Harvey. The latter decided to pay a special visit to Dorchester, where he found the watch and various other articles belonging to May in the prisoner's lodgings. These proved sufficient to incriminate him.

Edmund Galley, a brickmaker, was well known around fairs in the south-east of England as a rogue and he was nicknamed Dick Turpin, after the notorious

The gravestone of Jonathan May,
Dunsford Church. (© Dr Ian Mortimer)

highwayman. A description of him was widely circulated, and although he lay low for a while, he was apprehended when Thomas McGill, a London police sergeant, went to Coldbath Fields Gaol to interview him while he was being held there on a charge of vagrancy. Galley told him he had been born at Kingston-upon-Thames and claimed he had never been in Devon. He said he was at the races in Reigate when the murder took place, but later he changed his story to say he was at Dartford, working at the Windmill public house. The police ignored his second statement. His supposed employer, Mr Rowe, had no recollection of Galley's working for him, and it turned out that Galley had only been employed casually by the carpenter for beer money.

At the expiry of his sentence for vagrancy on 30 April, Galley was arrested by McGill and taken to Bow Street, where he saw a handbill on the walls giving details of May's murder. He then realised that this must be the reason for his arrest. Shortly after his arrival in Exeter, Elizabeth Harris was brought in to identify him. She had described him as being well built with bushy whiskers, and at first she thought this puny-looking whiskerless man was somebody different. Gradually she reached the decision that although he was 'strangely altered', he must be the one. Others came forward to say that they had seen both Oliver and Galley in the area at the time of the murder, and swore that Galley was the man they had seen with Oliver at Moretonhampstead the previous year.

Edmund Galley and Thomas Oliver, whose real name was Thomas Infield but who was generally known as Buckingham Joe, were charged with the murder. The case came to trial before Mr Justice Williams at the Crown Court, Exeter, on 28 July 1836. The judge was already notorious for having ordered a sentence of transportation on the 'Tolpuddle Martyrs' two years earlier for forming a trade union in Dorset.

The greatest stir in the courtroom occurred when Harris came to give evidence for the prosecution. She claimed to have been at Moretonhampstead on the eve of the fair and to have seen the prisoners entering the Bell Inn together on the following afternoon. She knew them by sight as she had seen them at earlier fairs at Bromhill, near Taunton, and at Dorchester and Weymouth. She also claimed to have heard them talking in travellers' slang. Buckingham said to Turpin, 'It's a fine-looking gaff, and there's some crusty looking blocks in it, and we must have some gilt in the rot.' Elizabeth thought this meant that it was a large fair with some wealthy-looking farmers present, and that they were planning to rob some of them that very evening.

She said she had had an argument with her lover after tea, and she set off to try and cadge a lift on a cart out of Moretonhampstead at about 10 p.m., but could not catch up with it so she turned back. The two prisoners passed her on the road outside the town where there was a steep hill and a sharp bend. She had stopped to loosen her bootlace, and heard somebody say goodnight to the turnpike gatekeeper shortly before May rode into view. Recalling what the two men had been saying, she turned and followed May from a distance, and as he reached the top of the hill by the milestone, she said that she saw Oliver leap from the hedge and grab his horse by the head.

'You're just going home, farmer', was what she thought she heard him say. 'I am,' replied May. At this point, Turpin emerged from the shadows behind the farmer, carrying a stick. He struck May on the left side of the head with two blows, but the farmer stayed on his horse until Oliver dragged him on to the ground. They fought for about five minutes, Turpin continuing to hit May. 'If you rob me, for God's sake don't take my life' were his last words before Turpin kicked him hard twice and he lost consciousness. Both men climbed over a gate into a cornfield with a pocket-book and what looked like either a watch or a seal for fastening letters. Elizabeth said she was too scared to move, and stood still in the shadow of the hedge for what seemed a very long time, then went back to George Avery's house at Moretonhampstead.

At 6 a.m. the next morning, at the lodging house of Mary Splatt, Elizabeth was taken into custody on suspicion of murder, along with several of her travelling companions, including Avery, 'Black Soph' (Elizabeth Weeks), Andrew Carpenter, who was kept in custody for nine months and then released as he was dying, and Arthur Pardew. Elizabeth Harris spent a month in prison at Exeter before being released to spend some time with her sister in Taunton. Four months later she was arrested again, tried and sentenced for a theft in North Devon. On that occasion, in February 1836, she told Tryphoena Lampen, the Matron Turnkey of Exeter Bridewell, that she had witnessed the murder of Jonathan May. She claimed she had not even told George Avery what she had seen, and that she did not expect nor ask for a pardon in return for giving evidence against the prisoners.

In court Galley directed his questions to her in some disbelief. 'Can you look at me with a clear conscience,' he asked her, 'and say you saw me do what you say to this man?' She replied, 'I did, and you know that I did, by what I have told you since.'

'Did you ever see me in company with this man,' he asked again, pointing to Oliver, 'till you see me in gaol?' 'Yes, at Bromhill Fair.' Galley asserted that she had never seen him there, nor anywhere in Devonshire before. 'I did, and at Bridgwater Fair together,' she said. Galley turned to the judge. 'My Lord, she mistakes me for another man, I never was in Devonshire in my life, till I was brought to the prison; I know I am not the man my Lord, and God Almighty knows I am not the man; she swears in the name they have given me my Lord, and not my body.' Elizabeth insisted that he was the man. 'If you know me to be the man,' he asked, 'why did you not mention this before?' 'Because I am afraid if I am out, but I am not afraid when I am in there,' she said, meaning the gaol. 'I think you should be glad I have told of it, as I'm sure you can have no peace nor rest on account of it. I had not.'

Galley was highly suspicious of Harris's motives, as he pointed out to the judge. He told the latter that 'she might get her freedom, she swears my life away. I know I am not the man, and God Almighty knows it. I am not the person who did this, thanks be to God. I was brought down to Exeter on the 1st May last, and never was in the county in all my life before. I never saw that woman in all my life, my Lord, till I saw her in the gaol.' The judge asked Harris if she had any doubt that these were the men she saw commit the murder. She assured him that she had none. Turpin was definitely the man who came out of the hedge and passed behind the farmer towards the left side of the horse. He was the one who struck the blow with the stick, she said.

Two local residents, Ann Carpenter and her daughter Jane, recalled staying at a boarding house in Butchers Row, Exeter, on 13 July. They thought they saw the two prisoners there with a woman whom they knew as 'Black Ann'. In August they saw Oliver at Wilton after the Salisbury races. He was with 'Black Ann' and Elizabeth McKinley, but all of them denied at first having been in Exeter in July. 'Black Ann' later admitted to Ann Carpenter that she had been in Exeter, but she was not with Oliver at the time. 'Black Ann' had washed Oliver's smock coat in the courtyard, but was unable to remove a suspicious-looking stain. They had a violent argument, attacked each other, and 'Black Ann' ended up with a nosebleed. Elizabeth McKinley remarked loudly, so that Oliver could hear, that the stain must have been the blood of Jonathan May. The coat was produced in court and a rusty-coloured stain was still visible. Oliver said he had already been convicted because the mark had been taken as evidence.

Catherine Gaffrey, Mary Smith and Mary Marengo all testified in court that the prisoners before them at the assizes were the same men who had stayed at Mrs Marengo's house the previous July, though Gaffrey retracted her statement after the trial. The two men had been studying a booklet giving dates of the local fairs and decided they would go to Moretonhampstead, but did not appear concerned that they were unlikely to arrive before it was dark. They paid for their lodgings with a gold ring and a silver snuffbox.

A lace-seller, Charlotte Clarke, said she saw two men with 'Black Ann' at the Lamb Inn on the road from Exeter to Moretonhampstead. One of them she knew to be Buckingham Joe and the other one she recognised as Turpin, who had previously tried to persuade her to buy a gold ring at Taunton. She was sure that this Turpin was not the man now facing her across the courtroom. The man she saw at the Lamb Inn had a full set of teeth – Galley had two upper teeth missing – and his dark whiskers met at the chin. He was quite respectable-looking compared to the man she now saw in court who had just served a sentence for vagrancy.

Charlotte Clarke recalled leaving the inn at the same time as the two men and 'Black Ann' at midday on the opening day of the Moretonhampstead Fair. She reached the town in the early hours of the evening, but the other three had stopped to rest about 2 miles away and she had not seen them since. She was positive that Oliver was Buckingham Joe and that he was on the Exeter Road at around the time of the murder. The landlady of the Lamb Inn felt that Galley was the other man, as did other witnesses who claimed they had seen the two robbers in Moretonhampstead during

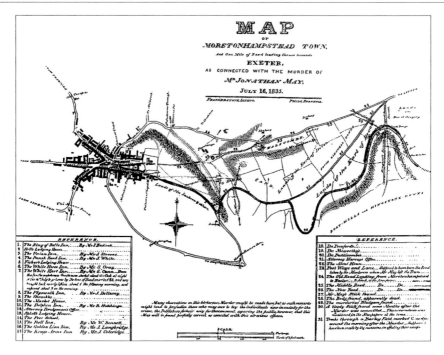

Map of Moretonhampstead, showing areas connected with the murder of Jonathan May, 1835. (Moretonhampstead History Society)

the fair. Betty Croot said she had seen him in the White Hart Inn, playing a pub game with the local apprentices and doing rather well financially in the process.

John Hiscox, a convicted thief, was serving a sentence at Dorchester Gaol in September 1835. He told the court that his fellow-prisoner, Oliver, had often boasted how he and a man named Turpin had robbed a Moretonhampstead farmer before heading back through Taunton on the way to London. At the time Oliver was awaiting transportation for life for his part in three highway robberies in Dorset. Hiscox was reminded of these conversations in prison by a handbill that he was shown in the governor's office when he was being released the following January. This bill offered a reward for the capture of May's killers. At the trial Oliver was indignant about Hiscox's testimony, accusing him of 'swearing false in every word you say, and you are trying to take away my life for gain'.

At the end of the prosecution's case, Galley repeated that he was in Reigate at the time of the murder, and that the finger of suspicion had pointed at him merely because he had the misfortune to share the same nickname as one of the murderers. Had he been able to afford it, he would have obtained the services of a good lawyer who would prove his innocence beyond the shadow of a doubt. His lover, Jane Cording, had tried to obtain money from his family to help him, but only his sister was able to contribute anything – the princely sum of 5s. Mr Justice Williams had not assigned him any counsel, but had he done so, the outcome of the case might have been very different. Galley appealed to the judge: 'I am as innocent as a baby just born, and if I do suffer here through false swearing, and by persons who know nothing of me, and never saw me before, God knows that I am innocent, and I hope he will receive my soul.'

Oliver hoped that some attention would be given to Avery's comment to a fellow prisoner, William Rattenbury, who was under sentence of transportation for rum-running and assault on a coastguard officer, that Elizabeth Harris, who claimed to have witnessed the murder, had been in bed with him all night, so she could not possibly have been at Jacob's Well. Most of the information she gave about the murder could have been gleaned from the newspapers at the time, and also from her fellow rogues in prison. Avery was brought from gaol to confirm that she had been with him from just before 10 p.m. on the night of the murder, thus throwing some doubt on all her evidence. He had been meticulous in creating his own alibi at the lodgings that night, and took particular care to ask people the time throughout the evening. He was known to have sworn vengeance against May, yet he knew better than to be implicated in any physical attack on him. As he was with Oliver and Turpin at the fair, he may have had some hand in instigating the crime.

In summing up the case, Mr Justice Williams said that the jury's decision rested largely upon their opinion as to the quality of Elizabeth Harris's testimony and way of life. If the jury believed her evidence, they must convict the prisoners. He hinted that their identities had been corroborated by several of the witnesses. Significantly, he had apparently misunderstood one vital point – namely, what Charlotte Clarke had actually said when giving evidence to the effect that the man called Turpin, whom she had seen at the Lamb Inn and previously at Taunton, was definitely not the Turpin she now saw in the dock. Her words evidently had two meanings: 'this Turpin was not one of the men,' she said. She was referring to the unfortunate Galley and this should have been the main point in his defence, if only he had had any counsel to defend him.

At 9.45 p.m. the judge left the matter in the hands of the jury. Sixteen minutes later, they returned to give their verdict. Both prisoners were found guilty of murder.

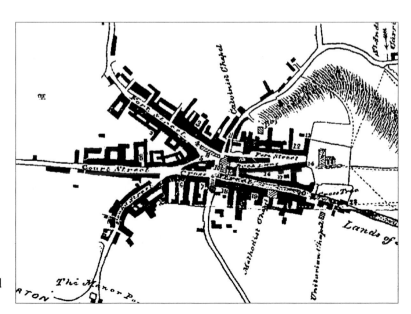

An enlargement of the map of the main street. (Moretonhampstead History Society)

Galley shouted that he was innocent, and the judge paused before donning the black cap. At some length he explained to the court that the jury must have felt that the weight of Elizabeth Harris's testimony was so great that they had to convict, despite what he regarded as a suitably impartial summing up on his part. If there was any doubt, he seemed to be saying, it was not for him to decide but for the jury, thus absolving himself of responsibility in the case after the conviction had duly been given.

As he reached the part where he was about to pronounce sentence, Oliver could hold back no longer. 'My Lord,' he said, 'do not, I hope you will not, send an innocent man to the trap. The man by my side is as innocent as you are, I never saw him in my life till I saw him in gaol. I was there but this young man was not. The man who did this is known by the name of the Young Hero, or the Kentish Youth; he is also known by the name of Turpin.'

The judge replied that it was 'only on proof that we can proceed here, and we must be regulated by the evidence given. On this the jury have found you both guilty.' Oliver insisted that his partner in crime was a better-looking man than Galley, and taller. Galley continued to protest his innocence, claiming that if he had had the money, he would have been able to prove it. He could not understand why the witnesses had sworn falsely against him, and hoped God would forgive them. The judge said that if what he claimed was true, Galley must be the unhappiest man alive, a sentiment with which the prisoner must surely have agreed. He reminded them that the jury had been persuaded of his guilt and that, though human nature meant it was possible they could have been deceived, there could be no better system of justice than that under which they had been tried. He recommended that Galley should obtain his mercy and forgiveness from God in the time remaining to him, rather than from the court whose decision had been made.

Again Oliver begged the judge not to hang an innocent man, saying that all the witnesses had been deceived and mistaken in identifying a man he had never seen as his partner in Jonathan May's murder. Both men protested Galley's innocence, and the judge took several minutes before he directed that the prisoners should be taken back to the gaol to await execution without hope of mercy.

Galley had one remarkable stroke of good luck, however. During the week of the trial, a statute requiring that death sentences had to be carried out within forty-eight hours was repealed. Had this not been the case, he would have gone to the gallows then. As a result of deputations from certain well-placed people, Mr Justice Williams was persuaded that certain aspects of the case against Galley needed further investigation, and so the executions were set for Friday week.

Both men were interviewed in prison, and Oliver repeatedly swore that Galley was innocent. He also said that his partner in crime had been a man called Longley, who killed May after Oliver had pulled him from his horse. After May had been attacked, Oliver said, they both fought for the money but Longley won as he was larger and much stronger.

While awaiting execution, the deeply distressed Galley almost went to pieces. The answers he gave to the investigators were very confused at first, and he said he could not recollect where he had been on 16 July the previous year. After a day or two he calmed down, and repeated that he had been at Dartford that day. Certain details of his visit to the fair came back to him, such as an argument he had had with a man over a wager of half a crown, which led to a fight and his losing the money. He later won it back by a card trick. He named three men whom he had seen at the fair; letters were sent to them, and they replied that they all recalled seeing him there.

Thomas Oliver was hanged at Exeter Gaol on 12 August 1836. He had made a strong impression on everyone at the prison with his courage, especially in his efforts to help Galley escape what he considered to be an unjust conviction. He had come to terms with his own fate. Asked at the last moment whether he had anything else to say, he said, 'All I have to say is to inform this congregation that I am a guilty man; the other is an innocent man.' Before the noose was placed around his neck, he dropped a red handkerchief, a custom which signified to the crowds that he had not betrayed his associate. He had already named Longley as the murderer, and had no reason to show him any loyalty because Longley had beaten him and taken the prize. The associate he had not implicated was probably Avery.

A few days later, a student doctor in Exeter told the prison governor that his father, a magistrate in Bath, had written to say that the Bath magistrates had remanded a man whom they believed to be Longley. They were holding him to give the Devonshire authorities a chance to take action, but they did nothing. Harvey was asked to intervene, but refused to prosecute the man, who was later released.

Galley was granted another stay of execution, until 23 September. From Exeter gaol he was taken to Woolwich and placed on the prison hulk *Ganymede*. His hair cropped and his face freshly shaven, he was placed in convict's clothes along with the other prisoners, and four key witnesses were brought to the ship to see if they could identify him. All could do so without difficulty, thus effectively proving his alibi that he was far away from Moretonhampstead at the time of the murder. A full pardon was expected by some, but instead, because of the doubts that remained as to his innocence, the sentence was commuted to transportation for life. For two years he waited for news of his release, but in vain. In May 1839 he was sent to New South Wales on HMS *Parkfield*, and arrived there four months later.

The fact that a potentially innocent man had almost gone to the gallows added weight to the arguments of those in authority who were calling for the abolition of capital punishment in England. Judges in Devon were so mindful of the case and the possible miscarriage of justice that no executions were carried out in Exeter for another thirteen years after Oliver was hanged.

Soon after reaching Australia, Galley was given the position of overseer on a chain-gang working at Cook's River for six months. Afterwards he worked alternately as a farm servant and at his old trade of brickmaking. A campaign in England to clear his name eventually succeeded, and he was granted a Queen's Pardon in October 1879. In 1881 after a debate in the House of Commons, an agreement was made for him to be awarded compensation to let him return to England if he wished, and live out his remaining days in comfort. However, he chose to stay in New South Wales, where he had long since happily settled with his wife and children. He died peacefully in November 1885, aged about seventy.

13
THE GLOVE-MAKER AND THE CHIMNEY SWEEP

Langtree, 1854

As the crime historian Colin Wilson observed in *Murder in the Westcountry*, because nearly everybody knows everybody else in such close-knit communities, rural crimes tend to be solved more quickly. However, the police in Victorian Devon often found it helpful that some areas within their jurisdiction were so remote that there was always somebody who knew other people's business and movements, especially if they were suspicious. If any strangers were in the area, a description could normally be supplied, and if a crime was committed, the miscreant would probably find no hiding place. This was what happened in 1854 when Mary Richards was raped and murdered in a relatively remote part of North Devon – the guilty man was remanded in custody within hours.

Mary Richards was a quiet, God-fearing girl of about twenty-one. She lived with her mother, Betty, at Langtree and helped to support her by making gloves for Agnes Wills, a shopkeeper at Torrington, 5 miles away. At around midday on 16 May 1854 Mary left her home for the shop, carrying the few pairs of gloves she had just finished. She also took with her two baskets, two dresses, a collecting card for the chapel and a shopping list including sugar, currants and saffron, to buy for a neighbour, Mary Ann Tucker. Arriving at Torrington, she did her errands, collected some belongings she had left at a friend's cottage, and at about 4 p.m. she set out for home with the shopping, walking up the long, steep Croft Hill.

She never reached her destination. At about 5 a.m. next day a shoemaker, William Milford, was walking past a row of fir trees at the top of the hill and heard groaning coming from a field adjoining the road. Going to investigate, he found Mary, her face and clothes covered with blood, lying in a ditch. Her dress was torn and one shoe was missing.

At that point another man, William Ward, drove by in a cart. Milford stopped him and between them they lifted her up carefully. As they moved Mary, the crown of her bonnet fell from her head and they were horrified to see the brain oozing from a large wound in the skull. They asked her who she was, and though very weak, she was able to tell them she was the daughter of Betty Richards. She was trembling and suddenly became violently sick.

Meanwhile, Betty had been sitting up all night, waiting for her daughter's return. At about the same time as the men found Mary she left the house to look for the girl, reaching the field shortly after Milford and Ward. Horrified by their discovery, she spoke to Mary, who asked her in a weak voice if she could have some warm tea. Having probably been lying in the ditch for at least twelve hours overnight and in a state of extreme shock, she was very cold. Other people arrived and one went to fetch a surgeon, Dr John Oliver Rouse. After he had examined her, she was gently lifted into the cart and taken to the union workhouse. So far she had been unable to say what had happened to her, or by whom she had been injured.

On further examination Dr Rouse found Mary's hair was clotted with blood, and when he cut a large amount out, he saw thirteen wounds on her head. The bone was broken on the temple, there was an extensive scar 1 inch in diameter and a heavy bruise on the right side of the head. Her skull was smashed, and after he removed a piece of straw bonnet from her wound, he discovered that the membranes that covered her brain were broken. A blow must have been inflicted with a heavy blunt instrument. Further examination revealed that she had also been raped.

When she came round, the doctor told her that her condition was hopeless and that she would not recover from her injuries. (One might think that in a similar case today, he would be a little less honest and try to give her some hope of survival, even if he knew she had no chance.) Though she was barely able to speak, somehow she found the strength to tell her mother the names of the people she wanted to bear her to her grave and the hymns she would like for her funeral. She then recited the verse of a hymn which she wanted engraved on her headstone.

Suspicion fell immediately on a chimney sweep, Llewellyn Garret Talmage Harvey, a distinctive-looking man with long sandy whiskers who had been in the vicinity of Torrington on the afternoon of 16 May. He had been born in the Oxford area, the illegitimate child of a tradesman, and received a good education. As a young adult he had visited the United States of America and claimed that while he was there he had taken part in activities with the Bible Christians, but later admitted this to be untrue. He was married, though there was no record of any children. He had a history of petty theft and his living as a chimney sweep gave him ample opportunity to identify suitable properties for future burglaries. Shortly after moving to Devon he had been imprisoned for sheep stealing. One account says that he was transported to Australia for the offence, but had this been carried into effect he would not have returned so quickly, if at all. It is more likely that he was threatened with such a sentence, which was then commuted to imprisonment. He had been seen speaking to Mary when she entered the cottage on the road home to collect her things and again in Torrington later that same day.

Abraham Oldham, police superintendent at Barnstaple, was put in charge of the case, and on 17 May he went round various lodging and public houses in the town to check on any strangers who might have arrived within the previous twenty-four hours. At 1 a.m. he went to investigate a brothel where he found Harvey standing naked by the bed with a handkerchief round his head. Oldham asked him who he was, to be told brusquely, 'That's my business and not yours.' 'I must know something about you,' Oldham insisted. 'If you must know, I came last from South Molton,' was the answer. Noticing that the man looked as if he had recently sported whiskers but was freshly shaved, Oldham asked him where he had visited a barber, to be told 'at Porlock'. Then he arrested him on suspicion of 'an aggravated outrage'. Harvey denied knowing anything about the attack on Mary Richards, but he was made to get dressed, taken downstairs and handed over to one of the policemen who had accompanied Oldham. He tried to escape, but after a scuffle he was recaptured.

The same day he was taken before the magistrate. At first he refused to give his name or say anything about himself. After considering his position, he gave in and supplied his name and address. Oldham then took him to see Mary Richards, where she lay helpless in her bed at the workhouse, and she confirmed that he was the last man she had seen. She fixed her eyes on him while he stood there and, not surprisingly, she seemed afraid of him. He was present at Rouse's examination. Another constable, James Terrell, went to search Harvey's home on 18 May, and found a hammer with bloodstains on it and a few blades of fresh grass between the claws.

During the next few days Mary drifted in and out of consciousness. At times she was quite lucid and made an effort to carry on normal conversation. George Henry Sellick, master of the union, saw her on 19 May. She said she had sent for him so he could take down in writing what she could remember about Harvey. She proceeded to give a detailed account of his attack on her. At one time Rouse thought she might make a reasonable recovery, or at least live for about another year, but it was not to be. In a few days she took a turn for the worse, and her mother stayed by her bedside for most of the time as she lingered, her periods of unconsciousness becoming longer, until she died on 30 May. A post-mortem found that the rest of her body was perfectly healthy and death was caused by injuries to the brain.

The case came to trial at Exeter Summer Assizes on 24 July. The first witnesses to be called by the prosecution were Milford and Ward. Among those who followed were surgeon Rouse, Sellick and Betty Richards. A blacksmith from Little Torrington, George Gribble, said he had been on the town bridge on the day of the attack and saw the prisoner; at first he thought he was fishing, but then he noticed he appeared to be doing nothing. He saw something projecting from his right-hand trouser pocket, which he thought must have been a stick, until he looked more carefully and noticed it was a knife.

Mary Allen, another glove-maker, lived at Sutcombe, 12 miles from Torrington. She said she had come into the town that day with some gloves, and that she knew Harvey fairly well. When she saw him sitting on a bank by the roadside they exchanged a few words, and he asked her how long it would be before she returned. She said it would not be for a while. At first he started to follow her, then said he would wait for her. He looked at what she was carrying, said it was a fine basket of work and added she was bound to get paid well for it. She found something disquieting about his manner, then saw what she assumed to be a knife in his pocket – only now did she realise it must have been the hammer. Nervously she humoured him before hurrying away.

Agnes Wills confirmed that Mary Richards had brought her some gloves on 16 May between 10 a.m. and 2 p.m. She paid her 4s 7½d, and gave her some leather to make up a few more pairs. On the next day she saw the prisoner at her shop, bringing in some gloves made by his sister-in-law, Agnes Dale. As she paid him, she asked if he had heard about the sad news in the area and he told her he had not. Policemen had been at her house just before he called at the shop and she mentioned that constables were out in full force, looking for a man whom she described as having the appearance of an Irish vagrant with sandy whiskers. With this he said 'Good morning' and left the shop. He told her he was a chimney sweep and she observed that his linen seemed unusually clean for somebody in that particular trade.

Grace Short, a widow who lived at Taddiport, said that on 16 May she saw a young woman walk past her shop carrying two baskets. She also noticed a man following her up the hill and was sure the prisoner was that same man. Another resident of Taddiport, Mary Haywood, recalled having seen Mary at about 3.30 that afternoon. A man in a black long-tailed coat and black high-crowned hat was following her. She heard him say to her, 'You have got to journey's end', to which she assured him that she had several miles to go. She then turned into the house of Haywood's next-door neighbour, Mary Martin.

Several other witnesses came forward to confirm that they had seen Harvey in the area that day. Among them was Thomas Stacey, who had been walking past the fir trees at the scene of the attack. Rather oddly, he noticed what he described as fresh blood, but heard no crying, nor anything else suspicious, and he saw no reason to make a search of the area.

Abraham Lamb, a barber at Barnstaple, recalled the prisoner coming to him in the afternoon and asking to be shaved. As Lamb was putting the lather on the prisoner's face, Harvey asked for his whiskers to be shaved off, high under the hair on his head. While the barber did so, he asked him about the distances to Wiveliscombe and Ilfracombe. On the following day Lamb identified him at the station house as the man he had shaved. After this the prisoner's statement was read out to the court. It was a long, rambling account, which said nothing about meeting the deceased, and only asserted his innocence.

At 6.30 p.m. the trial was adjourned. Throughout the proceedings Harvey was seen continually making notes in pencil to send to his counsel. They were written at high speed, which impressed the spectators in court. The sitting was resumed by Mr Justice Wightman at 9 a.m. on 25 July. Mr John Coleridge addressed the jury on the prisoner's behalf, but his task was a hard one. All he could do was express general observations on the brutality of the crime and the disgust that every man must feel. Though there can scarcely have been a man in court who had not made up his mind on a conviction, he continued, he asked the jury 'to dismiss from their minds anything they had heard or read on the subject'. Mr Justice Wightman summed up the case, but it only took the jury a few minutes to arrive at their verdict of guilty.

In prison awaiting execution, Harvey confessed that he was guilty of the murder and acknowledged that the sentence was a just and righteous one. He stated that he had left his house with the hammer in his pocket and had gone out determined to kill a woman or young girl at random. Mary Allen had had a fortunate escape because he had initially resolved to make her his victim, but somehow he lost his nerve. It was the tragedy of Mary Richards to cross his path by chance later that day and to pay the ultimate penalty of fate.

After he had been convicted, he sought the attendance of several local ministers of the Wesleyan Methodists, to which body he represented himself as belonging. Accordingly three of them attended him constantly until the day of his trial, after which they handed him over into the spiritual care of the chaplain of the gaol. He behaved himself well and hoped that he might still be acquitted. Once it was made clear that there would be no reprieve from his sentence, he resigned himself to his fate and asked the ministers to apologise to Mr Justice Wightman for 'the bold conduct which he displayed during his trial'. He likewise expressed his indebtedness for the powerful and eloquent speech made on his behalf by Mr Coleridge for the defence, and then had a last farewell meeting with his wife.

The last execution at Exeter Gaol had been that of convicted murderer George Sparks, sixteen months earlier, while Harvey had been there serving a sentence for stealing sheep. On Friday 4 August 1854, he was the next person to go to the gallows at the same premises.

14
THE SHOEMAKER, HIS WIFE AND HER LOVER

Clyst Honiton, 1865

In 1840 William and Mary Ann Ashford were married, both being around twenty-one years of age at the time. They lived in Clyst Honiton, a small, quiet village about 4 miles east of Exeter, where they had a shoemaker's business. According to the census returns of 1851, their address was 4 Victoria Cottages, though the Clyst Honiton burial records for 1865 give it as Duke of York Cottage. There appear to have been no children of the marriage.

William Ashford was a successful, thrifty and hard-working man of business, who had managed to save a considerable sum of money over the years. For much of the time he employed an apprentice. Census records for 1851 show that sixteen-year-old William Walrond was registered at the Ashfords' address in the capacity of 'cordwiner apprentice', as was bootmaker William Fish, aged thirty-two, although the latter is listed as merely a lodger. Walrond and Fish were reliable, hard-working young men who caused the Ashfords no problems. The same could not be said of a later live-in apprentice, William Pratt, who was appointed in about 1859.

After nearly twenty years of marriage Mary was becoming bored with her conscientious but perhaps rather dull husband, whom she sometimes felt paid more attention to his trade than to her. The arrival of good-looking, young William Pratt proved a temptation impossible for Mary to resist. As the newspapers were later to report, there could be 'no doubt that a criminal intimacy existed between them'. Aware that his wife and his employee were misbehaving behind his back, sometime around the end of 1863 William dismissed Pratt from his employment and ordered him to leave the house. Furious with his cheating spouse, William made a will in which he left all his property to his father and brother. Mary, meanwhile, continued a clandestine correspondence with Pratt, who had by now moved to Dawlish.

After eight months William Ashford reconsidered their position, and either realised that Pratt was too good a worker to lose, or was persuaded by his wife to let him return – perhaps a combination of both. By late 1864 Pratt was back at the cottage, and this time he was more circumspect in his behaviour. Having been given a second chance, he had seen the error of his ways, and 'his guilty passion seems to have cooled', no doubt much to the relief of his employer and presumably to the bitter disappointment of his employer's wife. Mary must have been even more mortified to learn that Pratt had recently become engaged to be married to a young woman in the village.

However, Mary and Pratt were both regularly seen together in public around Clyst Honiton, and their liaison was an open secret. She was still prepared to think she could win back his affections and get her hands on her husband's money. Already she had protested bitterly at being excluded from her husband's will, and this led to quarrels between them, as a result of which he reluctantly revoked the document. On 28 June 1865 he made another last will and testament which named her as the sole beneficiary.

On Wednesday 25 October 1865 Mary sent Selina Ann Ponsford, a young girl who lived nearby, to the chemist for some jalap, a drug which was then in common use as a laxative. The following Sunday, William Ashford had tea with a friend in the village, and in the course of conversation repeatedly expressed disgust with his wife's misconduct. Did he return home in a mood of bitterness and give her a piece of his mind? It was at this time that they were quarrelling, and not only in private. Angry scenes were seen and heard by others in the village. It may have been coincidence, but that evening Mary remarked with apparent concern to one of her neighbours, Police Constable Butt, that her husband had just become very ill with diarrhoea and general sickness. Next day he seemed a little better, but on the Tuesday he had deteriorated and she went to see Dr Lionel Roberts, a surgeon at Exeter. She described the symptoms to him, and he prescribed some medicine. That evening Emily Butt, the policeman's wife, called round to see how William was.

On the following morning Mary asked Dr Roberts to come and see her husband. He found the patient very weak and ill, constantly being sick, and complaining of great pain and thirst. He decided to change the medicine. On Thursday 2 November Roberts called again, and found the symptoms were just as bad as ever. That evening another neighbour, Mary Brewer, came to see them. While she was in the house Mary Ann mixed some medicine in the kitchen downstairs before bringing it up to William. Mary Brewer later said she thought there was nothing unusual in such an action.

On Friday William asked for a cup of tea, and his wife went downstairs to fetch him some. Mrs Butt had called again, and was sitting beside him in the bedroom.

Mary brought the tea up, but then heard a knock at the door and went downstairs to answer it. While she did so Mrs Butt got up to pour out the tea, and on lifting the spoon she was surprised to notice signs of a bluish-white powder attached to it. She thought it was probably arrowroot and expected it would thicken the tea, so she gave William a cup. However, one sip was enough for him to decide he did not want any more. Afterwards, she took some of the powder in her fingers, and was concerned to discover that it felt rather gritty.

Later that same day Dr Roberts saw William Ashford for a third time, and decided he would seek a second opinion. William asked for Dr Miles of Heavitree, whom he had seen before. Dr Miles arrived to find the patient in bed, his eyes protruding, his head bent backwards, his back arched and his limbs very stiff. He was just as puzzled by the case as his colleague, and could suggest no medicine other that that which had already been prescribed. Another visitor to the sickbed was William's younger brother, Thomas, who lived at St Thomas, Exeter. He had just received a letter from PC Butt warning him of the severity of William's condition. Mary took Thomas upstairs, and William greeted him sombrely with the words, 'Oh, I'm so very, very ill.' Thomas gave him some gin and peppermint, and stayed to talk to him for a while.

That night the patient had several seizures, and was in increasing agony throughout Saturday morning. He asked at least once for Dr Roberts, but either his wife delayed sending the message, or the doctor was too busy to come immediately. In view of the patient's serious condition, the latter is unlikely. It must be assumed that Mary did not want him to appear too promptly lest he should suspect what she was doing to the hapless patient. All the same, she invited Mrs Butt to come and stay at the house. During one of William's attacks Mrs Butt saw Mary sitting by the fire, saying nonchalantly, 'Stand back, let me look at him. Don't deceive me; one of those fits will carry him off.' On reflection it struck her as an unusually callous remark for a wife to make. She also noticed on the washstand a wine glass with a small deposit of powder settled at the bottom, similar to the substance she had found in William's tea. It looked rather suspicious, so when Mary was out of the room she scraped some out, putting it carefully in a piece of paper. Later she showed it to his brother, Thomas, and they guessed that it must be arsenic.

Mrs Butt stayed in the house to help, and during the afternoon she was in the kitchen cooking a meal for Mary when she heard what sounded like bumping going on upstairs. She went to the bedroom to check, and saw William out of bed having a fit, with Mary and another neighbour attending to him. Moments later Dr Roberts arrived. 'The man's dying,' he told them. 'What did you get him out of bed for?' 'He would get out,' they answered, as if unable to prevent him. At around 5 p.m. William's earthly sufferings were over.

Even after a post-mortem examination, two other doctors were unable to find any natural causes to account for the death. The deceased man's stomach, liver and samples of his vomit were placed in jars, sealed up and sent for further analysis to Mr Herapath at Bristol, after which he was given a funeral at St Michael's Church in the village. Mr Herapath discovered traces of arsenic and strychnine in the various samples, and gave his verdict that the symptoms were consistent with death

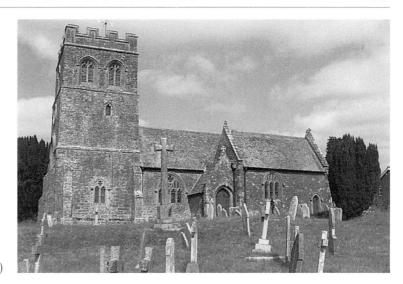

St Michael's Church, Clyst Honiton.
(© Kim Van der Kiste)

occasioned by such poisons. The powder in the paper which Mrs Butt had discreetly taken from the wine glass was sent to him and also proved to be arsenic.

Only one person had been in attendance on William Ashford when his illness began. PC Butt took Mary into custody that evening. When he asked her to come with him, she looked at him in horror and said, 'There is something, something; lock the door and tell me here.' He told her that he was not at liberty to explain any further while they were at her house, and she had to come to his place instead. When she agreed to accompany him, he charged her formally with causing her husband's death by administering poison. 'You cannot prove where I bought my arsenic,' she said. 'Oh, Mr Butt, I didn't do it.'

As he began to search her, she took from the pocket of her dress a prayer book, a purse, a pocket handkerchief and a small packet, which she threw into the fire. She had spilt part of the powder on her clothes, and wiped it off with the handkerchief. On examination this, too, turned out to be arsenic. White powder on the clasp of the purse was found to be strychnine mixed with starch. A further sample came to light on 10 November, six days after William's death, when Mrs Brewer was helping to clean the house. In the bedroom she found a screwed-up packet, clearly marked 'POISON'.

On 15 March Mary Ann Ashford went on trial at Exeter Assizes before Mr Justice Byles. For the prosecution, Mr Kingdon said that 'the prisoner was charged with one of the foulest offences that could be named – that of wilfully, with malice aforethought, poisoning her husband, who of all persons in the world should have been the nearest and dearest to her.' Leading the case for the defence was John Coleridge, who had been elected MP for Exeter the previous year. He told the court that it was unlikely the prisoner, 'however inconsistently she might have acted, would have poisoned her husband like a rat, before the eyes of several persons who had had their suspicions aroused against her. The matter was one of inference and suspicion, but was that sufficient ground upon which to take away the life of a fellow creature?'

The Ashfords' neighbour, Mary Brewer, had been summoned to attend as a witness, but was unable to be present through illness. One of those who took the witness stand was the deceased's brother, Thomas, who confirmed that William was forty-four years of age. He himself was forty: 'my brother was healthy, and a broader, stiffer man than I am.' William Pratt admitted that he had been on very familiar terms with the prisoner, but the relationship was over as he was now engaged. The prisoner had spoken to him about the last will at the time it was made, and when cross-examined, he said he had never known her and her husband quarrel about anything but the will. In view of the Ashfords' altercations in front of other people in the village, this remark seems hard to credit. The document was produced by the executors at the trial and revealed that the deceased had £123, plus effects amounting to £200 or so. Mr Chitty, the Clerk of Arraigns, read several letters written to Mr Pratt by the prisoner, making clear beyond doubt her passion for him, the fact that 'criminal intimacies' had existed between them, and that she had been indifferent towards her husband to the point of callousness.

It took the jury only ten minutes to reach a verdict of guilty. 'Anybody who has heard this evidence cannot entertain the particle of a doubt that you are guilty of that atrocious crime of which the jury has just found you guilty,' remarked the judge. 'You undoubtedly assassinated your own husband by poison, with a view, I fear, of obtaining his little property and returning to the embrace of your paramour.' On being returned to custody under sentence of death, Mary Ann Ashford confessed her guilt and the justice of the verdict. While in her cell at Exeter Gaol she tried to strangle herself with a handkerchief, but was prevented just in time by the female warders.

On 18 March her widowed mother-in-law, another Mary Ashford, died at the village poor house, aged seventy-four. Ten days later Mary Ann was hanged at Exeter by William Calcraft. Around 20,000 people were present, it was reported, 'to gratify their morbid curiosity'. Among those were presumably several friends and former clients of her late husband. None of them had ever been in any doubt as to Mary's guilt. Her blatant flaunting of her liaison with William Pratt and her husband's subsequent death in agony told them all they needed to know about her character.

In the normally sleepy little village the event attracted considerable local interest, even to the extent of being immortalised in a local ballad widely circulated on a broadsheet at the time. The verses run as follows:

Good people all both far and near
Pray listen unto me
Mary Ashford she did die
On Exeter's Gallows tree.

For the murder of her husband dear,
William Ashford was his name.
She poisoned him at Clist Honiton,
And died the death of shame.

In the year 1866
On March the 28th
Around the prison of Exeter
Many hundreds there did wait.

In expectation every moment
A dreadful sight to see
A female – Mary Ashford
Die on the fatal tree.

'Twas lust and money caused me
My husband dear to slay
For another man who worked for him
I took his life away.

May the Lord have mercy on his soul
I treated him so drear
I hope he's gone to the realm above
My murdered husband dear.

Mary Ann Ashford was the last woman but one to be hanged in public in England. Two years later the Capital Punishment Amendment Act was passed by parliament, and from August 1868 onwards all executions were privately conducted behind prison walls.

15
EXTRA DRILL LED HIM TO KILL

Devonport, 1869

In 1869 William Taylor, aged about twenty-two and a member of the 57th Regiment quartered at Raglan Barracks, Devonport, was like many other young soldiers serving in the British Army. He was married with a wife and baby, and most people who knew him considered he was of good character. In the army he had the small but noteworthy distinction of being awarded a badge for good service. Yet he had from time to time shown signs of mental instability as a child and as an adult. Some of those who had seen him behave peculiarly might not have been altogether surprised that his life was fated to end in tragedy.

On the evening of Tuesday 27 July he committed a serious breach of military discipline by scaling the wall in order to leave his barracks secretly for a few hours.

Raglan Barracks, Devonport, in the late nineteenth century.

Having won his temporary freedom, he visited a woman's house for, one assumes, the usual kind of assignation. While he was there he met a sailor, who was probably there for the same reason. A very merry evening was apparently had by all, not least Taylor, who ended up full of brandy and in no state to return discreetly to barracks that night.

Shortly after getting back the following morning, he was sentenced to be confined to barracks and given extra drill for seven days, which was considered a relatively light punishment. Corporal Arthur Skullin was appointed to see the exercise was carried out, and Taylor was accordingly put on his extra drill with Moses Jaques and Edward Randall, two other defaulters from the same regiment.

On the morning of Saturday 31 July drill was scheduled to start at 6.30. First, Sergeant William Bailey inspected the defaulters and made a remark to Skullin, who asked Bailey if he would inspect each man's kit. Jaques and Randall laid down their knapsacks and passed the test, but Taylor's was found to be empty. He was told that he would be reported to the sergeant-major, and his name sent to the adjutant for further punishment. Taylor said he had got another man's knapsack by mistake, and to give him a second chance Skullin sent him to the barrack-room for his own kit. As Taylor started to walk away, he was called back by Skullin who told him to take his rifle with him.

Lance-Corporal Patrick Burns, of the same regiment, went into the barrack-room at about that time, and noticed Taylor putting on another knapsack. At about 7.20 a.m. Burns returned to the barrack square, and found Skullin drilling all three defaulters together. Each of them, he noticed, had his rifle. The exercises went on for about ten minutes, after which the corporal dismissed the men and went towards his barrack-room. Taylor followed him, and they walked about thirty paces, Taylor being about seven paces behind all the way. Suddenly Taylor halted, took his rifle, put it to his shoulder and fired at Skullin's back. The latter fell immediately to the ground, dead.

When he saw what had happened Burns immediately ran towards Taylor, seized him and took his rifle away. He asked what on earth the soldier thought he was doing, but Taylor made no reply. Burns then took him to the guardroom. At that stage he recalled Taylor having said the previous evening that Corporal Skullin was drilling him 'very hard'.

Taylor was taken to Sergeant Edward Green, who was on duty at the barrack yard. He had heard the shot. Green examined Taylor's rifle, which contained a cartridge case and appeared to be dirty from powder at the muzzle. The barrel was warm, and in Green's mind there was no doubt that it had been recently fired. He handcuffed Taylor, and asked him what had made him do it. Taylor replied that he did not care; it would end his life, and that was what he wanted. 'You don't know everything,' he went on. 'I have a wife and child, and I have behaved very badly to them.' He said nothing more, and Sergeant Green left him in the charge of a sentry.

Police Constable David Shoebert found Taylor in the guardroom, and told him it was his duty to charge him with killing Corporal Skullin. As he was being led to the police station, Taylor said to him, 'It is curious what things come into a man's mind. He was the drill corporal, and he was annoying me the whole morning. I had seven days to barracks. I had not my kit in my knapsack, and he took my name down to report me. It must have been the drill that tempted me.'

George Bell Popplewell, the regiment's surgeon, was summoned to carry out an inspection of the dead man. He found two wounds in the head, one behind the left ear and the other through the left eye. The base of the skull and face on that side were broken, and the brain protruded. The ball had entered the left ear and come out at the left eye, and death must have been instantaneous. Later that day Mr Bone,

Raglan Barracks, Devonport, Plymouth. (Courtesy of Tom Bowden)

the Borough Coroner, met a jury at the Stoke Military Hospital, and they then went to Devonport Guildhall where Taylor was formally charged before the Mayor, Dr Rolston. Bone remarked to the jury that the case appeared to him to be as plain as it was melancholy, and a verdict of wilful murder was returned.

Taylor was remanded in custody at Exeter Gaol and on 13 August Robert Rainsford, the head warder, took him to Newgate, London, to await trial. The case was considered sufficiently serious to be tried not locally, but at the Central Criminal Court at the Old Bailey. On the journey Taylor made a full confession of his crime. He admitted having escaped from barracks to go out and visit a female companion. He said he had had too much to drink and had no idea what he was doing. Next morning he was ordered to do extra drill, and it only occurred to him on the spur of the moment to shoot the hapless corporal who had been placed in charge of him.

The trial was held on 22 September, the Attorney-General, Sir R.P. Collier, conducting the prosecution on behalf of the Crown, with Mr Molesworth St Aubyn defending. Various personnel from the 57th Regiment, including Colour-Sergeant John English, Lance-Corporal Patrick Burns, John Walsh (the drummer), Privates John Balston and Edward Randall, and Sergeant Bailey, were among those called by the prosecution to give their eye-witness accounts of events immediately before, during and after the killing. Rainsford and Popplewell were also called to corroborate their statements regarding the prisoner's confession and medical details.

For the defence, St Aubyn made much of the likelihood that Taylor was of unsound mind. The question of who was sane and who was not, and where the line was to be drawn 'when reason ceased to assert her sway', he said, 'had been a fascination for mankind from the remotest time'. Witnesses were to be called, St Aubyn went on, to prove that the prisoner's grandmother was mad, that his father had died in a lunatic asylum, and that he himself had exhibited signs of insanity during his boyhood. Only three days before he shot Skullin he had apparently attempted to drown himself at Devonport.

To support his view, St Aubyn quoted from a textbook:

Homicidal mania is commonly defined to be a state of partial insanity accompanied by an impulse to the perpetration of murder. Occasionally the act of murder is perpetrated with great deliberation, and occasionally with all the marks of sanity. Those cases are rendered difficult by the fact that there may be no distinct proof of the existence, past or present, of any disorder of the mind, so that the chief evidence of mental disorder is the act itself.

He proceeded to call several witnesses who could testify to Taylor's recurring mental problems throughout his short life. First was John Cook, a dyer at Kidderminster, who had known Taylor's late grandmother for several years. He averred that she had been completely insane, and could not be left on her own for even an hour. She used to climb a wall stark naked, shouting 'Murder' and 'Fire' for no apparent reason. An uncle was similarly deranged, and had a habit of taking pieces of live coal to set his hair alight for the price of half a pint of ale. The Attorney-General added that the grandmother was never in a lunatic asylum, but lived with her husband, a carpet weaver, until her death. The uncle was an imbecile, who had a well-known drinking problem.

Another witness, Charles Poole, the town crier at Kidderminster, said his wife was an aunt of the prisoner, being Taylor's mother's sister. He had known the prisoner since he was six or seven, and always considered him to be potentially dangerous. On one occasion the lad had been left in charge of Poole's much younger son and threw him down a railway embankment, as a result of which he cut his head badly. His wife Betsy said she had known the prisoner from birth up to about his fourteenth year; once or twice he told her he was going to drown himself. Once he threw himself into a river, and several times he had taken a knife and threatened to cut his throat. He had always been very odd, and once threatened to burn his house down. Her husband, she believed, was afraid of him, and on one occasion sent him to stay with his aunt at Birmingham because they could not put up with him any longer. Taylor's father, she said, died in a lunatic asylum.

The Attorney-General gave evidence that the prisoner had been put to carpet weaving, but would not work. He confirmed that he had often told others he was going to cut his throat, first when he was about thirteen and had been supposed to run an errand for Mrs Poole, but refused and without any warning suddenly turned suicidal.

Thomas Taylor, a carpet weaver at Kidderminster (and no relation), said he had known the prisoner when he was a boy in the Kidderminster Union Workhouse. The other boys used to put him under the pump and douse him with water, after which he would seize a knife or a fork, and the governor would put him in a ward for a time. The prisoner was subject to epileptic fits, and Thomas Taylor had helped in taking his father from the workhouse to a lunatic asylum.

This tendency to mental instability was also borne out by Richard Quigley, a fellow private in the 57th Regiment. He said he had known the prisoner for sixteen months. On 28 July he went with several other soldiers to bathe near Devonport. Without warning Taylor jumped out of his depth and then shouted, 'Save my life!'. Quigley and another man promptly swam up to him and prevented him from going under. Later that morning, Taylor told Quigley rather ungraciously that he was not going to thank him, as he might as well be in the water as anywhere else. Another private from the same swimming party reported that Taylor had said in the barrack-room that 'they might as well have let him do it, for he would do it some time or other'. Two other privates from the regiment spoke briefly for the defence, giving additional weight to the argument that Taylor's sanity was in question.

The first witness to be called by the Attorney-General for the prosecution was Hubbard Rose, the Governor of Exeter Gaol. He said the prisoner was taken there on 3 August and stayed for ten days, until he was taken to Newgate. He saw him each day, and never noticed anything in his conduct to induce him to believe that Taylor was insane. The prisoner observed the rules faithfully and 'conducted himself in a regular way'.

The chaplain of Exeter Gaol, the Revd John Hollins, mentioned seeing and speaking to the prisoner. Once he said the conversation lasted about half an hour, and had reference to the charge against Taylor and the danger he was in. Hollins did not discover any symptom of the prisoner not being in his right mind, though he thought him a rather stupid man. He wrote a letter which the prisoner dictated to him, putting it in witness's language. The subject of the letter seemed rational enough.

The gaol surgeon, Thomas Wilson Caird, and the governor of Newgate, Edmund James Jonas, had both seen the prisoner daily for the last six weeks, and talked to him from time to time, but not longer than five minutes on any occasion. As a prisoner he seemed quiet and well conducted, and showed no signs of insanity. This was substantiated by John Rowland Gibson, the Newgate Gaol surgeon, who had had several long interviews with Taylor in order to ascertain the state of his mind. On the subject of crime 'and on other subjects' he always spoke rationally.

On the part of the defence, Mr St Aubyn urged that there was no evidence of malice aforethought on the part of the prisoner, but that with the strong taint of insanity in the family, it might be that the taunts of his corporal and the effects of a sudden paroxysm were too much, 'and his cup of reason overflowed'.

The case for the defence was strong and eloquently argued. In his summing up Attorney-General Collier complimented St Aubyn on his ingenuity, and said how satisfactory it would have been to him if he could have adopted the theory of the defence, for the duty which he and the jury had to discharge was a painful one. However, he could not escape from his duty, which was to impress on them all that in his view the defence of insanity had entirely failed. He dwelt on what had been laid down by the highest authority on the plea of insanity, namely the judges in reply to questions by the House of Lords, and they had said in effect that:

> a jury ought to be told in all cases that every man was presumed to be sane, and to possess a sufficient degree of reason to be answerable for his crimes, unless the contrary was proved to their satisfaction; and that to establish a defence on the grounds of insanity it must be clearly proved that at the time of committing the act, the party accused was labouring under such a defect of reason as not to know the quality of the act.

He did not think that the prisoner was mad; the jury had to be satisfied that he was, and that he was so insane that he was unaware of what he was doing. Where, he asked, was the evidence of that? Nobody, he advised, had even suggested that the prisoner had any delusion at the time he committed the crime. The delusion, if any, existed nowhere except in the imagination of Taylor's counsel. He did not know what could countervail such a body of evidence as had been given by the governors, surgeons and chaplains of the prisons in which the prisoner had been confined since committing his crime. While it must be admitted that his father was at one time in an asylum, and madness was in some cases hereditary, so were other afflictions such as gout. A man was not necessarily mad, he said, because his father may have been insane at one time. Supposing, he asked the court, a man was forbidden to make a will because his father had once been in a madhouse; such a theory would be preposterous. The prisoner's grandmother was an eccentric, maybe an alcoholic, but she was never in a lunatic asylum, and she lived with her husband until her death. The uncle too was a drunkard, who had weakened whatever little intellect he ever had. Yet there was no evidence of any insane delusion under which he ever laboured during his life, boy or man.

The jury, he feared, must come to the conclusion that the prisoner had contemplated the crime for some time, and that it was executed with more deliberation and with more malice aforethought than Taylor was willing to confess. He had loaded his rifle some time before he went to drill, and before the corporal was shot. In all probability he loaded it when he went back to fill his knapsack, and it had to be remembered he said to one of the witnesses that he would 'put him out of his mess before night'. It must be assumed that having made such a declaration, Taylor loaded the rifle, and it was probably at this stage that he had the idea of shooting Corporal Skullin. That, Collier submitted, was what the law called malice aforethought.

His learned friend Mr St Aubyn had said the crime was murder or it was nothing, and it would be up to the jury to decide whether it was murder. If the prisoner was held to be mad, it was difficult to say what innocent person was safe from being killed by anyone who could be absolved from blame on grounds of insanity. Had there been fair or reasonable grounds for acquitting the prisoner, Collier should have sincerely rejoiced; but he felt bound to say that he saw no such reason, and he left it to the jury to perform their duty to the public.

In summing up the case for the jury, Mr Justice Brett reminded them first of the solemnity of the duty they had to discharge, and the fact that upon them rested the responsibility of deciding what was the law. If the prisoner was sane at the time, was he guilty of intentional murder? Did he deliberately take aim at the deceased? If he did so, whether it was premeditated or on a sudden impulse, there was nothing which in point of law could reduce the crime to manslaughter. Such an outcome was only possible if they could show that there had been undue provocation on the part of the corporal. While the latter may have acted harshly to the prisoner, this in itself did not provide sufficient grounds for calling the crime manslaughter instead of murder.

It took the jury only five minutes to bring in a verdict of guilty. As the judge put on the black cap and proceeded to pass sentence, he said that the prisoner had committed a grave military offence. He had been properly subjected to a military punishment and it had been the duty of the deceased, Corporal Skullin, to see that he did not evade it. In anger the prisoner had shot him, taking him at a base and cowardly disadvantage. It was to be regretted that such a crime was not so uncommon in the army as it had once been, but it had to be established that whoever was guilty of such an offence would meet with an inevitable doom, and that was the doom of death. Despite assertions made to the contrary, the judge could see no grounds for believing that the convict was not sane at the time of the crime, and he could therefore not escape the ultimate sentence.

Taylor was disowned by his unforgiving relatives, including his wife and young son, and received no visitors in his cell during his last days. On 11 October he was led to the scaffold with faltering steps, sobbing loudly as William Calcraft carried out the full penalty of the law.

16
THE MAN THEY COULD NOT HANG

Torquay, 1884

British murderers have achieved notoriety for various reasons. One Victorian villain has done so for one of the strangest reasons of all: he was 'the man they could not hang'. Three times the executioner tried to carry out his duty, and three times he failed before his 'client's' sentence was commuted to life imprisonment. After serving twenty-two years in prison, the villain of the piece emigrated and lived to a serene old age, dying thirty-eight years after release and exactly sixty years after he had gone to the gallows. As he wrote and published his memoirs shortly after release in 1908, the story and his thoughts on subsequent events are uniquely well documented.

John Henry George Lee was born at Abbotskerswell in August 1864, the son of a farmer. His parents, John and Mary, had already had a daughter, Amelia, and Mary also had an illegitimate daughter from a previous relationship. This girl, Elizabeth Harris, was raised by her grandparents in Kingsteignton. At the age of fifteen John became a junior servant at The Glen, a seaside house at Babbacombe, Torquay, which belonged to Emma Keyse, an elderly spinster. During boyhood he had always been fascinated by the sea, and despite parental opposition he joined the Royal Navy in October 1879. He proved a promising cadet, and just over a year later he was awarded an Admiralty Prize for good progress. However, any hopes of promotion and foreign travel were dashed when he was stricken with pneumonia at the age of eighteen, and after a spell at the Royal Naval Hospital in Plymouth, where his illness

The Glen, Babbacombe, Torquay. (From *Executioner*, Stewart P. Evans, Sutton Publishing)

was at one stage thought to be life-threatening, he was invalided out of the service. He found it hard to settle down to civilian life, and within a year he had had three jobs, none of which he really enjoyed.

By the end of 1882, thanks partly to a reference from Miss Keyse, he was employed as a servant by Colonel Edward Brownlow in Torquay. Six months into this post, he took advantage of the colonel's absence on holiday by stealing some of the family silver and trying to sell it to a pawnbroker in Devonport. He was arrested, found guilty and sentenced to six months' imprisonment in Exeter Gaol. Before his release the chaplain received a letter from Miss Keyse, explaining that she had always found the prisoner honest, truthful and obedient. If Lee was prepared to give her an undertaking as to his future good conduct, she would gladly employ him again as her gardener.

He accepted the position and returned to work for her in the spring of 1884. Meanwhile, she assured him she would do what she could to find him a more remunerative position elsewhere. As he now had a criminal record, Lee would find it difficult to obtain employment with anyone else, but Miss Keyse planned to put The Glen on the market and hoped to place her small number of devoted servants with other households as soon as she reasonably could. It may or may not have been a coincidence that at this time Lee began to do less and less around the house and garden. He remained impervious to her speaking to him on the subject. As she was reluctant to dismiss him, Miss Keyse told him instead that she would reduce his weekly wages from 2s 6d to 2s. He became surly, argumentative with everyone and made no secret of his lack of respect for 'the old woman'. Soon after this he became engaged to a local dressmaker, Kate Farmer, but realised he was not earning enough to support a wife. Frustrated by his lack of prospects, in October he briefly broke off the engagement, but Kate entreated him to reconsider, and they were reunited.

On 28 October Miss Keyse found a buyer for her estate at an auction in London. Later that day she paid her servants their quarterly salaries, owed in arrears, and Lee was furious to discover that she had carried out her intention to reduce his wages. She still assured him she would ask the new owners of the house to keep him on, but he evidently took the attitude that if he was receiving less money, he was obliged to work less hard. The atmosphere at The Glen became increasingly volatile.

Less than three weeks later, in the small hours of 15 November, the maid, Jane Neck, took Miss Keyse her nightly cup of cocoa and went to bed as usual. At some stage within the next two or three hours, Miss Keyse got up, went out into the hall and was savagely attacked. Her assailant bludgeoned her skull, slit her throat and then dragged her body into the dining-room where he attempted to burn it. He also lit other fires indoors. Between 3 and 4 a.m. the cook, Lee's half-sister Elizabeth Harris, woke up, smelled burning, and got up to rouse Jane and her sister Eliza, the only other servants in the house apart from Lee. When he appeared in response to her frightened cries, he was partly dressed. The house was full of smoke and he led her downstairs.

Coastguards and fishermen were summoned to help put out the blaze. On investigation it was discovered that five separate fires had been started in different places in the house, which smelled strongly of paraffin. In the hall was a pool of blood, and in the dining-room lay the body of Miss Keyse. Everyone thought at first that she had succumbed to the effects of smoke, and they were astonished to find that the cause of her death was something very different. The extent of her injuries was immediately apparent; newspapers had been spread around her body and set alight but had merely smouldered.

A window in the dining-room was broken, and when questioned Lee admitted he had smashed it. He had cut his arm, he said, while trying to let smoke out of the house. It was then realised that his hand had touched Elizabeth's nightdress before he broke the window, which explained the bloodstains on her garment, and more blood was found on the oil-can containing the paraffin used to light the fire. A towel and knife, which Lee kept to use for gardening, and a pair of trousers, all stained and smelling of paraffin, were also found in his quarters. The police superintendent warned him that as he was the only man in the house, he would be 'apprehended on suspicion' of murder.

An inquest was held at the town hall in St Marychurch and Lee was brought before Torquay magistrates. On 3 December, at Torquay police station, he was formally charged with the murder of Miss Keyse and committed for trial at Exeter Assizes.

Miss Keyse had been much loved and respected by local residents, and there was considerable indignation against the man whom they believed had killed her so callously. The vicar of St Marychurch preached a sermon to his congregation on Sunday 23 November, dwelling on the tragedy that had befallen them as a community, and how terrible it was that 'the one who served God so well should have fallen the victim of a heartless, cold-blooded, stealthy murder.'

The trial began on 2 February 1885 before Mr Justice Manisty, with Mr A. Collins and Mr Vigor conducting the case for the prosecution, and Mr Molesworth St Aubyn for the defence. Maintaining his innocence throughout the three-day proceedings, Lee pleaded not guilty. Among witnesses for the prosecution were Elizabeth Harris and a postman, both of whom said they had heard Lee make threats against Miss Keyse. The postman said that Lee had vowed to 'put an end to someone in the house before long,' and that if she 'did not soon get him a better place she would wish she had'. Harris repeated similar remarks, and said that Lee had threatened several times to burn down the house, especially after Miss Keyse had told him she was going to reduce his wages. At the time Harris was expecting a child, and she gave birth to a daughter, Beatrice, in the Newton Abbot workhouse six weeks later. The father was never named, but there was speculation that Beatrice was the result of an incestuous relationship between Harris and her half-brother. This was possibly no more than hearsay on the part of those who had already made up their minds that a fiend capable of beating an elderly lady to death could be responsible for anything.

The case against Lee looked reasonably straightforward, and it took the jury only forty minutes to reach a verdict of guilty. The judge told the prisoner that he had 'maintained a calm appearance' throughout the case, which did not surprise him. Even so, he had been 'found guilty of the murder upon evidence so clear to my mind, and so absolutely conclusive, that I am sorry to say I cannot entertain a doubt of the correctness of their verdict.' Lee was strangely unmoved by the verdict. 'The reason, my Lord,' he answered, 'why I am so calm and collected is because I trust in my Lord, and He knows I am innocent.' The *Western Morning News* thought otherwise, noting on 5 February that it was 'difficult to contemplate without a shudder the guilt which was brought home with absolute conclusiveness against him.' *The Times* was equally virulent in its condemnation of the prisoner, thundering in similar vein that 'the man who ought to have been her protector slew her in a barbarous and fiendish fashion, and added to his crime by endangering the lives of his three fellow servants, one of whom was his own sister.'

According to usual custom, there was a period of three clear Sundays between the judge's pronouncement of the death sentence and the execution itself. In his memoirs, Lee wrote that those three weeks were generally more terrible than the actual execution itself, but not in his case; he felt relieved because he knew what to expect. When the governor came to his cell to tell him the date fixed for the execution, he turned round and smiled. The governor told him in a very shocked voice that it was 'nothing to laugh at'.

On 23 February Lee went to the gallows at Exeter Gaol. Next day the *Dartmouth & Brixham Chronicle* told its readers that 'the culprit died easily'. It can only be assumed that the reporter did his work earlier that morning and took the rest of the day off, for the culprit did not die easily; in fact, he did not die at all. What happened was one of the most bizarre episodes ever recorded in the history of British justice.

During the night, Lee had written farewell letters to his parents and sister, received the Last Sacrament, and settled down to what should have been his final rest on earth, 'the last before the long, peaceful sleep of death.' He dreamed that he was on the scaffold and heard the bolt drawn three times but it failed to operate. On the morning of 23 February the Revd John Pitkin entered the cell, and stayed with Lee until the executioner, James Berry, arrived to pinion him and prepare him for the end.

Lee walked without assistance to the correct place beneath the beam, his legs were fastened, the rope was adjusted around his neck and the white cap drawn over his head. While the chaplain finished intoning the service for the burial of the dead, Berry pulled the lever, which should have freed the bolts on the trapdoors beneath the prisoner. Instead of the sharp jerk that should have launched Lee into eternity, the boards merely quivered. Berry tugged the lever again, thinking he had not pulled hard enough, while the attendant warders each used a foot to give added weight to the drop. Again, nothing happened. With the rope still around his neck and the hood still over his head, Lee was quickly escorted away as the warders set about searching for any obstruction that might have affected the working of the apparatus. Berry tested everything quickly and found that the doors were in working order. Lee was brought forward again and the chaplain repeated the last sentences of the service. Again Berry pulled the lever, but again the equipment failed to work.

It was six minutes since the procession had walked from the prison. Displaying astonishing fortitude and self-control, Lee stood as the rope was removed from around his neck and the white cap from his head, and he was escorted back to the main part of the prison. The structure on the scaffold was carefully examined and tested, and

John Lee.

Lee was brought out for a third attempt. As Berry pulled the lever once more, the structure quivered visibly – but the trapdoors remained firmly closed. Twenty minutes had elapsed since the first attempt. Lee was led back to the prison once more, and the increasingly embarrassed prison staff brought saws, chisels and other tools in an effort to make the equipment work. They were forestalled when the sheriff, acting on his own authority, ordered a stay of execution pending instructions from the Home Secretary, Sir William Harcourt. As Berry returned home to await his next job, having been paid his fee in full despite having failed to discharge his duty, local and national newspapers rang with the headline that would be eternally associated with the day's events – 'THE MAN THEY COULD NOT HANG'.

Lee had apparently taken this turn of events with equanimity. If he is to be believed – and naturally it is easier to be wise after the event – he seems to have had a touching faith in his dream that he would survive the attempts to put him to death. His Christian beliefs, he was sure, had sustained him. When he wrote to his sister twenty-four hours later, he told her that 'it was the Lord's will' that he should not die at the time appointed by man.

Newspaper reports of his being on the verge of collapse were credible enough, but he denied them. The cap on his head, he said, was slowly smothering him, so he tried to push it off by bending his head down and raising his manacled hands. The officials who saw him thought he was on the point of fainting. Once he was back in his cell, he proved that his appetite had not been affected. The doctor told him he could eat anything he wanted, so he promptly asked for a second breakfast of ham and eggs, to be followed by a beefsteak with half a pint of port for dinner. As he had already had one breakfast, not even the superhuman achievement of besting the hangman's noose

James Berry's lantern slide depicting his attempted execution of John Lee. (© Madame Tussaud, from Executioner, *Stewart P. Evans, Sutton Publishing)*

three times in a row was enough to qualify him for a second sitting and he had to wait until the following morning.

The apparatus had been thoroughly examined and tested on the previous Saturday, and its failure to work was never satisfactorily explained. The main theory advanced, but not conclusively proved, was that heavy rainfall on the Saturday night had caused the woodwork to swell.

Even Queen Victoria was horrified enough to intervene personally in the case. Within hours she had heard the extraordinary news, and from Windsor Castle she sent a telegraph to Harcourt expressing her horror at 'the disgraceful scenes at Exeter' at the execution:

Surely he cannot *now* be executed? It would be *too* cruel. Imprisonment for life seems the only alternative. But since this new executioner has taken it in hand there have been several accidents. Surely some safe and certain means could be devised which would make it quite sure. It should be of *iron* not wood, and such scenes must not recur.

For a month Lee was given to understand that his stay of execution was no more than that, and not until March was he informed that his death sentence would be commuted to life imprisonment. Penal servitude for life, the governor of Exeter Prison told him, would mean twenty years, though Harcourt had recommended that he should never be released.

Although (or perhaps because) his defence was thought to have been rather half-hearted, Mr Molesworth St Aubyn was cheered by this turn of events. On 24 February he wrote to Pitkin that he was among those who had never been fully satisfied as to Lee's guilt: 'What a marvellous thing if he turns out to be innocent!'

But if Lee was not the murderer of Miss Keyse, who was? It was said that Elizabeth Harris had a lover, a man prominent in London society, who sometimes slipped into the kitchen at night after Miss Keyse had gone to bed. On the night in question, she came down to speak to Lee, who slept in the pantry, and when she opened the kitchen door and saw what was happening, she recognised the man and fainted from shock. The man feared scandal, killed her, started the fire and bribed Lee handsomely to take the blame, assuring him that he had friends in high places who would somehow ensure that the gallows would not work.

Initially after the failed execution Lee had to spend a short period in solitary confinement, which in his case was at Pentonville for three months and then Wormwood Scrubs for another four. After this he was transferred to Portsmouth Prison, where he was employed making hammocks and working on the construction of new docks in the seaport. He then spent six and a half years in the prison laundry. When Portsmouth Prison was closed in 1892, he was moved to Portland, where inmates worked in the local quarries and stone-cutting sheds. For some time he was punishment orderly and had an exemplary record for good behaviour.

Each year he petitioned the Home Secretary to release him, protesting his innocence and citing his ordeal on the scaffold as extenuating grounds in his favour. For twenty years he was to be disappointed. However, in 1906 a Liberal government came to power, and the new Home Secretary, Herbert Gladstone – whose father, William Ewart Gladstone, was Prime Minister when Lee had begun his sentence – reviewed the case and decided that it was in Lee's best interests to set him free. Imprisonment for life, he wrote in a letter to one of his under-secretaries, would inevitably mean 'mental and bodily decay', and if he was to be allowed out, 'it is best to do it at once'.

The Home Office agreed that Lee should be allowed to sell his story by writing his memoirs, something which officials believed would be no more than a passing sensation. Lee's notoriety, it was assumed, would be a short-lived phenomenon and he would soon be forgotten. It was decided that he should be freed on licence, among the conditions set being that he should 'not habitually associate with notoriously bad characters, such as reputed thieves and prostitutes', nor 'lead an idle and dissolute life, without visible means of obtaining an honest livelihood'. Most important of all, a clause was added which forbade him from trading on his notoriety by taking part in any public performances, delivering any lectures or speeches, or exhibiting 'himself at any meeting, assembly or place of entertainment'. The previous government had been alarmed by rumours of his imminent release, and not surprisingly also by an offer from the owner of a music hall in Middlesex for Lee and Berry, the hangman who had failed to kill him, to appear on stage together for a fee of £100 per week. Trying to create a theatrical double act out of such a macabre event was surely stretching the bounds of good taste a little too far.

Berry, who resigned his position as executioner in 1892 after a few other botched executions (in one of which the murderer was decapitated by the rope), had displayed a wonderful talent for opportunism. Having executed 134 men and women during his eight-year career, he publicly came out against the death penalty, not only publishing his memoirs but also embarking on lucrative tours, lecturing on his experiences in a talk entitled 'From Public Executioner to Preacher of the Gospel'. During his period of office he had sold to a Nottingham publican the complete length of rope with which he tried to hang Lee. For some years afterwards he charged buyers 1s for a piece of the noose allegedly used on Lee – though the genuine article had long since been elsewhere.

Lee walked out of prison a free man in the utmost secrecy on 18 December 1907. He was escorted by a chief warder and his wife, who were going to spend Christmas in Torquay. Lee's father had died five years previously, but his mother was still living at Abbotskerswell, and he chose to pay her a surprise visit. Somehow rumours had preceded him, and several pressmen had gathered to wait outside the family home. He had barely arrived before editors were competing for the rights to print his story. On 29 December 1907 the mass circulation *Lloyd's Weekly News* began a series of episodes on the murder, Lee's experiences on the scaffold and his years in prison. The deal was said to have gained him £240, a handsome sum which precluded any urgent need to look for work.

In January 1909 Lee married Jessie Bulleid at a secret ceremony at Newton Abbot. One year later she gave birth to their son, also named John. Thirteen months later, in February 1911, he abandoned Jessie – who was expecting a second child – and their son when he sailed for New York with a woman whom he described as his wife. This was Adelina Gibbs, whom he met while they were working together at a public house in London and whom he probably never married but stayed with for the rest of his life.

A silent film based on his story, *The Man They Could Not Hang*, was made in Australia in 1912. Because of its poor technical quality, it was shelved by the producer, who passed it on to one of his employees. The man thought this was too good an opportunity to miss. Within a few years, he and an associate had enjoyed considerable success by showing it in cinemas throughout Australia and New Zealand. An expanded version was produced in 1921 and shown widely throughout Britain, and it was said, though never proved, that Lee made personal appearances at some of the cinemas concerned.

The rest of Lee's life is shrouded in some mystery. John Lee is a common name, and it is probable that others tried to pass themselves off as 'the man they could not hang'. His mother died in 1918 and ten wreaths were laid at her grave, but none of them on behalf of her son. One report says that he emigrated to Australia and died in Melbourne the same year as his mother. Another suggests that he went to Canada and died in an unspecified part of the country in 1921. According to another, he stayed in or came back to England, and took over a furniture shop in Plymouth in about 1920, shortly before committing suicide.

The most likely version seems to be that he and Adelina stayed in America and settled in Milwaukee. They had a daughter, Evelyn, who was employed as a maid but died in October 1933 at the age of nineteen after suffocating from naphtha fumes while cleaning her employer's apartment. Assuming this was the same John Lee, then he was still alive for many years after those scenes on the scaffold at Exeter were but a distant memory. On 19 March 1945, at the age of eighty, he succumbed to a heart attack at his home. Adelina survived him by twenty-three years, dying at the age of ninety-four on 9 January 1969.

17
ATROCITY AT PETER TAVY

Peter Tavy, 1892

Rarely did anything disturb the tranquility of Peter Tavy, a small close-knit village about 3 miles from Tavistock. But the gruesome events of a winter's evening late in 1892 temporarily shattered that peace in no uncertain fashion.

Among the families who lived in the community were the Williamses, the Doidges and the Rowes. William Williams, the eighteen-year-old son of the village miller, had become thoroughly smitten with Emma Doidge, a girl of seventeen, whose family

*Peter Tavy Mill,
the home and
workplace of
William Williams
and his family.*

lived at Cox Tor Farm. As well as farming at the property, her father John was a
churchwarden. For a while Emma was happy to spend time with William, but before
long she found his constant attention tiresome. He wrote her a couple of letters
begging her to take him back, but she replied with brief notes, telling him firstly that
she could only look on him as a brother, and secondly that she did not want him to
communicate with her any more. He was nothing if not persistent, and he still hoped
that she would eventually change her mind. Soon he became increasingly jealous of
any other young men whom he thought might be getting too friendly with Emma, and
when it seemed that she was becoming rather fond of William Rowe, whose family
lived at Lucy Cottage, he decided to act.

On 8 November Williams went to Tavistock to buy a revolver for 5s from Samuel
Blanchard, who ran an ironmonger's shop in Brook Street. Blanchard knew Williams
well, as he had often bought rifle cartridges at the shop. In spite of the fact that his
trade might suffer slightly as a result, Blanchard had recently discussed with Williams
the possibility that he might make his own cartridges to save money. When Blanchard
asked him why he needed the revolver, Williams said that he wanted to shoot a dog.
He also asked Blanchard if the weapon 'would kill across the street', and was told
that it would. Despite this conversation, not for one moment did it apparently cross
the vendor's mind that his customer had any more sinister motive in mind.

Williams had the forethought to keep it carefully concealed about his person, and
on Sunday 13 November he put it in his coat pocket before going to attend evening
service at St Peter's Church. All the families were pillars of the local church: William
Rowe worked the bellows for his organist father, Joseph; Emma Doidge and her
younger sister, Elizabeth, sang in the church choir; William Williams himself was one
of the bellringers, and had taken his part in ringing that afternoon.

Emma's brother, also called William, was a regular churchgoer too. Some of the
villagers thought that he attended services mainly so he could keep an eye on her and
shield her from Williams's unsolicited attentions, but as the family was so committed

to church activities, he would almost certainly have taken his place in the pews each Sunday anyway. After the service, Williams walked over to William Rowe, and evidently got the message that his presence was unwelcome. 'I'll knock your block off,' Williams said to Emma. 'You shan't touch her while I'm here,' William immediately told him. As Williams left, he was heard to mutter under his breath that somebody would 'fall tonight'. He also mumbled something to the effect that as they all had their Sunday clothes on, he would wait until the morning and then fight William Doidge.

As usual, William Rowe, Emma and her brother were among a large group of young people going home from church together in the direction of Cox Tor Farm. Others in the group included Emma's sister Elizabeth, and Annie, daughter of local farmer William Mudge. These girls, like Emma, all belonged to the choir. On this occasion, William Rowe and Emma had been delayed for a few moments because the vicar, the Revd Dr Bryant, had left his umbrella behind at the church and asked William if he would mind going back for it. When they came out with the umbrella, little did they know that Williams had gone ahead and was hiding behind a tree in Creedy Lane, waiting for them. As William Doidge was entering their house, Elizabeth was just behind him. She heard four shots. They walked back down the road, about 500yds, and could not believe what they saw.

While William Rowe and Emma Doidge were on their way home not far behind, Williams had jumped out at them and taken the revolver out of his pocket. A terrified William Rowe tried to run away but was shot in the head and fell to the ground unconscious as Emma tried to go to Sowtontown Farm for help. Williams seized her and she struggled to get away from him, tearing her jacket badly in the process. He fired at her and she was killed instantly. When their bodies were found, William Rowe's was about 12yds in front of Emma's. Next Williams turned the gun on himself, and the bullet struck him in the head but did no more than knock him off his feet. He tried to shoot himself again and this time the bullet took out one of his eyes.

After taking the service, Dr Bryant was sitting by the fire in his drawing room, reading, but was soon roused by the general commotion. A grief-stricken Mr Rowe ran in to tell him that his son and Emma Doidge had just been shot. The vicar had prepared Emma for confirmation, and this grim news came almost on the exact anniversary of the day that she had been confirmed. He paid a visit to Cox Tor Farm to offer his condolences.

By this time Emma's father had reached Creedy Lane, with Mr Mudge from Sowtontown Farm. The police had already been called to the scene of the crimes, and after they had concluded their investigations, the distraught Mr Doidge took his daughter's body to Cox Tor Farm in his trap, while Mr Mudge took the still unconscious William Rowe to Lucy Cottage. Dr Broderick went to Cox Tor and confirmed that Emma was dead. Next he visited Lucy Cottage, but after examining William Rowe, he sadly told his parents that he could hold out no hope. William lingered until 9 a.m. the next day and died without regaining consciousness.

Meanwhile, on the Sunday evening Williams bled profusely from his self-inflicted wounds as he staggered across the fields to the bank of the River Tavy and threw himself in. Either his attempt to drown himself proved as futile as the suicide bid with his revolver, or else he had second thoughts. After floating some distance downstream, he hauled himself out and staggered to a house at Harford Bridge, the home of George Doidge, a mason, who was not related to Emma's family. Mr Doidge was awakened about half an hour after midnight by the sound of loud knocking at his door. At first his wife thought it must be a passing drunk, but he went downstairs to investigate.

Though he knew Williams, at first he did not recognise the dishevelled figure with blood pouring from his head. When he asked Williams what the matter was, the latter said, 'Go and tell my father where I am. He will know all about it by this time. This is not the worst of it yet.' One of Doidge's daughters made a cup of tea for Williams, who drank it but refused to give any explanation for his condition. A little later, Williams's father and a policeman arrived at Doidge's house at the same time, and he was taken to Tavistock Cottage Hospital for treatment. When Dr Broderick extracted the bullet from his neck, he compared it with those taken from the heads of the victims and found they corresponded. At the hospital on Monday Williams said all he wanted to do was to see his parents. After that, the doctors could do what they pleased with him.

An inquest into both deaths was held on Tuesday 15 November at Cox Tor Farm. Among those present were Mr R.R. Dodd, the County Coroner; Mr T. Martin Rogers, the foreman; Superintendent Nicholls and Sergeant Pike, representing the police; Dr Bryant; Mr Holmes, Emma's maternal grandfather; and her father. After the formal identification of her body, they went to the village, passing the spot where the deed had taken place. Traces of blood were still to be seen and a large clot under a piece of timber marked the spot where Emma had died. After pausing at the Peter Tavy Inn to register their names, they went to Lucy Cottage for the formal identification of William Rowe's body. His father Joseph was there, and though he had maintained his composure till then, at the ceremony he collapsed, overcome with grief, crying out, 'My poor boy! My poor boy!' On their return to the inn, a unanimous decision was taken to adjourn the inquest until all the evidence had been gathered and post-mortem reports finalised by Dr Broderick.

On 16 November Police Constable Callard visited Williams at the cottage hospital. Mr Williams later came to see his son. 'Father, will you tell me the sense and truth of what has happened?' the young man asked. Mr Williams told him that William Rowe and Emma Doidge were going to be buried. 'Then they are dead?' his son asked him, still evidently a little confused. Then William Williams made a statement which the policeman recorded:

Father, I loved her dearly and it is all through the love and affection I had for her, and the provocation that I have received from other young men of the village that has led me to do what I have. It has been playing on my mind for the last four or five weeks, and, do whatever I could, I could not drive it off. They have trifled with me terribly. My intention to her was good, and I knew one or two others that used to go home with her, and that troubled me terribly. They have trifled with me so long until it has come to this. I have often had something to drink lately, thinking that would ease my mind, but no, it was all no good. Then I got to a terrible pitch, that I thought I would buy a revolver.

He went on to say that after he had bought the weapon he was afraid of it, as he had never seen one before. In order to try it out he fired at some birds, but did not think he succeeded in hitting any. 'I was not sure exactly whether it would kill or not. My mind was not easy then; I could not sleep at night; I was always thinking about it.'

A double funeral was held at the church on 17 November. The coffins were covered with floral tributes, and about 700 people attended. Both victims had been well-respected members of much-loved families who had long been known to the community, and many people at the church were weeping, still stunned at the horror of the incident which seemed so hard to comprehend.

Two days later, at 10 a.m., the inquest was resumed and concluded at the village school. The causes of both deaths were formally recorded, and a report on Williams's condition was also given. The remains of his wounded eye had been removed, and his bullet injuries were healing, though he was still in hospital and would probably not be well enough to be discharged for at least a month. Dr Bryant gave him what was described as 'a good character reference', though this was contested by some of the villagers, who said – perhaps with hindsight – that he had always had a shifty appearance which did not invite trust.

The grave of William Rowe, his parents and sister at St Peter's Church, Peter Tavy.

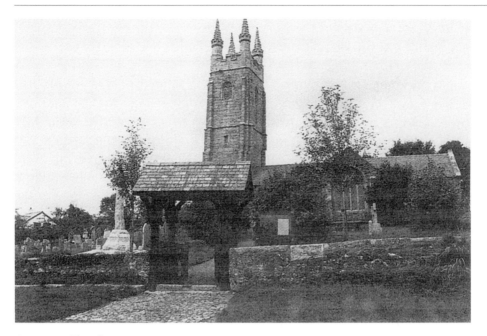

St Peter's Church, Peter Tavy.

Yet another untimely death was reported in the village that week. A friend of the Williams family, Mr Maddock, a man of thirty with a wife and small child, called at the house to express his sympathy to the parents. After leaving, he had only walked a few yards when he collapsed with a burst blood vessel. He was only saved from falling into the stream by the quick-witted presence of another man nearby. A policeman took him home just before he expired.

Williams recovered more quickly from his wounds than everyone had anticipated. Though still not completely better, he was allowed out of hospital in time for a two-day trial before the magistrates at Tavistock Guildhall on 29 and 30 November. Such was the interest in the case that the crowd gathering outside before the investigation began was estimated to have been enough to fill the hall ten times over. When the doors were opened to the public, after the magistrates had taken their seats and the prisoner was in the dock, there was such an unseemly scramble for the best seats that the police had to restore order and stop the fighting that broke out. Many of those who had to be excluded for lack of room then blockaded the doorway, and business was delayed so that silence and decorum could be restored.

That Williams's recovery was not complete soon became clear. He was still so weak that he was allowed to sit. He had to be helped in and out of the dock by policemen, and he wore a flesh-coloured shade over his face where the right eye had been. Throughout the hearing he betrayed no emotion, but kept pressing his hands against his head in pain. On the second day of the trial he fainted, and the hearing had to be suspended until he came round. After the trial he was taken back to the hospital and on the following day – 1 December, his nineteenth birthday – he was remanded at Exeter Gaol.

On 9 March 1893 he appeared at the Lent Assizes in Exeter before Mr Justice Lawrance, charged with 'feloniously, wilfully and of malice aforethought killing and murdering William Frederick Rowe and Emma Holmes Doidge at Peter Tavy'. The Hon. Bernard Coleridge MP and Mr Henry Lopez were counsel for the prosecution, and Mr H.E. Duke appeared for the defence. According to a possibly very short-sighted reporter from the *Western Morning News*, the prisoner, dressed in a light tweed suit with white cravat, 'had a smart, healthy and intelligent appearance'. Such a description of a youth who had narrowly survived a suicide attempt and become grotesquely disfigured in the process hardly rings true. Though he had already confessed to his crime, committed out of jealousy, before the Tavistock police and magistrate, Williams pleaded not guilty in court, hoping to get a reduced sentence on the grounds of insanity.

The prosecution opened by stating that the prisoner had gone about his work at his father's mill with the revolver in his pocket for several days before the incident in November, and therefore had the deliberate intention of taking life. The statement he made to his father at the hospital was then read out. It concluded with Williams's description of how he threw himself in the river, found himself on a stone and called to the Lord for mercy, and ended with the hope that his parents would forgive him. In short, Coleridge said, there was 'great design, great determination, and continued forethought' prior to the murders.

Among the witnesses called were Emma's brother William and sister Elizabeth, who gave their version of the events of that horrific evening. Mark Bellamy, a farm servant, told the court that he had seen a man with his collar pulled over his head soon after the shots were fired and was sure it was 'Blucher' Williams, the nickname by which he was known by the other boys in the village, after the Prussian general at the battle of Waterloo whose name was a byword for boorishness. Superintendent Nicholls said that he had found the prisoner's coat in the River Tavy between Tavistock and Harford Bridge. In the pocket were a prayer book and a cartridge.

The defence made the best of the mental incapacity argument. Dr Broderick said he could not say in all honesty that there were symptoms consistent with the prisoner having suffered from epilepsy, but he had been given to believe that there was a history of insanity in the family. First and second cousins had been admitted to mental asylums. Dr Peter Dens, medical superintendent of Wonford Asylum, Exeter, had made enquiries as to the prisoner's background and had personally examined him, but concluded he was of sound mind and understanding. He saw no evidence of insanity.

Mr Williams, the prisoner's father, said that his son had always been delicate, and at seven or eight years of age he had had a severe illness of an epileptic nature. Since that time he had often complained of severe headaches. Earlier in 1892 he had an attack of influenza and never seemed quite the same afterwards. In the weeks preceding the murders, his behaviour was very strange. Two villagers in Peter Tavy testified to the latter. One said that Williams had a tendency to glare and look excited for no apparent reason, and another thought he looked half-dazed much of the time, as if he had just recovered from a fit.

'Murder must be the deliberate act of a man in the full possession of his senses,' the defence remarked in summing up, suggesting that Williams was not of sound mind at the time. The judge elaborated, saying, 'The law on this point was that a person to be excused for such a crime must be in a state of mind which rendered him not able to distinguish between right and wrong.' If the jury had reasonable doubt as to whether Williams was responsible for his actions, if he was acting under some sudden and uncontrollable impulse, he must be given the benefit of the doubt.

The jury took only twenty-two minutes to return a verdict of guilty, adding that they considered the defendant to have been perfectly sane when he committed the crimes. 'I trust the jury will forgive me', the judge addressed the prisoner, 'if I think that had they come to any other conclusion they would have been wanting in their duty. A more cruel and deliberate murder I have never heard of.' As Williams had planned the deed and purchased the revolver a few days earlier with that very purpose in mind, it was difficult to argue that he had merely acted on impulse.

While Williams was awaiting execution, a petition for his reprieve was organised by the Revd A. Harvie of Christ Church, Devonport. Harvie had obtained 12,522 signatories and the petition was presented to Queen Victoria, but the Secretary of State could find no grounds for reprieve. Williams probably never knew of the petition's existence. While in Exeter Gaol he expressed some concern for the families of both his victims, and wrote long letters to his parents apologising for what he had done. In view of the circumstances of his deliberate cold-blooded double killing, it might not be too cynical to suggest that any belated penitence had a somewhat hollow ring. He found some consolation in reading the Bible and receiving religious instruction. On Thursday 23 March he was confirmed in the prison chapel.

On 27 March, the eve of his execution, he wrote a farewell letter to his parents, in which penitence and a startling certainty of going to heaven were equally apparent:

You must not trouble about me, I shall be far happier. I shall soon be where no troubles come. . . . I am very comfortable under present circumstances. My time is very short, but it does not trouble me much. I feel how I deserve my punishment, and all I have been through seems like a dream. I have been for a walk this morning. It seems very beautiful to me, but heaven will be far brighter.

It was signed, 'From your loving son, WILLIE IN CHRIST. Goodbye.'

On the following morning crowds gathered outside the gaol. 'An air of depression seemed to come over many of those who were waiting to see the message of death hoisted on the black staff temporarily erected over the entrance,' the press noted. '"Will the bolt fail?" seemed to be the thought uppermost in everyone's mind, so deep was the impression made upon the public by the futile attempt in 1885 to execute Lee.' Memories of that notorious failure probably loomed large in the authorities' minds too, and no effort had been spared to ensure that the fiasco would not be repeated. At 8 a.m. the warder whose duty it was to hoist the flag over the parapet was seen to lift his hat, and this was accepted as confirmation that the procession was approaching the scaffold. Williams, it was said, 'displayed the greatest fortitude' as he walked with a firm step the few yards from the condemned cell to the scaffold. The hangman, James Billington, assisted by Thomas Scott, placed the rope around his neck, a burial service was read by the chaplain, and a white cap was pulled down over the prisoner's face. As the black flag was drawn into position, there was a sigh of relief among the crowds who then dispersed, 'satisfied that the executioner had done his work with promptness and despatch'.

Within six months another member of the families involved had died prematurely. Joseph Rowe had been shattered by his son's murder; his health rapidly deteriorated, and he was admitted to the Cottage Hospital at Tavistock where he died on 1 September at the early age of forty-seven. The official cause of death was a heart and lung complaint, but nobody doubted for a moment that a broken heart had hastened his end. He was laid to rest in the churchyard beside his son. His wife, Emma, was buried there on her death in 1912, and their daughter Alice in 1940.

The shock of the murders continued to reverberate around Peter Tavy for some time to come. Constable Callard, who had been involved in the investigation, was so distressed by the case that he had a nervous breakdown and moved away from the area a few months later.

18
AN UNSUITABLE YOUTH

Plymouth, 1908

Edmund Walter Elliott did not have a particularly promising start in life. He was born in about 1889 to an unmarried mother of sixteen, whose own mother had also been born outside wedlock. On two separate occasions Edmund's mother had been convicted for keeping a brothel at their home, 46 Well Street, Plymouth. In spite of this he did well at school, achieved good results in his examinations, and decided he wanted to enter the Royal Navy. This ambition did not last long, and soon after leaving school he was apprenticed to a hairdresser, Mr Atrill of King Street, at his mother's request. After completing his term or being dismissed, depending on whose version of events is to be believed, he was unemployed for some time, and planned to join the army.

As a small boy he had played from time to time with a group of youngsters in the district, one of whom was Clara Jane Hannaford, a girl three years younger than Edmund, who lived at 2 Henry Street with her parents, George, an artisan, and Fanny, and her four younger siblings. As the eldest child Clara was expected to help her mother around the house, and in this she proved herself to be a model daughter.

When Edmund was eighteen he became rather attached to her. Her parents never really approved of him or of their liaison, largely as they thought Edmund was an idler who seemed incapable of holding down a steady job. When they found out that he had probably fathered a child with another girl who lived in the next street, they decided he was a bad character and thought Clara could do much better for herself. In the spring of 1908 they told her they did not want her to see him again. She apparently agreed to break off the relationship, which had never been very strong. As she was still only fifteen, she was hardly old enough to have a serious boyfriend.

George and Fanny's dismay when they found out in the summer that Clara and Edmund had resumed their friendship can be imagined. That they started seeing each other again may have been anything but a voluntary decision on Clara's part, as the family thought she was afraid of Edmund and felt it would be unwise to do anything that might provoke him to violence against her. After her parents had prohibited her from seeing him again, he frequently threatened to 'do for her'.

An incident in July 1908, the month Clara celebrated her sixteenth birthday, suggested that this was not necessarily an idle threat. One night he climbed in through her bedroom window to where she was sleeping in the same bed as her younger adopted sister, Elsie Gill. Edmund woke her and said he had come 'with the full determination of doing for you with a knife'. Although she must have been more scared than amused, she told him not to be so silly because he would wake Elsie. 'Very well,' he retorted, 'if she screams I will do the same to her.' At this point he evidently thought better of it and went away again.

When Fanny Hannaford heard that Elliott had broken into her daughters' room and threatened them, she vowed to give him a piece of her mind. She came round to his house looking for him, and when he came out to see her she hit him in the face and knocked him down. A policeman had to be called to separate them.

At this time Clara's uncle was serving in the Royal Navy aboard HMS *Leviathan*. He became friends with another young seaman, William Johnstone Lilley, who lived six doors down from Elliott in Well Street, and took him back to the house at Henry Street to introduce him to the family. They took an immediate liking to him, and George and Fanny probably thought that he would be far better company for their eldest daughter than the ne'er-do-well of Well Street. On the evening of 17 November Lilley was ashore, and he asked Clara if she would accompany him to the Palace Theatre of Varieties. She said she would prefer the show at the Theatre Royal, to which he agreed. When he came to the house early that evening to collect her, he arranged to meet her parents at the Athenaeum Hotel after the show, and they left the house at about 7.30 p.m.

They left the Theatre Royal after the performance finished about three hours later. As they were walking back to the hotel, Elliott approached Clara in the street and whispered something to her. She spoke to him for a few minutes, and Lilley clearly heard his last words to her – 'If you come up the lane, I'll prove it.' Clara and Lilley went into the hotel, where they met her parents and he bought himself a glass of ale. She told him she was going home to take her hat off, which struck him as a rather odd excuse for leaving, but she assured him she would be back in a few minutes.

There were at least two witnesses to what happened next. At about 10.45 John Tremlett, a labourer, heard a scream, and saw Elliott with his arm locked around

The Theatre Royal, Plymouth, behind Derry's Clock, 1907. Clara Hannaford and William Lilley saw a show at the theatre on the evening she was murdered, 17 November 1908. The theatre was demolished in 1937 and the present Theatre Royal, which occupies a nearby site next to the clock, was opened in 1982.

Clara's throat. He followed a trace of blood which led to the rear of 25 Queen Lane. Another person in the area, Mary Seccombe, whose husband Fred was a professional boxer, had known the Hannaford family for some years. She recognised them, and heard Elliott say, 'I want to speak to you a minute, Clara.' 'I will come down if you won't touch me,' she replied. Mary then watched in horror as they walked together, before he violently attacked Clara and knocked her hat off. She ran after them, picked Clara's hat up and made sure that the girl was not seriously hurt. She then handed the hat to her and asked Elliott what he thought he was doing. 'It is nothing to do with you,' he answered brusquely. She told him that she would tell the Hannafords what he had done.

True to her word, a few minutes after leaving the hotel, Clara returned. She was staggering, and a gaping wound in her throat bled profusely. She tried to speak to her mother, but her injuries were so severe that no words came out. Lilley bound a handkerchief round her throat in an effort to stop the flow of blood and covered her with his coat, while he and Fanny got ready to take her to the Homoeopathic Hospital at Lockyer Street. Two officers, Sergeant Beer and Police Constable Quantick, were on duty outside in George Street, and they phoned the station for an ambulance.

People had realised that something unpleasant was going on, and a large crowd was gathering to see exactly what was happening. Had they not tried to satisfy their curiosity, the poor girl might have been saved, as the policemen had to spend several minutes keeping them back and getting through to the victim. It was to no avail, for Clara collapsed and died from loss of blood before they could get to the hospital. Her body was taken to the mortuary at Vauxhall Street, where it was seen that the larynx was cut right across and the wound on her throat went from ear to ear.

After the crowds had dispersed, Mr Tremlett followed the trail of blood to Queen Lane and the spot where Clara had been attacked. Searching with the aid of lighted matches, outside one of the doors to a back entrance in the lane he found a large quantity of blood and near it a heavily stained razor, which he picked up carefully and took to the police station.

Having had his revenge, the murderer went back to his home at Well Street, changed his bloodstained coat and then walked to the Central Police Station where he arrived at about 11.30 p.m. and asked Inspector Hitchcock if they were looking for 'Ted Elliott'. He was arrested on a charge of murder, warned and cautioned, to which his reaction was, 'Is she dead?' On being told that she was, he confessed that he had cut her throat with a razor. 'She has been out with another young man tonight,' he added. 'I met her and did it, and put her to rights.' When questioned further, he said the crime had not been premeditated, but done on the spur of the moment. He was searched and formally charged with wilful and malicious murder.

A friend of Edmund's family went to tell the news to his mother and stepfather, a dock labourer, who had only been married since August 1907. They said that he generally seemed quiet but happy at home, especially as he had just finished his hairdressing apprenticeship satisfactorily. The stepfather was aware that he had quarrelled with Miss Hannaford, but was amazed that he should have resorted to such violence. The police later came and searched the house, and found Elliott's bloodstained coat. As for the Hannaford family, when she was told her daughter was dead, Fanny broke down and wept, then said she must go to the scene of the tragedy. One of Clara's sisters and her grandmother, both weeping bitterly, went straight to the hospital to ask if she really was dead, unable to believe that such a dreadful thing had happened.

Over the next two or three days the scene at Queen Lane became a magnet for sightseers. So many people came to look that a number of constables had to be placed on special duty. Though all tell-tale signs of the gory event had been cleared up, public curiosity was slow to diminish.

An inquest was held at Vauxhall Street on 19 November. Such was the public interest in the tragedy that an hour before proceedings were due to open, a large crowd consisting mainly of women and children had gathered outside the premises. Once again police had to be summoned to keep everyone under control. The main witnesses drove to the mortuary in a cab, which was immediately surrounded. If onlookers had come for a sight of the murderer himself, they were disappointed, for Elliott was given the opportunity of attending but chose not to, and was instead represented by John Ickle from solicitors Bicke & Wilcocks. The foreman asked why the accused was not present, as he certainly ought to be there. The coroner said he had been in touch with the prison governor, who told him that Elliott could have come if he wanted to, but 'I think he is just as well out of it'. Among those who had come to the inquest were George Hannaford, the victim's father, William Lilley, Mary Seccombe, John Tremlett, Dr Parsloe, Sergeant Beer and Inspector Hitchcock, who had prepared a detailed plan of the streets and lanes surrounding the scene of the attack. The jury took only two minutes to consider their verdict,

PLYMOUTH TRAGEDY.

STRUGGLE IN THE LANE SEEN BY A WOMAN.

ACCUSED'S THREATS.

VERDICT OF "WILFUL MURDER" AGAINST ELLIOTT.

Detail from the Western Morning News, *20 November 1908, reporting the murder of Clara Hannaford.*

and unanimously decided that it was wilful murder. At the same time, they also passed a vote of condolence to the parents of the victim.

That evening Clara's body was placed in a coffin and taken to her parents' house. Her funeral took place at the Plymouth Cemetery, Ford Park, on the morning of Sunday 22 November.

Elliott went on trial at Exeter Assizes on 11 March 1909. His case was heard by Mr Justice Ridley, with John O'Connor and Raymond Asquith as counsel for the prosecution, and Mr W.T. Lawrance for the defence. When called to the witness box, Fanny Hannaford said that she had known Elliott for nearly two years. Though he had been a barber's assistant part of the time, she had the impression that he would not work and that he was 'of bad character', citing his illegitimate child in the next street as proof. When the defence asked her about the courtship between her daughter and the prisoner, she denied that their relationship was ever anything more than a brief friendship, as her daughter was only fourteen when they first knew each other. Pressed to admit that such an age was a little young for her daughter to be going out with a boyfriend, she asserted indignantly that they never went out, and 'it was only girl and boy play'.

While there was never any doubt as to the outcome, Mr Lawrance suggested that in view of the lack of forethought, it might have been more accurate for them to call the crime manslaughter rather than murder. Much was made of the prisoner's bad start in life and his mother's character: 'A more squalid and a more unhappy condition than the birth of this young fellow could not possibly be imagined.'

Moreover, as a child Elliott had often suffered from fits and there was a history of insanity in the family – his great-grandmother had died in a lunatic asylum seven years previously. His mother, Mrs Emma Bryce, said that he had been subject to fits until he was five and a half years old. On the day before Clara's death he had been very unwell with pains in his head and all over his body, and on the day itself he had stayed in bed until about 6 p.m. She added that he had always been most industrious when not unwell. He had only lost his job as a hairdresser because of pains in his head and shaking, which made customers reluctant to be shaved by him.

In summing up for the prosecution, O'Connor said that the prisoner's mind was full of malice. He was consumed with jealousy because the deceased was going out with another young man, and he had waylaid her with the intention of taking her life. As he was carrying a razor at the time and had had it in his pocket the whole evening, and as he had already once threatened to kill her, this was a crime nothing short of wilful and malicious murder.

In conclusion, the judge called it a lamentable case, especially in view of the prisoner's family background. Nevertheless, there was another, more serious consideration – the nature of the crime itself. Edmund Elliott had clearly intended to kill the deceased, and the jury had to make up their own minds as to whether he was insane. If not, he was responsible for his actions.

The jury delivered their verdict of guilty after just fifteen minutes. As Elliott was only nineteen years old, they made a recommendation for mercy on account of his youth, but it had no effect. Passing sentence of death, Mr Justice Ridley told Elliott he should not place any hope in being reprieved. Standing in the dock, the prisoner seemed totally unmoved. He was hanged by John Ellis and William Willis on 30 March, the first murderer to die on the gallows at Exeter in the twentieth century.

Broken-hearted George Hannaford did not survive his eldest daughter for long. He died on 21 December 1910 at the early age of forty-seven. At the time of his death, his address was given as 3 Trafalgar Place. Fanny lived for nearly thirty years after the tragedy, dying on 23 January 1938 aged seventy-one. Both were laid to rest in the same grave as Clara at Ford Park Cemetery.

Ford Park Cemetery, Plymouth. (© Hannah Lindsey-Clark)

19

THE FATAL ATTRACTION OF TWO COUSINS

Plymouth, 1920

At the age of twenty-one, Cyril Victor Tennyson Saunders was a lance-corporal in the Royal Engineers, stationed at Crowborough in Surrey. For the previous two years he had been going out with his cousin, Dorothy Mary Saunders. Aged sixteen, she was also from an army family, born in India, where her father had served with the Royal Fusiliers. After he retired from the forces, the family returned to England, settling in Southampton. Dorothy's parents died within a few months of each other, and in June 1920 she came to Plymouth to live with another cousin, Mrs Elizabeth Lawrence. The latter had a tobacconist and confectionery shop at Percy Terrace in the Lipson Vale area of the town, and Dorothy regularly worked behind the counter. Cyril was falling deeply in love with her, and decided that he wanted them to become husband and wife.

Until now, Cyril had shown every sign of becoming a promising soldier. He had been briefly on active service in Russia, and was well liked and respected by everyone. His senior officers found him cheerful, good tempered and one of the smartest NCOs in his unit. Off the parade ground he had several interests, and particularly enjoyed singing, sports and reading.

Everything started to go wrong on 24 July 1920 when he was accidentally struck on the head with the butt of a rifle while on guard duty. Had it been a direct blow, the doctors thought, he would probably have been killed, or at least left with severe brain damage. As a result of the injury he was in hospital for about ten days, and on his discharge he was very changed in his manner. He 'flared up' at the smallest thing, often stared around with a vacant expression and was startled by sudden noises. On one occasion he and Lance-Corporal Tilford heard a dog howling at the camp. Saunders grabbed Tilford's arm in horror, 'For Christ's sake, what was that?' Tilford had to reassure him that it did not necessarily signify impending death. When he was giving evidence at a military court against the man who had hit him with the rifle, he was very nervous, fumbled with his hands, and seemed quite different in his demeanour from the normal self-confident soul of a few weeks previously.

Worse was to come. Early in September, while he was on leave, Cyril came to Plymouth to visit Dorothy. Whether they were officially engaged by now is open to doubt. He had certainly set his heart on marrying her, and she may have agreed to do so, later telling him that she wanted to break it off. On the other hand, she might

Percy Terrace, Plymouth, 2006, little altered since 1920 when Dorothy May Saunders was murdered at her cousin's shop. (© John Stapley)

have denied ever having agreed to become his wife, and sometime after that told him that she never promised him anything more than friendship. He suspected that while he was in Surrey she was seeing somebody else, something she fervently denied.

Though she was reluctant to admit it at first, Dorothy had discovered to her horror that she was probably carrying Cyril's child. Convinced that he had been supplanted in her affections, a furious Cyril asked for 'his' name, saying that he did not intend to hurt the boy, but (rather contradicting himself) he would surely kill anybody else who dared to come between them. When Dorothy remained adamant that it was all over between them, Cyril returned to Surrey after his leave was over. He hoped that the rejection of his affections had been an isolated aberration on her part, and he intended to get her to change her mind.

If this was his hope, he was doomed to bitter disappointment. A few days later Dorothy wrote to reiterate that she did not wish to marry him. He replied on 14 September:

> I warn you, if I do not hear tomorrow, I shall be in Plymouth on Thursday, and although I hope it will not be necessary yet, possibly, there will also be trouble coming for someone. Perhaps it is unfortunate, but I happen to love you a good deal more than you may think, and remembering your promises, I don't intend to stand anyone fooling around and helping you to break them.

He followed this letter with another three days later, in which he addressed her by her pet-name of Bubbles:

You need not be afraid that I will make trouble if you tell me his name. This is the second time I have stopped myself from fulfilling my vow; but, Bubbles, as surely as any other fellow ever attempts to come between us again, I shall murder him in cold blood with my own hands. All the pleadings, tears, or explanations will not save him. That is my oath, which I swear on the Bible before me now. Bubbles, my precious, write soon, my beloved, for my heart is breaking, with the torture of this last two days. Answer my questions and make your promises again, for your old boy has forgiven you, darling. G.B.Y. [God be with you], and help you to keep true and loving to me. My darling, I am more unhappy today that I think I have ever been in my life before. It seems all my world is crumbling around me. All my heart's deepest love and devotion, and my most tender kisses, dearest love of my heart.

Ever your own true and devoted boy, Cyril

She answered on 20 September, making it clear that as far as she was concerned, it was all over between them:

Dearest Cyril, It's no good, Cyril, I must tell you. I know I'll just about break your heart, but I don't feel at all now as though I could get married. You have spoilt all my trust in you, dear. Don't think, Cyril, there is any other boy, for there isn't. My heart will always be turning to you, but it's no good when you have lost all trust in me. If it is God's will that I should have a baby I'll let you know, but I must bear the brunt myself. Don't do anything rash, Cyril, look after yourself, and please answer this.

Yours, Bubbles

On receipt of this letter Cyril sent her a telegram warning her of his imminent return, and he was back on the train to Plymouth within a few hours. He took a taxi from North Road station straight to Mrs Lawrence's house, and begged Dorothy to reconsider. She refused, telling him it was no use his coming to see her as she was 'still of the same mind'. Mrs Lawrence left them talking in the kitchen while she went to serve in the shop. In the course of conversation Cyril became desperate, and threatened to go and put his head on the railway line. At this, an unnerved Dorothy called Mrs Lawrence back to talk some sense into him. As Mrs Lawrence came into the kitchen, Cyril walked out but she followed him, caught him up, and told him firmly not to do anything silly as there was not only himself and Bubbles to consider. How would his parents feel if he killed himself? Having talked him out of it, she invited him back to the house for a cup of tea, and he accepted. While they were drinking she admonished him: 'Buck up and be a man! In a couple of months you will think of what a fool you've been!' At this he burst into tears.

While Dorothy said she did not want to be friends with him any longer, she agreed that she would go to the cinema with him that night. They came back at about 10 p.m., and after their return Dorothy complained to Mrs Lawrence how tiresome he had been throughout the evening. Nevertheless, he was allowed to stay at the house that night, and as he said goodnight to his cousins, he told them he would turn the gas on. Mrs Lawrence was so uneasy about this that she went downstairs and turned the gas off at the mains. Dorothy then told him not to do anything silly that night, assuring him she would think it over and give him an answer in the morning.

Next day, 23 September, at about 9.30 a.m. she took him a cup of tea. Half an hour later he came downstairs and had breakfast, during which he read a newspaper, saying barely a word to the others. At 11 a.m. he went out, returning a couple of hours later. He had tried to buy a revolver, but was unable to do so. Instead he purchased a hunting knife for 8s 6d, telling the vendor that he was about to go abroad. He then went into a public house and had a couple of drinks.

What happened next was described by Mrs Lawrence to a newspaper reporter that afternoon:

They were quite friendly last night, and [Dorothy] told him that though she did not intend to marry him she would treat him just like the rest of the boys. He stayed here last night, and this morning went for a walk alone, returning for dinner about one o'clock. Dorothy was not here when he returned, as she had gone for a walk through the fields to keep out of his way. He promised me faithfully and on his oath that if she came back he would not lay a finger on her, and that neither would he do anything to himself, so I went out to find her and we returned to the shop together.

As long as she would let him see Bubbles once more, he said, he would go straight back to the camp afterwards, and promised he would not even write to her again.

All three went into the kitchen, and Dorothy asked Cyril if he was really going back to the camp. 'Yes,' he answered, 'by the 2.50 train, if you give me dinner.' At that stage a customer entered the shop and was attended to by Dorothy, followed by Cyril. He stayed in the shop until the customer was served and had left, and then there was a quiet conversation between them both which Mrs Lawrence could not hear. It continued for some time until a piercing cry of 'Betty! Betty!' startled the house.

Mrs Lawrence heard a scuffle, and on looking into the shop she saw Dorothy with her hands up to her throat. At first glance it looked as if Cyril was strangling her. Dorothy screamed again, and Mrs Lawrence saw blood coming from her mouth. She ran into the shop, shouting frantically, 'You brute! Don't touch her!' Cyril then laid Dorothy on the floor. Mrs Lawrence saw the bloodstained knife in his hand. She snatched up the scoop and scales from the counter and hurled them at his face, then ran into the street screaming 'Murder!' From the street she saw Cyril standing in the doorway of the shop, calmly smoking a cigarette. After a few minutes he turned as if to walk away and she shouted, 'Stop that man!' 'Did you think I was going to run away?' he asked her. When she said she thought he was, he said he never intended to, and went back into the shop.

Meanwhile, another soldier, James Boote, was sitting by an upstairs window in one of the houses opposite. At the sound of muffled screams he jumped up to see what was happening, saw Dorothy lying across the doorway of the shop, immediately telephoned for an ambulance, and then ran across the road. Cyril was still standing there, looking quite unconcerned. 'There is no use your doing anything,' he said calmly, 'because I have done her in; I have stabbed her through the heart.' A crowd was beginning to collect round the doorway, so Boote persuaded Cyril to come back to his house until the police arrived. As they crossed the road, Cyril told him, 'I have courted her for two years and she chucked me up.' When the police came he handed them the knife. 'You may as well have this,' he suggested, aware of what lay in store for him. 'I am not going to kill myself. Someone else will do it for me.'

PC Quantick was the first to arrive, and he formally arrested Cyril. When Deputy Chief Constable Martin charged him with murder and cautioned him, Cyril said, 'I have nothing to say. I had a couple of drinks this morning, and by telling you that it may help me a little.' When he was searched, a handkerchief stained with blood and an undated letter signed 'Bubbles' were found in his coat. He made a full statement to PC Dawe, starting with the morning's events and his going into town. At the time, he said, he was wearing Dorothy's watch and she was wearing his. When he returned to Percy Terrace he was told that she had gone out, so he waited for her, 'and when in the doorway of the shop we were in the act of changing watches, I took out the knife and stabbed her with it. She fell down. I placed the knife on the counter and one man who I do not know came in and took it away.'

Lipson Vale was normally one of the quieter residential areas of Plymouth, but the tragedy, reported the local press, turned it into 'the scene of much subdued excitement'. Several people were attracted to the vicinity of the shop, all gossiping about the crime. As the family was well known, several callers came to bring Mrs Lawrence their heartfelt sympathy in person.

On 9 November Cyril went for trial at Exeter Assizes, pleading not guilty to murder before Lord Justice Coleridge. Counsel for the prosecution were Mr Holman Gregory and Mr Edward Duke; for the defence were Mr W.T. Lawrance and Mr J.L. Pratt. Among the witnesses to be called were Mrs Lawrence, Private Boote and Dr Wolferstan, who confirmed that the injuries to the deceased would have caused her death within a few minutes.

Two other witnesses gave evidence suggesting that the prisoner was slightly abnormal. Sergeant McGregor of the Signal Corps gave him a good character reference, but after the incident in July when he was struck on the head, McGregor saw him wandering around the camp at Crowborough 'with a faraway look in his eye, and I reported the matter'. Dr H.G. Pinker, medical officer at Plymouth Gaol, said he examined the accused on his arrival. He considered him mentally normal and he remained thus all the time he was in his charge. On cross-examination, he said that a blow on the head 'might occasion cerebral mischief if the skull was injured. Following severe concussion mischief might occur periodically at times of excitement.'

Opening the case for the defence, Mr Lawrance said that it was impossible to contradict the facts of the tragedy. He intended to call evidence to show that the blow on the head had materially altered the accused's state of mind. Lance-Corporal Tilford and other colleagues from Crowborough all testified to the change for the worse in his demeanour.

Throughout most of the proceedings Cyril maintained his composure, but he had to work hard to control his emotions when his father, Mr T.B. Saunders of Camberley, told the court that after the blow, his son became irritable and listless. Dr Alfred

Turner, who maintained a private lunatic asylum at Plympton and had had many years' experience in mental cases, had examined the prisoner and considered that such an injury might produce insanity. The unhappy and tragic love affair through which he had just passed, he added, might predispose him to mental trouble, especially at his age. All that had been said pointed to the fact that the blow on the head, coupled with the affair, led the prisoner to become unbalanced and irresponsible. Such an insane state of mind might not be continuous, and it was possible the prisoner would become fairly sane after the murder. When cross-examined, he said that a superficial head wound would not be enough in itself to cause insanity.

Addressing the jury, Mr Lawrance said that they had to consider in what degree the accused was responsible for his actions. Did he know exactly what he was doing, and if so, did he know that he was doing wrong? Conceding it was difficult to establish insanity in a direct way, he told them it would be best to return a verdict of guilty but insane if there were any doubt. The prosecution, he averred, was possibly at fault in suggesting the murder was caused by a desire for revenge and prompted by jealousy, as the material change in the prisoner's mental condition after July was undoubtedly aggravated by the shock he received in Dorothy's letter on 20 September.

Summing up for the prosecution, Mr Holman Gregory said that the law dealt with insanity from a point of view different from the way in which it would be approached by a doctor in charge of a lunatic asylum. When the accused bought his knife, he had no doubt as to what he was going to do with it. There was no doubt that he was madly in love, desperately jealous, and in the eyes of the law he knew that he was going to kill his cousin. He had weighed the consequences, whatever they might be; he knew that he was doing wrong, and there was only one possible verdict.

Lord Justice Coleridge said there was merely one issue in the case, that of the responsibility of the accused for the act of which he was undoubtedly guilty. When he committed the act, did he know that it was contrary to the law? If he did, he was responsible; if he did not, then he was not. If he knew he was doing what was contrary to the law, then he was guilty in the eyes of the law. If the jury were of the other opinion, then their verdict would be one of guilty, but that the accused was insane at the time. He further directed that such a verdict was not to be returned merely on the grounds of sympathy or compassion.

After retiring for ten minutes the jury returned a verdict of guilty, the foreman adding that they were unanimous in their verdict of wilful murder.

'No one who has heard this case will doubt that the attempt to prove you were mentally insane has failed,' the judge remarked before passing the death sentence.

You knew well the difference between right and wrong, for the murder was premeditated. No sudden gust of passion carried you away. You bought the weapon wherewith to kill your victim. You determined that if she was not to be yours she should belong to no one else. With four determined strokes you slit the thread of a bright young life. Truly it has been said that jealousy is as cruel as the grave. The law is not vengeance; it is punishment with justice. There is one retribution that you can effect, and the way is by remorse, by sorrow, and I trust, by penitence.

Cyril Saunders received the verdict without flinching, though he was seen to shrug his shoulders as he was escorted away. While in custody he left a letter thanking the prison officers for the kindness they had shown him during his time in the condemned cell. He went to the scaffold on 30 November. The executioners once again were John Ellis and William Willis.

20

MASSACRE AT WEST CHARLETON

West Charleton, 1936

Most of the murders described in this book were relatively straightforward cases in which the culprits were swiftly apprehended and brought to justice. One of the most horrific, a triple killing, failed to lead to any conviction. What happened one summer evening at Croft Farm, in the small village of West Charleton, near Kingsbridge, will never be known for certain.

Thomas Maye, a 71-year-old farmer, his seventy-year-old wife Emily and their daughters (Emily) Joan, twenty-eight, and Gwyneth Florence, twenty-five, had lived there for some time, and the family had farmed at Croft for several generations. Mrs Maye was active in church affairs and the Mothers' Union, while the daughters had been Girl Guides and were members of the Kingsbridge Hockey Club. Joan was also a teacher at the local Sunday school. They seemed to be a normal, happy, churchgoing family, well liked in the area, comfortably off and apparently with no enemies. Two other children were married. Mary lived with her husband at Aveton Gifford a few miles away, and Jack, a civil engineer, lived in India with his wife and two children. Thomas, his wife and daughters were frequently seen in West Charleton and around the area, and everyone considered the farmer very active and healthy for his age.

Also living in the house was Charles Lockhart, the Mayes' general servant and gardener. Aged twenty-two, he was one of five orphaned children from a Modbury family whose father had been killed in an accident at the mill where he worked. He had been with the Mayes for three years, and had his own bedroom at the back of the house.

On the evening of 11 June 1936, Lockhart was going out to a dance at Stokenham. He went off duty at 7 p.m. After leaving the house, he returned briefly at about 9.30 p.m. to collect an overcoat, letting himself into the outer kitchen through the back door and going up the back stairs to his room. While he was there he heard voices in the dining-room, which he assumed were those of Mrs Maye and her daughters. He also noticed that two men, Mr Maye's accountant Victor Smith from

East Allington and a farrier, William Stear from Aveton Gifford, had called at the farm to discuss routine business.

At 2.45 the following morning Lockhart came back to a house of horror. As he opened the door he could hear feeble groaning, and he saw a stream of blood seeping into the kitchen under the closed door from the adjoining upper kitchen. Gwyneth was lying on the floor downstairs between the hall and the kitchen, bleeding profusely from severe injuries to her head and a deep cut in her shoulder. Her pet spaniel was licking her face. Beside her was a cushion or pillow which it was thought she may have used to shield herself from her attacker. Without stopping to investigate further, Lockhart went to fetch the village policeman, Constable William Mugridge. Frank Lee, another of the farm labourers, was still around, and he came back with them to help.

They found the house reeking of paraffin, with some of the furniture and beds ablaze. Fuel had been poured on the stairs as well as in the bedrooms, but Mugridge was able to put part of the fire out by himself. The carpet and window curtains in some of the rooms were still ablaze, and Lee and a couple of others set to work with buckets. They formed a chain of water carriers until the flames were under control. If Lockhart had not returned when he did, they all realised later with a shudder, the entire house might have been gutted.

Joan was lying dead upstairs in the passage outside her bedroom, her skull fractured. In her parents' room Thomas was lying semi-conscious on a burning bed with a deep cut on his forehead and injuries to his jaw. When Mugridge entered the room, Thomas asked, 'What are you doing? Where has my wife gone?' On the floor beside the bed was the partly burnt body of Emily, who had also died of a fractured skull.

Mugridge then committed two cardinal errors. First, he failed to caution Maye before he spoke, and second, he uttered words that, if they were not tantamount to an accusation, came uncomfortably close. When Maye asked the policeman what he was doing in his bedroom, Mugridge replied, 'Your wife has sent for me as the house is on fire.' Maye asked him next where all the blood was coming from, adding that his head was very sore. Mugridge said he had sent for the doctor, and then asked 'What have you done?' As time would show, the question was easily misconstrued.

A walling hammer (a hammer and an axe combined), minus part of its shaft, was found lying beside Gwyneth. The missing part of the shaft was later found next to Joan's body. Lockhart had been using it in the garden the previous day, and put it in a china cupboard in the kitchen. He had meant to return it to one of the outbuildings, but was distracted at the time by the need to look for some other tools. There were pools of blood in rooms both upstairs and down, and particularly on Joan's bed, where it was assumed she had sustained most of her injuries before staggering out to the passage to die. The immediate assumption was that Mrs Maye was the first to be attacked, and that her daughters had done their best to protect her, but ultimately met with the same fate.

At 4 a.m. Dr Robinson arrived, and first he examined Gwyneth. The smell of paraffin from her head and the coats that had been put over her to keep her warm was overpowering. He had her rushed to Kingsbridge Cottage Hospital, but the matron, Miss Duffy, took one look at her and guessed from the extent of her injuries

Kingsbridge Cottage Hospital, which was opened in Duncombe Street in 1898. (Courtesy of the Cookworthy Museum)

that she did not have long to live. Her face, legs and shoulder were very badly bruised, and she died at about 8.30 a.m. without regaining consciousness.

Maye was told by the doctor that he would be taken to hospital as well but he refused, saying that the men would be coming for milking and he was expecting a delivery of manure. He was well enough to get out of bed and dress unaided. When Robinson looked at Maye's injuries, he found three cuts on his head, under each of which there was a fracture to the skull. Such wounds, he said, could only have been caused by someone striking the farmer with the walling hammer which had killed the rest of his family, and they were sufficiently severe to precipitate immediate unconsciousness. Though initially Maye seemed well and determined enough to carry on about his business as normal, his loss of blood, his age and above all the fact that he was suffering from severe shock, had to be taken into consideration. Robinson told him he needed a complete rest, and he would require a prolonged period of convalescence.

When more police arrived at dawn, they searched the property and were convinced that there had been no intruder. Three out of four of the family were dead, and there was blood over much of the house, with several imprints of bare, bloodstained feet. Maye was questioned by Inspector West. He was very frank and open, giving complete details of what had happened earlier the previous evening, even down to what the family had eaten for supper. He mentioned that the girls had been out to watch some night filming at Blackpool Sands, had had a long day, were extremely tired and wanted an early night. When he was asked what occurred later on, he said, 'I can't tell you. I wish I could.'

That morning Maye was moved to Kingsbridge Infirmary. Dr Robinson found that he was still answering questions lucidly, but could give no explanation for his injuries. When questioned, he had a clear recollection of events of the Thursday evening up to 9.30 p.m. His last memory was of what turned out to be the final farewell to his wife. He was going upstairs to bed and they passed on the stairs as she was coming down.

She put her arm around him and gave him a kiss and a punch in the ribs as she told him she had some mending to do but would come up and join him shortly. 'That was the last time I saw her,' he added poignantly.

Though he had been able to dress unaided and read his watch at 5.20 at the farm that morning, his condition had deteriorated in the last few hours. As a result of haemorrhaging and swollen eyelids, now he could not even open his eyes. In the afternoon he was moved to a nursing home at Plymouth, where he spent the next few weeks under treatment. He regularly asked for his wife and daughters, as if unable to accept that they were dead.

As the only other surviving member of the family in the area, it fell to Thomas's daughter, Mary Wroth, to shoulder the sad burden of making arrangements for the triple funeral. Though the Maye family grave was some miles away at Staverton, near Totnes, on this occasion it was deemed appropriate for the service and burials to take place at St Mary's Church, West Charleton, on 16 June. Charles Lockhart was among the mourners, and eighteen farm workers from the neighbourhood acted as bearers. The three coffins, each surmounted by wreaths of roses and carnations, were laid in the chancel, while a psalm and the hymn 'Rock of Ages', a favourite of the family, were sung by the congregation. As Emily Maye and her daughters were interred in a single grave in the churchyard, within sight of Croft Farm, a guard of police officers was still clearly visible around the latter. The graves were lined with flowers by members of the Hockey Club, where Joan and Gwyneth had made so many friends.

On 15 July Maye was informed that he would be indicted on a charge of triple murder. He protested his innocence: 'I think it absurd making that accusation as I loved my wife and daughters too well.' At first a degree of suspicion also fell on Charles Lockhart, the only other person who was known to have entered the house during those hours. However, there was no reason to doubt his presence at the dance at Stokenham on the Thursday evening, especially as others had vouched for him.

Two weeks later Maye was formally charged at Kingsbridge Police Court. A model of a skull was displayed on the table for demonstration purposes; other exhibits included the walling hammer with broken shaft, bundles of clothing and stained carpet, and five bloodstained flagstones.

For the prosecution, Mr G. Roberts (who was later to become a judge himself) said that the prisoner was a man of exemplary character, and as far as everyone knew, he had always led a perfectly happy domestic life. After the murders, there was no sign of 'burglarious entry, and there was no sign of any robbery, although there was money, jewellery, and other articles of value in the house'. No motive could be suggested, no credible reason why he should have turned on his family, and his previous record rendered such crimes 'almost inconceivable on his part'. All Mr Roberts could suggest was that some trick of the mind, some temporary mental derangement, had suddenly changed a devoted husband and father into 'a homicidal maniac whose actions were controlled, not by reason, but by some murderous instinct'. It was perfectly clear, he went on, that Maye had not received his injuries in bed and remained there after being assaulted. His nightshirt was dirty with soot and charring, his feet were caked, bloodstained and dirty, and the dirt smelled of paraffin and blood, as if he had been walking for some considerable distance in such conditions. The filthy state of his hands seemed to confirm the same.

For the defence, Dr Robinson confirmed that Maye would have become unconscious almost immediately after being attacked. When counsel for the defence, Mr Laskey, asked if the injuries were consistent with the blows having been struck while the accused was in a lying position, the doctor said that they appeared thus to him, and it seemed impossible that any person could inflict such injuries on himself. When asked to suggest who had committed the murders, Maye was at a loss to say anything.

Further evidence was given at a second hearing the next day. Constable Mugridge reported that the spaniel belonging to Gwyneth smelled strongly of paraffin. One of the labourers brought back to the scene of the crime on the night, William Lamble, said that the constable left him to keep an eye on Maye's bedroom while he went to get help, and handed him a truncheon with the words, 'If he comes for you, knock him down.' Leonard Bevan, Master of Kingsbridge Public

The Maye family grave at St Mary's Church, West Charleton. The facing panel shows a dedication to Emily and Thomas; panels on the other side are inscribed with the names and dates of death of their daughters, Joan and Gwyneth. (© Kim Van der Kiste)

Assistance Institution, assured everyone that when Maye was brought there, his hands were covered with a substance which looked like lamp black and smelled of paraffin.

When asked for his own version of what had happened, the prisoner said that he and his family before him had lived at Croft Farm since 1840. He was on the best of terms with his wife and daughters, and as far as he knew he did not have an enemy in the world. He could not recall any conversation with police officers, and the first he knew of the fate of his family was when he learned from the solicitors of their deaths: 'I told the matron of the hospital that I knew something must be wrong, as my wife would be the first to come if she knew I was bad.' When asked if he had any financial worries, he said he did not. He had never seen the walling hammer, and declared that it did not belong to him. Pressed as to how his hands and feet could have become so dirty, or how blood came to be in various rooms, or who set fire to them, he could not explain. His mind was still a complete blank from 9.30 on the evening of 11 June, when he went to bed, until he found himself in a Plymouth nursing home.

Counsel for the defence, Mr F.S. Laskey, submitted that there was no case to answer. He asked the magistrates to believe the medical evidence that Maye had received his injuries while lying in bed, and that there was no considerable amount of blood anywhere in the house but on the bed itself. If Maye had been struck such severe blows while in the bed, they could not possibly be self-inflicted and he was surely not guilty of the charges of killing his wife and daughters. Nevertheless, after an adjournment of about fifteen minutes Mr Ashley Froude, Chairman of the Magistrates, announced that the bench had decided that the case should be submitted to a higher court.

On 9 November Maye, dressed in grey overcoat and black tie, still bearing scars on his face and forehead, appeared at Devon Assizes before Mr Justice Charles on three charges of murder. As the trial opened, Mr Roberts said that it would be part of the case for the prosecution that the individual who murdered Emily Maye also murdered her two daughters. The prosecution had no wish to press for a conviction, and did not intend to persuade the jury to find the prisoner guilty. Their sole duty and desire was to place the facts before the court. Mr Roberts's words seemed to anticipate the final outcome of the proceedings. He emphasised that 'the hand of the burglar or thief was entirely absent, and there was no sign of any entrance from outside', thus implying that the prisoner was the only person who could have perpetrated the crime.

Among witnesses called by the defence were accountant Victor Smith and farrier William Stear, who had visited Maye soon after 7 p.m. on the evening of 11 June. They agreed that everything at Croft Farm appeared perfectly normal. 'Do you know [Maye] as a kindly dispositioned old gentleman?' asked the judge. 'Yes, ever since I have known him,' was Stear's reply. 'Was he on affectionate terms with the family?' 'Yes.' A less affectionate portrait emerged from the testimony of others, who said that Maye was quick-tempered and mean with money. Walter Farr, a wheelwright who had worked for him for thirty years, told the court that he had been increasingly shaky and irritable of late. After a recent argument Maye had walked away, muttering angrily, 'If I were a younger man I should feel like hitting you.'

Constable Mugridge's question to the prisoner of 'What have you done?' at the scene of the attack, it was suggested, was out of order. 'Without any evidence whatsoever,' said Laskey, 'you made up your mind that my injured client was guilty of murdering his wife and daughters.' Roberts said he was sure the judge would realise the position with which the officer was faced.

When questioned about the medical evidence, Dr Robinson said that the bruises on Maye's jaw were consistent with his having been struck while under the bedclothes. 'Do you think it conceivable that he could have done it to himself?' asked the judge. 'Not the least bit,' Robinson replied. The judge said that he would feel bound to put to the jury that it was more likely, upon the evidence, that the prisoner had been attacked by someone else than that he had attacked his wife and daughters. Concluding the case for the prosecution, Mr Roberts said he would call no further evidence.

At the direction of the judge, the jury returned a verdict that Maye was not guilty of murdering his wife. He was then formally charged with murdering his daughters, and on each count the jury found him not guilty.

In summing up, Mr Justice Charles said that for the first time in the whole of his experience, the jury had been told at the opening of a murder trial that the case had only been lodged after the Chief Constable of the county and the Director of Public Prosecutions had most carefully considered the matter. 'Having made this a public matter in the opening to the jury, I feel bound to say that I think, after close consideration of the doctor's evidence, that the man might have been spared this ordeal.' He added that he wanted it to be understood that he was not attacking the prosecution, 'who appeared to have called every witness who could have been of any assistance to the defence, including the vital witness, Dr Robinson. If they had not called him, he could not have stopped the case, but the Crown, with that fairness with which it always acts, called the witness and put all the evidence before you to consider. I think we need discuss it no further.'

Maye looked dazed at the judge's words. When he had recovered from the shock, he waved a hand to somebody in court and was assisted from the dock. He left by a side entrance to be met by a couple of friends outside who congratulated him, and by his son, who led him to a car and swiftly drove him away. Later he spoke briefly to the press. 'Thank God that terrible time is over,' he said. 'I knew I would be proved innocent.'

As the case for the prosecution had been demolished so quickly, nobody had any chance to put forward possible alternative theories in court. A few years later, Roberts said that it was possible Gwyneth and her father might have had a struggle on the stairs for some unknown reason, and maybe she fell, thus receiving the injuries from which she died the following day. As she alone had had time to put on a dressing-gown and slippers, she was not attacked while still in bed. The hammer bore traces of hairs belonging to both of Gwyneth's parents and her sister, but not from Gwyneth herself. Another factor not taken into account was that someone – who, precisely, was never known – heard footsteps disappearing into the night during those fatal hours. Yet another theory is that Maye might have been sleepwalking and committed the murders while in that state, though that would not explain the blows he himself sustained.

Some years later, two local people who recalled the case well spoke to local historian Judy Chard. One was Leonard Pedrick, who brought the load of manure for which Maye had been waiting. According to him, Maye was known to have a quick temper and inclined to be unusually strict with his daughters. Nevertheless, there is some difference between a stern, unbending yet respectable patriarch and a psychopath hell-bent on eliminating his nearest and dearest. Even so, Pedrick had grave misgivings, remarking that he 'always felt there was an unhealthy atmosphere between himself and his daughters'. The other person was a lady who, like the Maye family, attended church regularly. She had sat in a pew with them on the Sunday before the killings and said that, despite the doctor's testimony, everyone was convinced that Maye was guilty as charged. Her own father knew him well and was never quite the same again after the case. Following the events of that night he had a nervous breakdown, and she was sure that it had been precipitated by the triple murder.

The 300 acres of land belonging to the farm were let to a Suffolk farmer, and in March 1937 the implements, equipment and some of the stock were sold. It was a sad end to a sorry and tragic case which left too many questions unanswered.

The police did not emerge from the business unscathed either. Young policemen joining the force in Devon for some years afterwards were lectured on the Maye case as a salutary lesson in how not to conduct a murder inquiry. Mugridge's errors of judgement and ill-considered words on arriving at the house had been counter-productive, and the judge admonished him in court for his having taken 'a view which might have been entirely wrong'.

According to one account, Maye left England and emigrated to Australia, where he died soon afterwards, though another says that he spent the rest of his life with his daughter Mary and her husband. The latter is more probable. He survived the terrible night of June 1936 by more than twenty years and died on 10 February 1957, aged ninety-one. As an inscription on the gravestone in St Mary's churchyard testifies, at last he could be reunited with his wife and daughters.

21
THE FATAL KISS

Plymouth, 1952

The Second World War placed a strain on many marriages, one typical casualty being that of Thomas Eames and his first wife. They tied the knot when he was in his late teens, shortly before the outbreak of hostilities in 1939. The following year he joined the army and his wife left him, though the marriage was never dissolved. After demobilisation he found himself work as a labourer. In 1947 he met Muriel Elsie Bent and went through a bigamous marriage with her. At the time he was aged twenty-six and she was five years younger. After being convicted of bigamy, he served two days in prison. On his release the couple lived with his parents until they found a house of their own at 3 Northumberland Terrace, West Hoe, in Plymouth, and had a child.

The relationship soon broke down – they quarrelled throughout most of the time they lived together – and at length Muriel decided she had had enough. When she found herself a boyfriend, she moved out of their home. Thomas saw her and her

*Northumberland Terrace, near
Plymouth Hoe.* (© Kim Van der Kiste)

new man together in Plymouth on at least a couple of occasions; jealous by nature, he could not put up with the situation indefinitely. On 23 February 1952 he called on his brother-in-law, Ronald William Greep, at Greenbank Avenue, and said there had been 'an upset' between them. Greep thought he seemed in a very nervous state, under great strain. He was unable to eat or sleep properly, and was suffering from severe stomach trouble. Three days later Eames asked Muriel to call round at the old house to collect a letter, and she readily agreed.

On the following day, 27 February, he took a 5½-inch table knife round to his place of work, borrowed a file from one of his workmates, and spent about half an hour sharpening what had been a single-bladed kitchen implement into a two-edged dagger. He then returned home and waited for her to call round. When she arrived, he asked Muriel if she was planning to marry her boyfriend. She said she was, and he told her she would not. According to a statement he later gave, 'I said: "If I cannot have you, nobody else will." She kissed me. As she was kissing me it flashed in my head, "Now is the time." I drew the knife out of my pocket and stabbed her in the back while kissing her. She said "Goodbye." I thought she was not quite dead so I stabbed her again so that she would not linger.'

Muriel's death was instantaneous. (Dr M.R. Thomas of Greenbank Hospital later recorded that there were two wounds on the deceased's body, and that death would have taken place within a few seconds.) Next Eames contacted his brother-in-law, Ronald William Greep, confessed to what he had done, and asked Greep to accompany him to the Octagon police station so that he could give himself up. After being cautioned, Eames admitted to Inspector Harold Poole that he had killed his wife by stabbing her. 'The knife is on top of the cupboard. It was jealousy made me do it. She left me for another man. I sharpened the knife this morning.' As he was unable to read or write, apart from signing his name, he dictated a full statement to Detective Superintendent W.A. McConnach.

Charged with murder, he appeared at Exeter Assizes on 23 June before Mr Justice Lynskey and pleaded not guilty. For the defence, Mr N.F. Fox Andrews and Mr H.S. Ruttle tried to show that he was insane at the time of the murder, owing to the effects of worry, stress and an inability to eat properly. Ronald Greep confirmed that he had seen his brother-in-law on several evenings, and had noticed a deterioration in him. He seemed to be increasingly worked up with each passing day, and had told Ronald of his insomnia and severe stomach pains. On the evening that Muriel was killed, he briefly seemed his old self again, said his stomach pain was gone, and then told Greep what he had done. Eames's brother, Cyril, who lived nearby at Clarence Street, said his brother had always been 'a kindly, decent fellow, affectionate by nature'.

Superintendent McConnach produced the statement that had been dictated by the prisoner, and said he had problems with expressing himself. When asked by the judge if he thought the prisoner knew what he was saying and doing, McConnach replied in the affirmative. Fox Andrews mentioned that Eames's relatives called him 'a quiet and gentle fellow, would you from what you have seen of him agree?' The superintendent again answered 'Yes'. 'He is the reverse of the violent character?' 'Yes.'

Next Fox Andrews cross-examined the prisoner, who said that he loved Muriel Bent and their child, and that he could not clearly remember the night she died. 'You don't dispute now that you killed her in fact?' 'No.' 'At the time when you struck her did you know what you were doing?' 'I did not know before, but I did after, sir.'

For the prosecution, the Hon. Ewan Montagu and Mr J.F.E. Stephenson described the case as 'rather a simple one as regards the actual killing'. According to Montagu, it was 'a perfectly clear, intentional, deliberate killing out of jealousy'. Detective Sergeant L.J. Isaacs, when cross-examined by Fox Andrews, read from a letter which he said he understood Eames had dictated and had written for him on 26 February, addressed to Muriel Bent's father. It explained that Eames had asked her to marry him again (even though in the eyes of the law he was still married to the first Mrs Eames), but she had said she did not want to be his wife any longer. He begged her father to come to Plymouth so he could explain the situation and prove to him that he had never ill-treated her, in spite of whatever she might have told him to the contrary. The letter concluded: 'If she does not take any notice of you I am afraid she will be lost to us both in the way she is carrying on.'

As in so many other murder cases, some of the evidence dwelt on the prisoner's state of mind at the time of the killing. Dr J.T. Dunkerley, a part-time medical officer at Exeter prison, said that while in his cell Eames had said that when he was a child, he saw a vision which he 'took to be Our Lord'. When he saw it he was suffering from sores on his foot, and when he went to bathe them the next morning after his visions, he found that they had completely healed. Nevertheless, this was hardly proof of insanity, and when he was cross-examined by Montagu, Dunkerley said that in his view Eames was sane. It was a view supported by Mr M.R.P. Williams, a medical officer at Bristol prison. He admitted that the prisoner had the average intelligence of a cross-section of the public over sixteen years of age, but he was more or less illiterate; this hardly amounted to insanity.

Mr Fox Andrews submitted that if the prisoner was unaware of the consequences of his actions when he drove the knife into the victim's back, it did not matter if he contemplated doing it or if the realisation came to him after the deed was done. 'The question is whether at the time he struck the blow he knew what he was doing,' he concluded. 'If, looking at the whole of the evidence, you take the view that at that moment he did not know what he was doing, then you will be entitled to and it would be your duty to return a verdict of guilty but insane.'

In his summing up the judge pointed out that Eames could have been temporarily insane at the time of the killing. Two doctors had given evidence that he was sane, but it was possible for people who were worried and sleepless and had not eaten properly to commit acts of violence without knowing it. The jury thought otherwise, and believed that Eames had planned to murder Muriel. As he had gone to such effort to prepare the weapon, such a claim was difficult to contest, and they found him guilty, but added a recommendation for mercy.

The case was referred to the Home Secretary, who maintained that there were 'insufficient grounds for recommending any interference with the due course of law'. When he went to the gallows at Bristol Gaol on 15 July, to be hanged by Albert Pierrepoint and Robert Stewart, Eames had to be dragged fighting and kicking, as he struggled all the way to the drop. To him belonged the dubious distinction of being the last Devon murderer to be executed.

chapter three

Somerset & Bristol MURDERS

22

'I HOPE GOD AND THE WORLD HAVE FORGIVEN ME'

Over Stowey, 1789

In the Quantock hills, high above the village of Over Stowey, threre is a well-known and popular beauty spot. However, its sinister name suggests anything but beauty. Since a shocking event that occurred there over two centuries ago, it has always been known as 'Dead Woman's Ditch'.

In 1765, John Walford was born at Over Stowey, the son of a collier (as the makers of charcoal from wood were then known). He grew up to be a good-looking, popular, even-tempered young man, and followed his father into the charcoal business, sometimes supplementing his income by working as a casual farm labourer in the summer. When he fell in love, the object of his affections could be said to have been a cut above the illiterate but hardworking manual worker. Ann Rice, who came from the neighbouring village of Nether Stowey, was the youngest of four daughters of a prosperous miller and his wife. She and John were very much in love and there was an understanding between them that one day they would be married.

Dead Woman's Ditch.
(© Nicola Sly)

The trade of charcoal maker was a lonely one, with little free time for courting. John spent most of the week living in the woods, in a makeshift shelter that he had constructed from poles and turf, rarely coming into contact with other people. He cut and collected timber, then closely supervised it as it burned in a turf-covered pit. The pit remained alight for four or five days, during which time it needed tending every couple of hours, and when he could snatch a little sleep, John simply curled up fully clothed on a bed of straw in his hut. His only food during the week was bread and cheese, his only drink, water from the streams. Every Monday he would carry a half-peck loaf weighing almost 9lbs and 2lbs of cheese into the forest for sustenance. He returned home every Saturday night to eat a hot meal, drink with his friends and catch up with some much needed sleep, before attending church on Sundays.

Into John's isolated life came Jane Shorney, the daughter of another charcoal burner. She was described as 'a poor stupid creature, almost an idiot; yet possessing a little kind of craftiness…an ordinary squat person, disgustingly dirty, and slovenly in her dress.' Jane set her cap at John and took to deliberately seeking him out in the woods while she was supposed to be gathering wood for the fire. For a lonely and virile young man, totally devoid of female company, the outcome of her visits was almost inevitable. She gave birth to a son in 1785 and named John as the baby's father. John was soon taken into custody by the parish officers and given an ultimatum; he must either marry Jane or pay for the child's support. His mother, Ann, stepped in and offered to help, thus effectively letting John off the hook. In the following year Jane gave birth to a daughter, allegedly fathered by John's brother, William.

Ann Rice was obviously prepared to forgive and forget, as the banns were read for her marriage to John in 1787. However, John's mother, who until then had approved of the match between her son and his socially superior girlfriend, now seemed jealous that Ann was replacing her in John's affections. Having previously welcomed the girl into her home, she suddenly took a violent dislike to her; a situation not helped by the fact that Ann's father, George, had relinquished his mill, and as a result lost some of his income and social standing. Perhaps she threatened to withdraw her support of John's illegitimate child, or maybe he simply did not want to go against his mother's wishes, but the engagement between John and Ann Rice was broken off and Ann went into service. However, she continued to meet John secretly and eventually she too became pregnant.

Meanwhile, no doubt heartened by the news of his broken engagement, Jane Shorney resumed her prolonged seduction of John. When she was expecting his second child, John had no choice but to marry her.

The wedding took place on 18 June 1789 and, once married, 24-year-old John took a new job as a husbandman, which left him free to return home to his wife every night at the cottage they shared in the nearby village of Biscombe. Although their union seemed peaceful on the surface, John felt so trapped by his marriage that he was soon contemplating either moving to London or emigrating to a foreign country. It was only a lack of ready money that kept him tied to Somerset and to a wife he resented, but he planned to sell his horse and his bed in order to raise funds to leave. According to William Bishop, a friend of John's who had given Jane away at their wedding, John told him that he would sooner see the Devil in his house than his new wife, saying, 'I must either murder her or go from her.' Jane, it is said, constantly taunted her husband about his true love, Ann, and her spiteful remarks and constant criticism of him made his life a misery.

Jane got into the habit of visiting either her mother or her nearby neighbours for long periods of time, leaving John alone in the house to brood. On 5 July, only three weeks after his wedding, he came home and once again found his wife absent. He went next door to see if she was with their neighbours and to pick up his door key, and was invited in for supper, passing a couple of hours with the Rich family before going home to wait for his wife. On her return, she suggested a visit to the Castle of Comfort public house in the nearby village of Doddington to buy cider. John gave her a shilling from his weekly wage of 6s to do so, but as she was afraid of walking in the dark and reluctant to go alone, Jane persuaded him to accompany her. He returned home alone at 12.30 a.m. the following morning, and he was observed creeping barefoot through the darkness by two of the Rich sisters who were waiting up for another sister.

The Castle of Comfort Inn, Doddington. (© Nicola Sly)

Memorial to Jane Walford at Doddington. (© Nicola Sly)

Early the following morning, two children noticed blood running from beneath a gate. They reported their find to two men who lived nearby, and soon the body of Jane Walford was found at the place now known as Dead Woman's Ditch.

When told of the gruesome discovery, John expressed shock and surprise. He was asked to view the body but declared that he could not bear to see it, so he set off in the opposite direction towards his mother-in-law's house, where he persuaded her to accompany him to the gruesome site. Arriving at the scene of the murder, he glanced briefly at the corpse before staggering back in distress. Questioned by a local businessman, Thomas Poole, Walford maintained that his wife had left their cottage the previous evening to buy cider. He was asked to search the body to see if the coin he had given her was still there and, having first been reluctant to approach his dead wife, eventually made a great show of searching her pockets for the shilling. When it could not be found, he suggested that his wife had been attacked and robbed. However, his actions that morning aroused considerable suspicion.

On leaving his house to view the body, he met his brother William, whom he told that his wife had 'cut her throat'. This detail had not yet been mentioned to the widower, and was something he would not have known if he had played no part in Jane's demise. A search of Walford's cottage produced a small bloodstained pocket knife. The breeches that he had been wearing on the previous night were also heavily stained with blood and there, forgotten in the pocket, was a shilling. A pair of mud-stained stockings was found concealed between the ceiling and thatch of the cottage.

Walford was questioned about his clasp knife, which he claimed to have lent to his brother, William. The latter vehemently denied this and immediately Walford changed his story, saying that he had given the knife to a little boy whose name he could not remember. The knife was found on the following day, bearing traces of dried blood, concealed beneath a window seat in the cottage.

Although he initially denied killing Jane, the evidence against Walford was overwhelming and he soon confessed to her murder. During their trip to the Castle of Comfort Inn, Jane had provoked yet another argument and pushed him too far.

Leigh Woods, near Bristol.

Ever mindful of having forsaken his beloved Ann for this nagging harridan, something inside him finally snapped. He grabbed her by the throat and shook her, then grabbed a post from a hedge and beat her until she fell unconscious, fracturing her skull in the process. Finally he pulled out a knife and slit her throat. Realising that he had killed her, he tried to drag her body to a disused mineshaft but, finding the pregnant corpse too heavy to move, he eventually left it in the ditch. Having first retrieved the shilling that he had given her earlier, he then proceeded to conceal Jane's body, covering it with stones, branches and leaves.

In the light of his confession to the murder, John's subsequent trial at Bridgwater, which opened on 18 August 1789, lasted only three hours before he was officially pronounced guilty and sentenced to death. The presiding judge, Lord Chief Justice Kenyon, was clearly sympathetic towards the prisoner, whom he appeared to view as a quiet and decent man pushed beyond his limits. While Walford showed no emotion, Kenyon wept as he pronounced the death sentence but, despite his obvious reticence, he was under pressure from local residents to punish Walford and deliver the ultimate penalty. Jane's murder came at a time when there had been several violent crimes in the area in the preceding few years. The community demanded that John Walford should be made an example of, asking that he should be hung from a gibbet at the place where his wife's body was found, his body subsequently caged and left for all to see. This, they felt, would act as a deterrent to anyone else contemplating violence in the future.

Accordingly, next day John was shackled around his neck, wrists and ankles and taken by cart to the execution site. A crowd of almost 3,000 villagers gathered to watch the hanging, but on John's arrival at Dead Woman's Ditch, it became apparent that the construction of the gibbet was not yet finished. He was taken to a nearby inn, The Globe at Nether Stowey, for a drink of ale and a meal of bread while the preparations for his death were completed.

As he waited, the crowd parted and a lone young woman approached the prisoner. It was John's first love, Ann Rice. Out of respect, the majority of the crowd turned their backs as a member of the execution party assisted her onto the cart. The couple were allowed to talk for a few minutes before Ann leaned forward, intending to give John a farewell kiss. The executioner would not allow this and placed his arm between them, and then lifted Ann gently from the cart.

John joined in a recital of the Lord's Prayer and the Apostles' Creed before finally confessing his guilt to the assembled crowd. He admitted murdering his wife but swore that the murder was done 'without foreintending it.' He then said, 'I hope God and the world have forgiven me', before a brisk slap to the horse's rump set the cart in motion, leaving his body dangling by the neck at the rope's end.

John's body was subsequently caged and hoisted to the top of the 30ft-high gibbet, where it remained as an example to others until exactly a year to the day after the murder, when the cage finally fell to the ground. Cruelly, this spectacle was within clear view of John's childhood home where his parents still lived. Every time they opened their front door, they were greeted by the sight of their son's body, slowly decaying as the days passed by. Ravaged by crows and blowflies, his remains were eventually buried, still in their metal cage, at the foot of the gibbet. The execution site is still marked on maps of the area as 'Walford's Gibbet'.

Ann Rice gave birth to Walford's daughter in November 1789, and named her Sarah. Within three months the young mother was dead.

Almost two centuries later, the site was associated with another murder. In 1988 the remains of a young Bristol woman, Shirley Banks, were located at Dead Woman's Ditch. They had been placed there by John David Guise Cannan, the man later found guilty of killing her in Leigh Woods near Bristol. In 2001 the same area was extensively searched in the hope of finding the body of Suzy Lamplugh, an estate agent missing since 1986 and now presumed dead. That search was not successful and Suzy remains officially missing.

23

'WHAT MARTHA'S ALREADY SAID GOES FOR NOTHING'

Crewkerne, 1843

Bachelor farmer Richard Alvin lived at Sheep Market Street, Crewkerne. In 1843, by the age of 30, he was said to be worth £18,000, an eccentric and something of a recluse, living with a spinster cousin Charlotte Coles and a servant, Martha Clarke, aged 20.

The household's apparently peaceful existence was soon to be hit by scandal. In May 1843, Martha accused 25-year-old Sarah Bulgin, an unmarried mother of two and Alvin's servant until about two years previously, of spreading false gossip about her, saying she had secretly borne an illegitimate child. Martha denied having done so and told Sarah to keep quiet, but not before rumours had reached the parish authorities. On 18 May, Martha was charged by John Turner, a local policeman, with having disposed of her infant. Protesting her innocence, she was lodged in custody at Turner's house.

One morning after breakfast, she broke down in tears. When Elizabeth, Turner's wife, tried to comfort her, she said that if she was had up before the magistrates, she would confess everything. Mrs Turner asked her what she meant, and Martha admitted to having borne a child. If she was to suffer for it, then Alvin would as well. He had made her pregnant the previous year, and on the afternoon of Sunday 18 December, she gave birth to a baby in the hay loft of the house in Sheep Market Street. She knew that the child, whose sex she did not know, had been born alive as she heard it cry. Alvin, she said bitterly, delivered it and took it away, then sent her back into his house with orders to say nothing and carry on as if nothing had happened. His bitch had produced a litter at the same time and he prepared gruel for the animals, paying more attention to his dog than the mother of his child.

On his return home, the story was repeated to Mr Turner. Martha was taken before the town magistrates and a warrant was issued for Alvin's house to be searched for the child, or any traces of it. Turner checked the garden, hay loft and stables, but found nothing. Nevertheless, Martha's statement was enough for her and Alvin to be taken into custody at Taunton for questioning. As Turner took his prisoners to gaol, Alvin said nonchalantly, 'Never mind, what Martha's said already goes for nothing.' About a mile on, he said, 'I know all about it.' 'I should like to know all about it too,' Turner replied.

On being questioned at the gaol Alvin protested his innocence in relation to the birth or disposal of an infant, but Martha swore she had told the truth. However, unless a body could soon be found, there would be no case to answer.

On 10 June, after a visit by Mr Loveridge, one of the divisional magistrates, Martha made a statement indicating where she thought the child might have been buried. The next day, Hugh Simmonds, the local constable, John Turner and another police officer, William Pottinger, started digging in Alvin's garden. Buried below the bushes, about a foot below the surface, they found some bones, a skull, 'and remains like dung'. It was almost certainly the decomposed body of a small child. As Simmonds and the surgeon, Emmanuel Bowdage, took the corpse carefully out of the hole, they saw a band of straw was wrapped around it. They took it to the Red Lion Inn and placed in a storeroom to await the coroner's arrival.

At an inquest on 12 June, the jury decided 'that the body now found is the body of a human being, an infant, but how or by whom placed there is not known.' The magistrates opened their inquiry four days later in the Crewkerne Justice Room, and Richard Alvin and Martha Clarke were brought from the gaol through streets packed with people eager to catch a glimpse of them. Counsel for the prosecution was Mr Langworthy of Ilminster, while Alvin was represented by Mr Lowman and Mr Sparks. Nobody represented Martha Clarke.

Hugh Simmonds and William Pottinger testified to having found the body, and Emmanuel Bowdage recalled that on the previous Sunday afternoon, he had been called to Alvin's garden to see the body of an infant. It was taken to the Red Lion Inn and the next morning he had examined it in the company of a fellow surgeon, Mr Wills. The body was of a 'full grown infant much decomposed', he said, and twisted around it was a band of hay and straw. There were traces of blood on the band which he believed came from the child, and he said it must have been born alive; if it was stillborn there would have been no blood. It was too decomposed for him to say whether it had been a boy or a girl.

Sarah Bulgin said that during the previous year, she had noticed Martha getting larger. For a while they had worked as servants together until Sarah left, and one day, as they were gleaning corn together at the harvest, she had joked about Martha's appearance, but there was no response. One day a little later, Sarah had visited Alvin's house to find Martha Clarke looking smaller and ill. She made a remark to her about having 'lost her belly', but again there was no answer.

The next two witnesses, Mary Fowler and Charlotte Coles, were asked to confirm Martha Clarke's statement about some events on the afternoon of Sunday 18 December. Mary Fowler said she had been a servant to Mr Alvin's late father and had since married a local farmer. She knew Martha Clarke, but on the few occasions she had seen her recently, had observed no signs of pregnancy. However, on the morning of the Sunday in question, Miss Coles had called on her and said she was concerned about a rumour that Martha was expecting. Although Martha had immediately denied it, Miss Coles was unconvinced, and asked Mary Fowler to come to the house later that afternoon and have a look at the girl.

Mary said that at about 4 p.m. she called at the house, and while talking to Miss Coles in the hall, Alvin had walked past them. As a rule, he said hello to her and invited her to see the cows and the garden, but this time he did not seem pleased to see her there. Soon afterwards he went back out again. Mary then said that Miss Coles told her Martha was out milking the cows, and both women chatted for a while. About an hour later, she heard Martha come into the kitchen and begin pouring milk into a pail. Miss Coles then went out into the passage, and soon afterwards, Mary Fowler heard someone go upstairs.

When Miss Coles returned, she said Martha was not well and had gone to her room. A few moments later, someone called at the back door asking for Martha but when Miss Coles called up and told her, Mary Fowler heard the girl reply that if anyone wanted to see her they would have to come upstairs. It was then, Mary Fowler said, that Miss Coles asked her to go up and see what was wrong. The farmer's wife found Martha lying in bed complaining she had been feeling poorly since last night, after being out the day before with the donkey cart, running about and getting very warm. Afterwards she had stood about and got cold.

Suddenly Martha exclaimed, 'You know it had been reported a good deal about me that I be in the family way. Well I'm not! Here! feel me belly to prove it'. Taking her hand, the girl passed it over her stomach. Miss Coles had now arrived on the landing outside the room and called out to Martha that if she did not go downstairs at once, she would call the doctor to see her. The farmer's wife suggested to Miss Coles that they talk about the servant's condition before doing anything, and both women went down to the parlour to find Alvin sitting at the table.

Market Street, Crewkerne.

The Square, Crewkerne, c. 1900.

When they discussed Martha's condition and the rumours of her pregnancy, Mary did not think Martha was with child. They wondered if she might have been confined elsewhere in the town but thought it unlikely, as her duties required her to be about the house and garden all day. Later, Mary continued, she took a cup of cocoa up to Martha and was followed by Miss Coles, carrying a candle. While the girl drank, Miss Coles had stood holding the candle at the half-opened door, but when Mary came back onto the landing with the empty cup, Miss Coles asked if anything was wrong. Mary said she could not be certain, so Miss Coles had told her to go back and check the bed. Mary Fowler did so, and examined Martha's day clothes, finding some marks of blood, but put this down to natural causes rather than a concealed confinement. On returning downstairs, she told Miss Coles that she was sure the servant was not in the family way and went home at about 6.30 p.m.

Charlotte Coles stated that she lived with her cousin and managed his household. Martha Clarke had been in service for about two years, and until the rumours began before Christmas last, she had given no cause for complaint. Her duties included watering, feeding, milking and bedding down the household cows, sometimes with Alvin's help. Early in December, it had been rumoured that Martha Clarke was with child, but when asked whether it was true the girl had strongly denied it. However, Miss Coles explained, she was not completely satisfied because she thought Martha was looking rather stout, but when she had told the girl to do up her coat, she was able to do so. She therefore decided to ask Mary Fowler, as a former family servant and a respectable married woman with children, to look at Martha and give her opinion.

Miss Coles recalled that on the Sunday in question, Martha Clarke had had her lunch at 1 p.m., and then went into the back premises. She did not see her again until the milk was brought in later in the afternoon and she helped the girl to strain it into pails. Then, she said, Martha had complained of feeling unwell, and as the milk was taken down into the cellar she heard the girl go upstairs. She then recounted the events described by Mary Fowler. With regard to her cousin's activities during the afternoon, Miss Coles remembered that he was in and about the house and garden and did not leave the premises. She could not recall whether he had helped with the cows or whether his behaviour to Mary Fowler was any different. Finally Edith Turner, the town policeman's wife, told of Martha Clarke's confession at her house but denied that she had induced the girl to make the statement.

After all the witnesses had been called, Richard Alvin was asked whether he wished to address the court. He said firmly that he was 'innocent of the charge.' Martha Clarke, sitting opposite, leapt to her feet and pointed at him, shouting, 'He is not innocent, gentlemen!' There was uproar in court for several minutes. When order had been restored, the chairman told Martha that if she wished to address the court, now was the time, but anything she said would be taken down and might be used against her 'in another place.' She told how she had given birth to a child, delivered by Alvin who then took it from her:

He never allowed me to see the child and he would never tell me whether it was a boy or a girl because if no one saw it I should never blush if accused by anyone. As soon as I was delivered he told me to go down. I heard the child cry before and after I went down. I was in the hayloft about 10 minutes after the child was born and about 10 minutes after I was confined I went down and fetched the milking pail and brought it up to milk the cows. Alvin carried the milk as far as the kitchen door and I took it up and carried it in and placed it on the table. I then went up stairs and went to bed. I asked Miss Coles for some more clothes which she denied me and she said I should have no more. Mary Fowler afterwards brought me some which Miss Coles gave her. I had been in bed about half an hour when Mary Fowler came up to me. She examined me and heaved up the bedclothes and did not think there was any more the matter with me than with any other woman. Miss Coles was standing outside my bedroom. I saw Alvin place the hayband round something and heard it cry. It was moonlight at the time and there are windows in the place. When he was twisting the hayband his back was towards me, and after it was tied he threw it amongst the reed. I heard the child cry after I came down from the loft. I left him there and he returned about 5 minutes afterwards. I never heard the child cry after Alvin came down. He never told me where the child was but I suspected it was somewhere in the garden. The day after I was confined I went into the garden and saw the ground had been removed at the top of the garden near the middle walk but I never examined the ground. I was in the stable at the time I was taken in labour, and Alvin told me to go up into the hay loft and he said it was the best place. I never asked him what had become of the child.

Mr Alvin, she maintained, was the child's father. He had spoken to her a good deal about it, and said he knew what was the matter with her, but never mentioned that he should deliver it himself. She had provided the clothes for it and planned to entrust it to her sister to keep until she could care for it herself, as Alvin never suggested getting any clothes. Finally, she said, she never left his service, and the gate of the garden door was secured so that nobody could enter from the street.

There was further uproar in court once she had finished, and after the noise died down, the magistrates committed both prisoners for trial at the next Assizes – Richard Alvin as principal in the murder and Martha Clarke as accessory after the fact. An application for bail for Alvin was refused, and both were taken to the County Gaol.

Alvin appeared before Mr Justice Coleridge at the Somerset Lammas Assizes in Bridgwater on 16 August 1843, indicted for 'the wilful murder of a child, name and sex unknown, on 18 December, 1842 in the Parish of Crewkerne, by tying a band of hay round its neck and thereby strangling it.' He pleaded not guilty. The charge against Martha of being an accessory after the fact had been dropped, and she was to be the prosecution's principal witness. Mr Kinglake and Mr Rawlinson appeared for the Crown and Mr Cockburn and Mr Stone defended.

Mr Kinglake opened for the prosecution by describing events leading up to Sunday 18 December. He told the court that the prisoner had lived in Crewkerne for some years and was a man of considerable property. The charge against him was that the female servant, who lived with the prisoner and his cousin, Miss Coles, was bearing his child, and that in December a child was born alive and he had killed it. The servant, Martha Clarke, affirmed that she was in the family way, the prisoner was the father and that on the afternoon of the Sunday before Christmas in 1842, she was delivered of a child. She would state that the prisoner knew she was expecting, that he had often spoken to her on the subject, and would give details of his actions on the afternoon in question. The substance of the indictment, Kinglake emphasised, depended upon the credit which the jury would place on the statement of Martha Clarke. The defence would doubtlessly seek to discredit her evidence as she had been an accomplice and party to the crime but, after hearing what she had to say, he would submit that she was not an accomplice.

The constable of Crewkerne and William Pottinger then gave evidence of finding the corpse. Mr Bowdage, the surgeon, spoke about its removal from the garden and his subsequent examination. Cross-examined by Mr Cockburn, he stated that he had not put the bones together or measured the child because it was too badly decomposed. He thought it had been in the ground for about six months, and he could not confirm whether it had been born alive. However, the blood found on the hayband might have flowed from the umbilical cord if it had been born alive, and it could also have been fatal if the cord had not been tied. He thought it unlikely that a woman just delivered of a child could carry a pail of milk, or even get up the next morning. In reply to a question from the judge, the surgeon conceded that 'women of the lower orders go to work sooner after delivery than those in the better classes of life.'

As principal witness, Martha repeated the evidence she had given at the previous proceedings. For the defence, Mr Cockburn subjected her to a searching cross-examination, and though she became confused about events in the hayloft, she stuck to her story. The remaining witnesses, Sarah Bulgin, Mary Fowler and Charlotte Coles, also repeated their evidence as given before the magistrates. Elizabeth Turner told of Martha's first statement and denied inducing or in any way encouraging the girl to confess.

Mr Cockburn then told the jury that the prisoner stood accused on the testimony of one witness, and he could not call evidence to prove that he was not a party to the 'transaction' with which he had been charged. His learned friend had pointed to the case depending entirely on the word of the principal witness, and if the jury did not believe her, that was the end as there was nothing in the rest of the evidence to fix guilt upon him. It was said that Martha Clarke was not an accomplice. What then was she? She had confessed to giving birth to a child and, when charged with having made away with it, blamed it on her master, the prisoner at the bar.

Taking each statement made by Martha Clarke in turn, he pointed out to the jury that there was no evidence as to the mode of death, and argued on the improbability of the mother of her firstborn child acquiescing in the contemplated murder of her infant in the hay loft, without remonstrating against the deed. Could a master have had so much influence over his servant to suppress a mother's feelings for her child and become a party to its death? The prisoner had no motive to kill the child; he was not poor and the expense of maintaining it would have been of no consequence. It might be said that his character was at stake, but he had no ground for fear of moral censure as he was unmarried and there was no reason why he should place himself in such dire peril of his life.

Cockburn suggested to the jury that there were three things on which they must be satisfied: first, that the child had been born alive; second, that the prisoner had killed it and third, that it was killed in the manner described in the indictment.

On the first point there was no evidence, except that of the witness, that the child had been born alive, and the surgeon could not be sure she was telling the truth. As to the second point, there was no evidence to connect the prisoner with the murder. With regard to the third, the jury must be satisfied that the death was occasioned in the manner described in the indictment, namely, that the prisoner had killed the child by tying a hayband around its neck, strangled and suffocated it. The evidence from the surgeon and the men who had discovered the body was that the hayband was tied round the body, but there was nothing to show that it had caused strangulation.

The defending counsel went on to say that that several actions by the prisoner proved his innocence. He had never tried to prevent Mary Fowler from examining Martha Clarke, even though he knew his cousin would be asking her to do so. Neither had the prisoner, after the first examination of his house and garden by the town policeman, removed the corpse to a more secret place. Mr Cockburn concluded by suggesting to the jury that the case was surrounded by great doubt and suspicion, and there was a total absence of motive for the prisoner to commit the crime.

In summing up, Mr Justice Coleridge told the jury that unless it was satisfactorily proved beyond all reasonable doubt that the death of the child had been caused in the manner described in the indictment, the prisoner could not be found guilty. If the jury believed that proof had not been given, it would be unnecessary for him to go through the whole of the evidence. It only took them a few minutes to decide that there was proof that the death had been caused by strangulation, and found Richard Alvin not guilty. Speculation remained as to whether Martha Clarke could have given birth to another man's child, on her own, in the hay loft, and buried the body under cover of darkness without anyone knowing.

24
'IT'S NO USE; I'VE DONE IT'

Weston-super-Mare, 1844

Joel Fisher of Weston-super-Mare was a veteran of the battle of Waterloo, having faced the Grand Army of Napoleon in 1815 as a member of the 7th Hussars. In 1844, aged 52 and back in civilian life, he had been the landlord of the Devonshire Inn on High Street for nearly three years. Born the son of a farm labourer in the nearby village of Wick St Lawrence, as a young man he had worked for Joseph Hewlett, a local farmer, before entering service with Mr Bisdee, a local surgeon. In 1811 he joined the army and served with honour until 1834 when the colonel of the regiment retired and he left the forces to act as the colonel's servant. He lived with him for nine months, before marrying a fellow servant. The couple set up home in Weston-super-Mare, where Fisher was re-employed by Mr Bisdee. Three children were born, but then the family was beset by tragedy. Mrs Fisher died, followed shortly afterwards by one of the children.

Fisher left Mr Bisdee, and soon afterwards, married Mary Hyatt, a widow with an adult son and daughter. The marriage was fiery from the outset. Mary had a violent, explosive temper and her children were prone to interfering. Within less than a year they parted for a few weeks, until Mary managed to persuade her husband to take her back, promising to behave better in the future.

For the next year the couple lived at Nailsea and Congresbury, but were soon quarrelling again. The fights were fuelled by Mary's daughter, who was living with the

High Street, Weston-super-Mare, 1920s.

couple and actively took her mother's part against Joel. He bought the Devonshire Inn in 1841, using the nest egg he had accumulated during his army years. The squabbling with his wife continued unabated and Mary frequently left her husband, only to persuade him to take her back yet again. In 1843 she packed her bags once more, this time leaving with £20 of Joel's money and some linen. Furious, Joel managed to track his errant wife to Bath, where he recovered his money. By now his patience was all but exhausted, and he took out an advertisement stating that he would no longer be responsible for her actions.

It took only three weeks for her to wheedle her way back to Joel with promises that, if he took her back, she would control her temper and never leave him again. Her promises lasted until the long-suffering Joel had agreed to take her back yet again, when arguments resumed almost instantly. Soon he was at breaking point. As he was illiterate, he depended on his wife to manage the pub accounts. The pressure of running a busy public house and looking after his two young sons grew too much to bear and, on Tuesday 4 June 1844, after one quarrel too many, he finally snapped.

On the previous evening, Joel and Mary had fought bitterly over Peter Baker, a lodger at the pub, who, according to Fisher, had left on account of Mary's conduct towards him. The argument blazed on, with Mary Fisher seemingly doing her best to antagonise her husband, blowing out his candles and erasing the details of the day's takings from the pub from the slate on which they were written. Throughout the argument, Fisher continually threatened to 'do for' Mary, and she refused to sleep with him, choosing instead to retire to bed with Ann Evans, a family servant, in the bedroom that the girl shared with Joel's two young children. Even after Mary had gone to bed, Joel continued to storm about in a state of rage, uttering threats that he would murder her and that that night would be her last. At one stage Fisher pounded on the bedroom door, ranting and raving, and Evans had to persuade his wife not to jump out of the bedroom window. Finally, at about 1 a.m., the fighting ceased and the pub fell quiet.

The silence was an uneasy one. Joel stayed awake throughout the night brooding until, at 5 a.m. the next day, he burst into the serving girl's bedroom, wielding an iron bar with which he had forced the door open. With his children, then aged about 10 and 12 years, screaming in the background and the servant girl begging him to go away, he dealt his wife several blows to the head with the iron bar, smashing her skull. He then left the room, returning shortly afterwards with a large carving knife and, standing on his wife's chest, proceeded to slash her throat so viciously that her head was almost severed. He then turned calmly to Ann Evans and reassured her that he would not hurt her – he had committed no sin, he maintained, merely removed a sinner from the world.

Satisfied that Mary was now dead, he left the room again and went immediately into the bedroom of William Upsall, one of the pub's lodgers, telling him exactly what he had just done. Upsall had been rudely awakened by the shouts and screams, followed by Joel Fisher rushing into his room, a bloody carving knife in his hands. Upsall asked if he had killed his children, to which Fisher jubilantly replied, 'No, but I've killed her!' He then asked Upsall to fetch a policeman.

By now the servant girl had alerted the neighbourhood to the situation at the inn. Meanwhile, Upsall had roused Mr Bernard, a local doctor and, having informed him of what had taken place, continued to the police station. Bernard arrived at the pub shortly before Constable Robert Hill, finding the door locked and one of Fisher's sons standing forlornly outside. Bernard had knocked on the door and Fisher had opened it. Seeing the boy, he had taken him gently back into the pub saying, 'Come in my son; it was for you I did it.' He had then bolted the door again behind him again, saying that he would admit nobody until the police arrived.

In answer to Constable Hill's knocking, Fisher had opened the door and led the two men to the bedroom where his wife's blood-soaked body still lay on the bed. As Mr Bernard bent over the corpse, Fisher began to mutter; 'I've done it; I've done it; it's no use; I've done it; I knew I should do it and I know I should be hung for it.' He was promptly arrested and taken to the police station at Weston-super-Mare. Hill then returned to the pub to carry out further investigations.

Having examined the dead woman, Bernard confirmed that the blows to the head had not killed her outright, but that the wound to her throat was the cause of death. Fisher later confirmed that he had cut his wife's throat because she was still breathing after his onslaught with the iron bar and he thought it best to put her out of her misery.

Fisher appeared at the Summer Assizes in Wells on 12 August 1844, charged with the wilful murder of his wife. Ann Evans, William Upsall, Constable Hill and Mr Bernard all testified before the court for the prosecution, and then it was the turn of Mr Cockburn, counsel for the defence to speak. He could not and would not deny that his client had committed the terrible act of murder, he said in his address to the jury, but he believed that certain features of the case should preclude a verdict of guilty of wilful murder which was not proven, he maintained, suggesting that the jury should consider instead a verdict of manslaughter.

He reminded the jury that Mary Fisher had had a violent and aggravating temper and that this may have provoked Joel Fisher to commit the crime. He pointed out that

Fisher's actions immediately following the murder could not be described as those of a sane man. He had not harmed Ann Evans, the woman who had just witnessed his acts – on the contrary, he had almost encouraged her to bear witness against him. Fisher had then specifically requested that his lodger fetch the police. When the surgeon had arrived, he had opened the door only for long enough to allow his son to enter the inn, telling the boy that he had done this for him, even though the act had nothing to do with the child. Cockburn told the jury that this behaviour was without reason or sanity and pointed to madness in the accused.

Cockburn then called two witnesses to testify that Fisher's past behaviour had not always been rational. Joseph Hewlett, a local farmer, told of paying ten pennies for five pints of ale in the pub. The landlord had only taken eight of the pennies and, when Hewlett pointed out his error, had flown into a tremendous rage and threatened him with a carving knife. Hewlett purported to have been in fear for his life, although he was sure that Fisher had not been in control of his senses at the time and had not realised what he was doing.

The second witness, James Bailey Smith, was an excise man who had carried out regular excise surveys at The Devonshire Inn over the past three years. A certain strangeness about the accused had prompted him to comment many a time, 'That Fisher's mad.'

It was left to the judge, Mr Justice Pattison, to sum up the facts of the case for the jury. He instructed them to consider whether Mary Fisher had died from her wounds and, if she had, had the prisoner inflicted them? With regard to the defence, he reminded them that in the eyes of the law, a man must be considered sane and to know the laws of the land unless the contrary was proven. If a man did not know that what he had done was wrong, then he could be considered insane. If, however, he was aware that he had committed an act that was against the law and wrong, then he must be assumed to be responsible for his actions.

Given that Fisher had been muttering about being hanged for his part in the death of his wife, even while her body was being examined by the attending doctor, it was hard for anyone to argue that he had not understood that what he had done was both against the law and wrong. Thus the jury retired for only a short period before returning a verdict of 'Guilty of Wilful Murder.'

Fisher was then asked if there were any reason why he should not be given the death penalty, to which he replied that nothing had been said that ought not to have been and he would rather hang than live with such a wicked woman. He was well aware of what he had done, and could only hope that the Lord would have mercy on him as a sinner.

Mr Justice Pattison donned the traditional black cap and passed the death sentence. He then told Fisher that he was sorry to hear his remarks which, he felt, showed a 'fearful state of mind'. If Mary Fisher had indeed been as wicked as her husband stated, then he had sent her out of this world without the chance to repent and make her peace with God. He believed the jury had given the right verdict, and he hoped that Fisher would use the time remaining to him to come to a better state of mind since there was no hope of any mercy being extended to him on this earth.

While waiting to be transported from Wells to Taunton Gaol, Fisher was allowed to see his sons. Their last meeting was a painful one, at which Joel passed on his treasured Waterloo medal to the oldest boy, wishing fervently as he did that he had been killed in the field of combat so that his sons would not have been born into such disgrace.

Fisher's accommodation at Taunton Gaol was relatively pleasant, considering his circumstances. His cell was light and airy and had a small yard in which he could exercise, and an officer in constant attendance. He spent his last days in prayer or in long discussions with the prison chaplain. Two days before his execution, he received two visitors, his brother and an old army comrade, with whom he had served for twenty years in the 7th Hussars.

On the night before his death, the prison chaplain gave Fisher a letter of forgiveness, written by Thomas Hyatt, the son of his deceased wife Mary, and it apparently brought him great comfort. On 4 September 1844, after eating a light breakfast, he spent his last hours in prayer in the company of the prison chaplain. Divine Service began at 10 a.m., during which Fisher received the Sacrament. Then, escorted by the chaplain, prison officials and several of his comrades from Waterloo, he walked calmly and steadily to the scaffold. A crowd of 3,000 people assembled outside the prison to watch as the rope was secured around his neck and a hood placed over his head. A hush descended as the Lord's Prayer was recited and then, as the bolts were drawn, Joel was heard to cry out, 'Oh God, pardon my sins and receive my soul.'

The local newspaper reported that the prison governor had received numerous requests from people who wanted the dead hand of Joel Fisher to be rubbed over parts of their bodies. According to folklore, this was a recognised cure for both rheumatism and 'King's Evil', another term for scrofula or tuberculosis of the lymph glands. The paper expressed surprise that such superstition still existed.

25

'YOU MUST HAVE THOUGHT WE WERE KILLING EACH OTHER'

St Augustines, 1849

Shortly after five o'clock on the morning of 3 March 1849, Mrs Isabella Fry woke suddenly to the sound of screams. Within moments her lodger, Mrs Anne Ham, had also been disturbed by the blood-curdling sounds. The two women agreed that the noise seemed to be coming from the house next door, 6 Trenchard Street, specifically from the bedroom where their neighbour and landlady, Elizabeth Jeffries, normally slept. At Mrs Fry's suggestion, Mrs Ham banged on the dividing wall with her walking stick and, as she did, the noise stopped abruptly, leaving the ladies to finish their sleep in peace.

Trenchard Street – now the site of a multi-storey car park. (© N. Sly)

Barely two hours later, there was a knock at the door. Mrs Ham answered, and on the doorstep stood a young girl, who introduced herself as Miss Jeffries's maid. Sarah Thomas said that she had been sent to apologise for the disturbance, explaining that a cat had jumped onto her mistress's bed, frightening her half to death. 'You must have thought we were killing each other' she joked. Mrs Ham was disbelieving. 'It was no cat', she argued, telling the maid that she had heard her crying in the yard before and thought that she had been making the noise because her mistress was trying to pull her out of bed. Sarah denied this, although she did confide that Miss Jeffries was 'such a good for nothing woman' that she couldn't live with her.

Sarah Harriet Thomas was, it seemed, the latest of numerous servants employed by Miss Jeffries, a woman who was so unpleasant that she rarely received any visitors and whose own brother deliberately gave her a wide berth. However, the elderly lady did have one friend, a Mrs Susan Miller. Mrs Miller had called at the house to see Miss Jeffries on the previous afternoon and had promised to return that day. However, when she did return, no amount of knocking at the door elicited any response from within – the house appeared shut up and empty.

Earlier that morning, it had been a different matter. A neighbour who lived across the street had watched Sarah and a male companion removing items from the house, eventually walking off together carrying a bundle.

This bundle was left at a confectioner's shop in nearby Maudlin Lane, to be called for later that day. Sarah unexpectedly turned up at the home of her parents, George and Ann Thomas, in Horfield. Her parents asked no questions as she carried her luggage into the house, leaving shortly afterwards to return to Bristol to collect her bundle and returning at around half past nine in the evening.

Sarah spent the next day with her parents, who were surprisingly reticent in asking her about the jewellery, money and silverware that had come home with her. Still, it was not the first time that Sarah had suddenly left her job and neither was it the first time that money and trinkets had left with her.

On Wednesday 7 March, the body of Miss Jeffries was found lying in her bedroom with numerous wounds to her head; her pillow and bolster completely soaked with

Host Street, early 1900s.
The Flitch of Bacon is on the
extreme left of the picture.
(Author's collection)

blood. The room was in some disarray and indeed, the whole house appeared to have been ransacked. The first persons to gain entry to the house included Miss Jeffries's brother, Henry, himself a retired surgeon, who quickly surmised that his sister had died from violence. Nearby lay a large stone, weighing around 4lbs, which was usually used as a doorstop and which bore traces of grey hair and clotted blood. The body of Miss Jeffries's dog, which was known to always bark at strangers, was found in the backyard privy.

Mr Ralph Bernard, a surgeon, later carried out a post-mortem examination and concluded that Miss Jeffries had died of concussion and compression of the brain. She had three contused wounds on the left-hand side of her forehead, and a 2in wound on the top of her head. Just to the right of this was a slightly smaller Y-shaped wound and there were numerous other contusions and skin abrasions, including one on her left hand. This, along with Miss Jeffries's position in the bed, which gave the impression that she was trying to get up at the time of her death, suggested that she may have attempted to defend herself against her attacker. The injuries had been caused by a blunt instrument and a closer examination of the large stone showed that it fitted the wounds exactly.

Police immediately set off in pursuit of the missing maid, their first port of call being her parents' cottage. Sarah's mother initially denied that her daughter was at home but the officers insisted on looking round anyway, eventually finding Sarah crouched, partially dressed, under the stairs in the coal-hole. A thorough search of the cottage revealed all sorts of treasures – jewellery, including a gold chain, foreign coins, twenty-seven sovereigns, four half-sovereigns and a quantity of silver and copper coins. Most damning were four shifts, each marked with the initials 'E.J.' and a petticoat belonging to Sarah, which bore bloodstains. Sarah was promptly arrested, as was her mother. When searched at the police station after her arrest, Sarah was found to have five silver teaspoons concealed in her stocking, all engraved with the letters 'E.J.'.

Initially, Sarah tried to lay the blame for her employer's death on Miss Jeffries's brother. Then, she abruptly changed her story, telling the police that a girl who said she was a former servant had arrived at the house on the Saturday morning, demanding a word with Miss Jeffries.

The visitor told Sarah that she was having problems obtaining references from her previous employer and had picked up the large stone from beside the kitchen door and gone upstairs to Miss Jeffries's bedroom, obviously with the intention of persuading her to co-operate. Sarah told police that she had gone up to the bedroom a little later and seen the elderly lady lying folded in her bedclothes. The former servant had given Sarah the money and jewellery as an inducement not to tell and told her to leave, promising to lock up after her. The girl's name, Sarah recalled, was either Maria Lewis or Maria Williams.

Strenuous efforts were made to identify the mysterious Maria. Susan Miller vaguely remembered a servant employed by her friend in the recent past, but believed that girl's name to be Rebecca. The proprietors of domestic staffing agencies (known as intelligence offices) were quizzed at length, but nobody could identify the young maid that Sarah swore had killed her mistress.

The last known servant of Miss Jeffries, prior to Sarah's appointment, was 16-year-old Lucy Chad. Lucy had had health problems but, having recovered, had travelled to Bristol to live with her aunt in Avon Street while looking for work. She was engaged by Miss Jeffries but spent only five weeks in her situation before she suffered a relapse, mainly, she claimed, due to the unkind treatment she received from her employer. Lucy also maintained that her mistress had always carefully locked the house every night and slept with the keys in her bedroom – if this was so, how could Sarah have opened the door to admit Maria?

Host Street, 2007. (© N. Sly)

Yet Lucy had left Trenchard Street on 24 January and Sarah Thomas didn't begin work until 5 February. This left a period of two weeks during which the mysterious Maria or Rebecca could have been in service to Miss Jeffries. One firm did recall supplying a servant for Miss Jeffries in early January but could not give her name. Miss Jeffries had dismissed this girl as unsatisfactory on account of her being too dozy and for wearing too many flounces on her gown. Another intelligence office recalled sending several servants for Miss Jeffries's approval during the week commencing 22 January. However, an inspection of the agency books showed that none of the girls' names had been recorded and none had been hired.

Then a new witness came forward, a 9-year-old girl called Mary Ann Sullivan. Mary Ann's uncle, John Collins, was a fiddler who played at the local pubs to supplement the relief money he received from the parish. He was blind and it was her job to lead him from pub to pub. Mary Ann knew Sarah Thomas quite well and told police that Sarah had been courting a rifleman for at least a month prior to the murder.

On the Saturday of the murder, Mary Ann claimed to have been in the Flitch of Bacon public house in Host Street with her uncle. There she had seen a young man whom she knew as Matthew Lyon, in the company of two riflemen, one of whom was Sarah's boyfriend. Mary claimed to have eavesdropped as the three men plotted the murder of Mrs Jeffries. According to Mary Ann, she had watched the three men climb over the wall separating the pub from Mrs Jeffries's yard at around midnight. She had then followed them through a door in the wall to see Lyon strike the elderly woman on the forehead, while one of the riflemen hit her with the side of his sword. Lyon had then killed the dog and thrown it into the yard.

Again, we must question why the men would climb a 20ft wall to gain access to Miss Jeffries's house if they could have simply walked through a door? The landlady of the pub denied knowing Mary Ann Sullivan but hinted that the girl came from a bad lot and was 'not quite in her senses'. Nevertheless, the keys to Miss Jeffries's home were found in a groove in a windowsill of the Flitch of Bacon on the very day that Mrs Jeffries's body was discovered. Had they lain there unnoticed since the murder or been placed there at a later date?

At the coroner's investigation into the murder, Mary Ann was accused of telling lies and threatened with punishment if she continued to do so. If her evidence was the truth, admonished the coroner, then she had nothing to fear but if she had lied, then she had better confess at once. Mary Ann insisted that she was telling the truth and signed her deposition accordingly. As it was being read to the court, Sarah Thomas laughed out loud several times.

In his summary of the facts for the jury, the coroner, Mr J.B. Grindon, discounted Mary Ann Sullivan's evidence as 'wholly unworthy of credit.' He told the jury that they would have to rely largely on circumstantial evidence in reaching their verdict, but that, in his opinion, the evidence was strong and appeared to point to Sarah Thomas alone as the murderess. The jury retired for fifteen minutes before returning with a verdict of wilful murder against Sarah Harriet Thomas.

At this, all traces of Sarah's former levity vanished and she burst into noisy tears, burying her face in her handkerchief. It seemed as if all her strength deserted her, since she had to be assisted from the court 'hanging like a dead weight on the arms of the policemen.' Outside the court, a large, angry crowd of people had gathered to hear the coroner's ruling and police had to struggle to protect Sarah from them as she was transported to gaol to await her forthcoming trial at the Gloucester Assizes.

The trial opened on 3 April, before Mr Baron Platt, with Mr Whitmore and Mr Skinner as counsel for the prosecution and Mr Serjeant Allen appearing for the defence. First the court heard the circumstances of the discovery of Miss Jeffries's body. Next came the statements from Miss Jeffries's next door neighbours, her brother and Mr Bernard, the police surgeon.

Sarah Harriet Thomas. (By kind permission of Bristol Central Library)

Numerous witnesses mentioned Miss Jeffries's character. She was described as not having an amiable disposition and as being a violent woman who was known to ill-treat her servants. Mrs Ham testified to hearing her neighbour call Sarah Thomas a 'dirty hussy' and complaining loudly that she was slow at her work. Lucy Chad and other previous servants spoke of being threatened with beatings, particularly when Miss Jeffries, who insisted that her servants rise at five o'clock every morning, considered that they hadn't got out of bed quickly or early enough.

Counsel for the defence did not dispute any of the facts put forward by the prosecution, but did dispute the inferences drawn from them. He did not deny that Miss Jeffries had met her death by his client's hand, nor that she had lied about her part in the murder, but did deny that Sarah Thomas had committed a premeditated murder with the intention of afterwards robbing her mistress. If that were the case, he maintained, then Thomas would have selected a more appropriate weapon and made better preparations for her escape. A hatchet, a poker, a hammer, several knives and other instruments of death had been readily available to her, some even in the bedroom where the killing occurred. A stone was the last weapon a cold-blooded, calculating killer would have chosen.

The clothes that Miss Jeffries was wearing when her body was discovered were not strictly nightclothes, indicating that she had already been up and about on the morning of her death. The screams heard by the neighbours were, according to their testimony, similar to the sounds of crying that they had heard Sarah Thomas make in the past.

Miss Jeffries was not in the habit of rising before ten or eleven o'clock in the morning, yet her servants had to be up at five. And it was shortly after five o'clock in the morning that neighbours reported hearing the sound of screaming coming from next door.

Mr Serjeant Allen asked the jury, was it not more probable that the deceased had risen from her bed to force Sarah Thomas to get up? That the two women had quarrelled and that Sarah had inflicted the fatal blows 'in a moment of rage, passion and ungovernable fury?' If the jury found Thomas guilty of murder, then her life would be sacrificed. At very least, there was sufficient doubt that there was any suggestion of malice aforethought and, in that case, the charge should be reduced to manslaughter. The defence counsel then reminded the jury that they would have to live with the consequences of their decision for the rest of their lives. Sarah wept continuously while her counsel spoke, showing her first signs of any emotion in the entire proceedings.

In summing up, the judge cautioned the jury against being led away from the facts of the case by what he called 'this strong, eloquent and pathetic appeal', while reminding them that if they had any doubts as to Sarah Thomas's guilt, they should give her the benefit of this doubt.

The jury retired, leaving just enough time for a charge of horse-stealing to be heard in their absence. In the course of this hearing, some amusing evidence was put forward, causing a good deal of laughter in the court, with Sarah Thomas laughing as heartily as anyone else.

When the jury returned after thirty minutes' deliberation, they announced a verdict of guilty, but with a recommendation for mercy on the grounds of the defendant's youth. Thomas showed no emotion at the verdict, but when the judge put on his black cap, she buried her face in her hands saying, 'Oh, I cannot stand that.'

In passing sentence of death, the judge said that he saw no reason for the jury's recommendation to be considered, although he promised to forward their concerns to the proper quarter. As a gaoler came to take Thomas after sentence was pronounced, she begged him to ask the judge to spare her life, saying that she would not leave the court until he had done so. A second gaoler was forced to assist in removing her and her sobbing as she left court affected many of those in attendance.

In the event, the recommendation for mercy came to nothing and Sarah Thomas was hanged at Bristol Prison on 20 April 1849. Her age at the time of her death was variously given as 17 and 19 years old.

[Note: In different contemporary accounts of the murder, there is some variation of names. Mrs Fry, who heard screaming from next door is referred to as either Isabella or Jane, while Susan Miller, friend of the deceased, is also referred to as Sarah.]

26
'I DID IT FOR LOVE'

Frome, 1851

John and Leah Watts were dairy farmers living at West Woodlands, 2 miles from Frome. Their daughter Sarah, aged 14, helped with the chores at home, and when they went to town on market day to sell their wares, Sarah stayed behind to look after the house and farm. On Wednesday 24 September 1851, John and Leah set out for Frome as usual. Returning at about 4 p.m. they called out, 'We're home', as John Watts opened the front door, but there was no answer. He saw signs of blood on the kitchen floor, called again for his daughter, and then went through to the adjoining dairy. One of the dogs was lapping blood from the floor, where her dead body lay battered and bruised with her clothes torn. The remains of several broken basins suggested that she had put up a fierce struggle.

The devastated John picked her up and carried her upstairs. The police were notified, while the surgeon, Mr Giles arrived to examine the body laid out on the bed, and noted the extent of scratches on the neck and general bruising, as well as the fact that she had also been raped.

On 29 September, a detective, Mr Smith, appointed by the Home Office, was put in charge of the case. Several loaves of bread, plus some butter and cheese had disappeared, suggesting that Sarah had surprised a burglar. An upstairs room had been ransacked, while clothes and a watch were missing. On the kitchen table lay a silk handkerchief belonging to nobody in the family. When Smith examined the blood on the dairy floor, he also saw some spilt whey, and on checking the whey tub, he found signs of blood. On the dairy door was a handprint with blood on the thumb. A shoe mark on the wall matched a scuff mark on the victim's shoe.

No neighbours or passers-by had heard anything unusual, but the house was about a hundred yards from the road. Sarah had last been seen, safe and sound, by neighbours at about 1 p.m. When others were questioned, it was revealed that three local men, Robert Hurd, William Sparrow and William Maggs, had all been drinking in a public house at around the time that John and Leah Watts were on their way to Frome. Sparrow knew the family well, and was probably aware of their market day routine, no least the time they were expected to return. He was therefore aware that Sarah would have been alone in the house at the time. At around midday, the three had been overheard making arrangements to meet in about an hour, and then went their separate ways.

Around 2 p.m. they were seen not far from, and in the direction of, the Watts' family home. Hurd was in front, encouraging the others on, but they were then seen without him. At about an hour later, a man was seen running away from the Watts' farm. Between then and the discovery of the body, they were noticed again but in different clothes, and Maggs was noticed passing something to Hurd. Later still they were all seen in the market place at Frome, and one of them was heard to mention 'a watch but no tin', which was taken as meaning that they had found a watch but no money somewhere. The other witnesses testified that a handkerchief left on the kitchen table belonged to Sparrow, though he denied having had a handkerchief for several years.

On 29 September, the day the detective started his investigation, there was a fair at North Bradley, 7 miles from Frome. Sparrow was there, and a Mrs Watson said to him that as he was from Frome, he must have heard about the murder. He told her that he knew about it, as he had seen the victim since she was killed. She had been lying near the whey tub with her dress over her head, and blows on her head had been inflicted by a stick, and she had been in the whey tub which had been covered with blood from her head, 'and that he did not think it would ever be found out, as only one man had done it, and he would never tell.' Amazed that he should know all these details, Mrs Watson asked if he knew how the murder had been committed. He then described to her how Sarah had been hit with a stick, held in the whey tub until dead, and then left on the floor. At the time, the detective had yet to discover all this for himself, and so naturally none of it was yet public knowledge. There was only one way that he would have known, and that was for him to have been there at the time – either as an accomplice, or as the killer himself.

At about the same time, Maggs was overheard telling somebody else that he knew Sparrow was going to 'peach' on his associates, so he could be pardoned and claim a £50 reward. Sparrow, Maggs said, would be unable to do so, as he had killed the girl when she recognised him. The detective also gathered that Hurd had been the mastermind of the bungled robbery, but after the initial planning, merely acted as an accomplice of the others.

On 30 September, Sparrow was arrested as he had a watch in his possession, assumed to be the one taken from the Watts' house. He claimed he had bought it from Hurd in the presence of Maggs, and this led to the arrest of all three. No owner for the watch was ever found, but it gave the police officer a good enough excuse to arrest them. Sparrow was further questioned by the detective, who noticed Sparrow's hand was bandaged. Asked how he had injured his hand, he said that it had been bitten in an argument he was involved in the previous day. When the wound was examined, it was apparent that it had been inflicted several days before.

Also on 30 September, the coroner, Mr Ashford, held an inquest at the George Inn, West Woodlands. Whether the cause of death was a blow to the head or strangulation was open to doubt, but after a further post-mortem, he deduced that pressure on the windpipe had killed her. When the coroner asked, rather oddly whether she could have strangled herself, Giles said that this was impossible, and the size of the bruises around her neck suggested the fingers of a man's hand. As yet, there was insufficient evidence to pin the murder on any individual, and the jury were instructed to return an open verdict that the deceased was wilfully murdered by person or persons unknown.

On 27 October, the three men were brought before the magistrates' office at Frome. Alongside them was a fourth, Sergeant, who had been seen with them and had been arrested by Smith that morning. Several witnesses were called, among them Sophia Cornish, whose husband William was an innkeeper at Frome, and Mary Francis, whose husband kept the Horse and Groom at West Woodlands. All of them could account for the movements of some, if not all four prisoners on the day of the murder, and the magistrates were left with the impression that each man had made a point of being seen, preferably with somebody else, in order to establish an alibi and thus be nowhere near the Watts' farm when Sarah was killed. No conclusive evidence was proven, but the prisoners were remanded in custody for a further period.

As the prosecution wished to call for forty-three witnesses, gathering the evidence proved a lengthy process and the case did not reach court for almost six months.

On 6 April, Sparrow, Maggs and Hurd were brought before Mr Justice Erle at Taunton Assizes, with Mr Edwards leading the case for the defence, Mr Moody and Mr Everitt, the counsel for the prosecution. The main facts of the case rested upon circumstantial evidence; the combined evidence of the witnesses for the prosecution proved inadequate, and they all swore to having seen the prisoners elsewhere in Frome at the time the murder was committed. When Mr Edwards addressed the court at the end, he said that in his view, a weaker case had never been submitted before a jury. Was there evidence, he asked, upon which they would even hang a dog? In particular, the watch that had led to the prisoners' arrest was not the one stolen from the Watts' house, and there was nothing to suggest that it had not been obtained in a perfectly legitimate manner. It took the jury little time to hand down a verdict of not guilty against all three.

The case against Hurd and Maggs was demonstrably lacking, but in view of what almost amounted to a confession at North Bradley fair, Sparrow was perhaps fortunate to be acquitted. He had been seen near the scene of the crime, had an unexplained bite mark on his hand, and had left his handkerchief on the kitchen table.

Yet the sad tale was not yet over. During the initial investigation, suspicion had fallen briefly on another youth, Joseph Seer. Soon after the murder, he left the area, joined the army, and was invalided out about ten years later. On the morning of 17 September 1861, he reported to the police station at Frome to have a form filled in which would enable him to get his three months' pay on being discharged. The magistrates' clerk, Mr Turner, thought he seemed very ill-at-ease while filling in the form. Asking if anything was the matter, Seer said he had a confession to make.

'I murdered Sarah Watts,' he told Turner and Superintendent Deggan, in the latter's office. 'I hope the God above will let me live to see her again in another world. I have [had] it on my mind a long time. I have been very unhappy ever since.' He said he had known her and played with her as a child. He knew that her parents would be out of the house as it was market day, and he thought her father was 'worth some money'. Going to the house at about 3 p.m., he asked her where to find the money, but she would not tell him. He offered to marry her and take her to America, but she told him firmly that the money did not belong to him. 'If you don't tell me where it is I will be the death of you,' he insisted, taking hold of her by the neck and striking her on the head with a poker. He then dragged her body into the dairy, and put her in the milk pail, leaving her for dead. He then removed 2s from a cup on the mantelpiece, searched the rest of the house, and helped himself to some clothes before leaving. As he knew he was under suspicion of murder, he ran away to sea, and later enlisted in the army. 'I have now got it off my mind,' he concluded. 'I killed her for love. I was very fond of her.'

Within a week, further information emerged. As he had given his age at the time of his discharge from the army as twenty-five, he could only have been about fifteen at the time Sarah was killed. He had evidently laid low for a few years afterwards, as he did not enlist until December 1857. In June 1859, he embarked with his regiment for Corfu, where he became mentally unbalanced and twice attempted suicide. He was sent home and in August 1861, admitted to Fort Pitt, a military mental hospital at Chatham. One month later he was discharged as 'a hopeless lunatic and unfit for further service', sent back to Frome under escort, and handed over to the care of friends.

After his confession, he was taken into custody at Shepton Mallet Gaol, and brought before Frome Magistrates' Court on 8 October. The main witness, an elderly cooper, James Payne, testified to having known Seer since the latter was a child. A few days after the murder, Payne went into the Castle Inn to meet his wife. Seer came in, evidently drunk. Mrs Payne and a friend were talking about the incident and Seer, overhearing them, said he 'had done all he could with the woman [sic] and then he murdered her because he should never be found out.' Payne should have told someone else about it at the time, but when he left the inn to look for a constable to whom to report the matter, his wife (now deceased) ran after him to warn him that if he did so, 'you will be murdered as sure as you be born.'

Further, but less conclusive, evidence came from four other witnesses. One recalled having seen a man who came to her house shortly after the murder, but she could not be certain whether the prisoner was the same man. The other three could add nothing of importance, being either reluctant to say anything at all, or else only having vague recollections of having ever seen the prisoner shortly before or after the murder. What purpose they served in being called at all was debatable. The chief constable applied for a remand and Seer was kept in custody.

When proceedings were resumed on 12 October, Mr Bartrum, defending, said that the prisoner, 'a hopeless lunatic', was 'not responsible for his own acts.' The bench said that that he 'had occasioned very considerable trouble', and Mr Simkins, the gaol surgeon, testified that he could not find in Seer any trace of insanity. However, Superintendent Deggan then produced a letter from the India Office, London, stating that Seer was apprenticed to the East India Company to serve in the Indian Navy in 1847 for seven years. He had arrived at Bombay in December 1847, and was discharged in July 1854. He was therefore not in England when Sarah Watts was murdered, and could have known nothing about the crime. His confession could only be explained by his 'diseased state of mind'. The Earl of Cork, chairman of the magistrates, concluded the trial by discharging him, admonishing him on his folly and the wickedness of his conduct, which had made so much trouble for the police and bench, and so great an expense at the county, and told him firmly never to repeat such conduct.

27

'OH NO, A CHILD COULD PLAY WITH IT'

Leigh Woods, 1857

On 11 September 1857, at about seven o'clock in the evening, gamekeeper George Worts was going about his normal daily routine on the estate of Leigh Court,

Above: *Clifton Suspension Bridge and Leigh Woods.
(Author's collection)*

Left: *Nightingale Valley. (Author's collection)*

situated close to the foot of the Clifton Suspension Bridge. In Nightingale Valley, he spotted what he believed to be a patch of blood, which somebody had evidently tried to conceal by kicking soil over it. Looking around, he noticed footprints, which he followed until he saw what appeared to be the body of a woman lying in a crumpled heap about 12ft below a large, overhanging rock. He rushed to Ashton police station for assistance, returning with Superintendent Jones. Between them, the men retrieved the body and it was taken to the nearby New Inn at Rownham Ferry to await an inquest.

The woman, her identity then unknown, had been shot in the right-hand side of her head and her throat bore two slash marks that were so deep that she was almost decapitated. Animals had torn away parts of her throat.

She was described as between 20 and 30 years of age, of diminutive stature and rather handsome, and was dressed in a dark grey dress trimmed with white lace. One pocket had been cut away from the dress. Near to the body lay a bloody, lace-trimmed handkerchief embroidered with the initials 'C.P.'.

As the county coroner, Mr B. Fry, lived some distance away, it took several days to arrange for a post-mortem examination. Meanwhile, the police made exhaustive efforts to identify the body.

At first it looked as though it would not be too difficult to name the young woman as, almost immediately after the news of the murder broke, a local innkeeper, Mrs Bowden came forward. She told police that a woman dressed in a similar grey outfit to the deceased had come into her inn in the company of a sailor. She remembered them particularly because they had asked for Devonshire cider, but had not liked the drink and had eventually exchanged it for beer. The woman had paid for the drink, taking some money from a purse that was brimming with sovereigns.

Mrs Bowden had engaged the woman in conversation and learned that she had come to Bristol from Hull and was on her way to Appledore in Devon to meet her

*Rownham Ferry. The New
Inn is the white building
to the left of the picture.
(Author's collection)*

husband, the captain and owner of a timber ship that had just docked from Quebec. It so happened that Mrs Bowden was herself a native of Appledore and was able to give the young woman details of a place where she might lodge. Having established that the sailor was only an acquaintance who was accompanying her on her journey, the innkeeper cautioned her customer about displaying her money so freely. The young woman reassured Mrs Bowden that the man had been very kind to her.

The two women discussed the grey alpaca dress, which the captain's wife said was very comfortable for travelling. She then went on to tell Mrs Bowden that she and her companion intended to spend the afternoon in Leigh Woods and to see the suspension bridge. She promised to call back at the inn on her way to catch her train, but never returned.

When the body was found in Leigh Woods, Mrs Bowden and another woman, who had been in the pub at the time, both felt that the description of the dress worn by the deceased sounded remarkably similar to that worn by the sea captain's wife. They contacted the police and Mrs Bowden was taken to view the body. The dead woman's face was too discoloured to allow Mrs Bowden to make a positive identification, although she felt that the dress was identical in appearance to that of her customer.

Hopes of an early identification of the body were dashed the following morning when, as a result of police enquiries, the captain's wife was found alive and well at Appledore. Another pub landlady, Mrs Caroline Green of the White Lion, Temple Street, told police that she believed that the woman could have recently lodged at her inn, again in the company of a sailor. Both Mrs Green and her servant viewed the body and both were positive that it was their lodger, who had told them that she had been fetched from her job in service at Clevedon by her husband and that they were going on to London, where his mother was going to set them up in business. Mrs Green recalled the woman saying that her own mother lived in Hotwell Road, Bristol, and police immediately began enquiries to try and find anyone who had recently left her job under the circumstances described.

A photograph was taken of the dead girl and handbills were printed and circulated. A plaster cast was also made of the head, but by this time the body had begun to decompose and it was felt that, rather than assisting in identifying the young woman, the cast would prove a hindrance. Hundreds of people flocked to see the body when it was placed on display, but to no avail. Miss C.P. – if those were indeed her initials – remained unidentified.

Eventually police looked to the dead woman's undergarments for further clues and found that her stays had been manufactured by Goodmans of Stall Street, Bath. A visit to the retailer elicited the information that the stays had been purchased by a young woman, who had told them that she was soon to be married and that she and her husband intended to emigrate to America. Then, laundry marks on the underwear were recognised by a laundress who had worked for the Honourable Mrs Hutchinson at Dorset House, Clifton. Mary Ann Kelston, a dressmaker eventually identified the dead woman's dress as her own work and Mr Burt, a shoemaker from Bath, was able to identify a repair to the boots that the dead woman was wearing as having been carried out by him. All identified the wearer of the clothes as Charlotte Pugsley.

These clues eventually led police to Hill House, the home of Samuel Bythsea in Freshford, near Bath, where, until the previous week, Charlotte had worked for three months as head cook. Then she had given notice, telling her employer that she was soon to marry. She withdrew her savings from the Bath Savings Bank and eventually left Freshford with her husband-to-be, John William Beale, on the evening of 9 September, seemingly under the impression that they were going to Southampton to be married, before sailing to America.

Beale was employed as a butler at Badbey House, Daventry, but on 6 September had requested compassionate leave from his employer, Captain Watkins, on account of a serious accident to his father. According to Beale, when the news of his father's accident had been brought to his home, his younger sister had been so affected that she had collapsed from shock and later died. Beale was a married man, who had met Charlotte when they had both worked at Dorset House. When Mrs Hutchinson, their employer, left Clifton to live in Ireland, Charlotte had moved in with Beale and his wife, but Mrs Beale had been jealous and Charlotte was forced to move out rather hurriedly. She had taken up a new position at Freshford, where it seems Beale often visited her, almost certainly without telling his wife!

Beale had arrived at Wine Street, Bristol, on Monday 7 September, calling in at Aplin's tailor's shop where his cousin worked. During his visit to the shop, Beale had asked to be measured for a new coat and it was noted that he carried a small pistol in his breast pocket. When warned by the tailor of the dangers of carrying a loaded pistol, Beale dismissed his concerns, saying, 'Oh no, a child could play with it.' For two days he remained in Bristol, drinking and playing bagatelle with his cousin and his cousin's workmates in the King's Head tavern in Wine Street and ordering a new hat from a shop in Clare Street. On the Wednesday, he had told his cousin that he was off to visit Bath, arriving at Freshford that afternoon. He had collected Charlotte and the three large bags containing her belongings, depositing the bags at Limpley Stoke station to be collected at a later date. He then returned to Bristol with Charlotte and was seen in the city by several acquaintances on the following day, each time accompanied by a woman matching Charlotte's description. He collected his new hat at about 1 o'clock on Saturday 12 September.

When a fellow servant of Charlotte Pugsley travelled from Bath to Bristol and positively identified her clothes, including a pair of stockings that she had personally mended for the deceased, police immediately circulated a description of John Beale. It was printed in *The Times* as:

About 30 years old, 5 feet 4 or 5 inches high, slight make, thin face, pale complexion, hair nearly black, worn long, and turned under at the back of the head, small black whiskers, dark eyes, good teeth, dressed in black frock jacket, with pocket outside the left breast, double-breasted black waistcoat and black or shepherd's plaid trousers made very large at the feet. He is flat-footed, has an awkward gait and turns his feet out very much when walking. He wore an old-fashioned silver watch and massive silver Albert chain and a ring set with red stones on the little finger. He has been a butler or single-handed servant in gentlemen's families and is supposed to have recently come from Daventry, near Northampton. He is well known in Bristol and the neighbourhoods of Clifton and Bath.

The Home Secretary authorised a reward of 100s for information leading to his capture, with a free pardon for any accomplice not being the actual perpetrator of the crime.

The fugitive was not at large for long, being apprehended at Daventry within days. Bristol police were notified of his capture by electric telegraph and Inspector Norris of the Bath police escorted him to Bristol by train. On his arrival, on the evening of 25 September, he was immediately taken before magistrates at Bourton Union workhouse. He gave a statement to the police admitting to meeting Charlotte at Freshford, but alleging that she was a married woman who went by her maiden name of Pugsley. He had escorted her to Bristol and handed her over to her husband, a man whose surname he didn't know, but whose Christian name was either George or Thomas. He was to have met with the couple the following day, but they hadn't turned up, so Beale had returned to his job at Daventry, taking Charlotte's luggage with him in the hope that she would arrange to collect it. However, he had told his colleagues that the boxes belonged to his sister, whose funeral he had applied for compassionate leave to attend.

Beale was charged with the wilful murder of Charlotte Pugsley and remanded at the Bourton Union workhouse until the following day, when he was again brought before magistrates. The chairman, the Revd Henry Morehouse, expressed concern that Beale was not defended. When he asked the prisoner if he would wish to be defended, Beale concurred that he would, so Morehouse proposed that he would only deal with items of evidence that were undisputed, that no counsel or solicitor in the world would attempt to disprove. Accordingly, magistrates heard only that the body of a woman had been discovered, the medical evidence on how she died and the evidence of the witnesses who would state what had happened at Daventry. Beale was given the opportunity to question the witnesses.

First came the evidence of Geroge Worts, who had found Pugsley's body. Since Worts had walked the same route on the previous evening and the body had not been there, it was fairly easy to establish the time of death to within twenty-four hours. Beale informed the court that he had witnesses who could prove that he was not in Bristol during this critical time.

Next, Mr J.R. Lucas, a surgeon of Long Ashton, gave evidence about the wounds on Charlotte's body, stating that they could have been inflicted by a clasp knife, such as the one later found in Beale's room at Badbey House, Daventry. The knife had what appeared to be a bloodstain on the blade, but, once again, Beale maintained that he had witnesses who could testify that the knife had remained on the pantry shelf in Daventry during his trip to Bristol. Here, the Revd Morehouse intervened, explaining to Beale that the surgeon was not stating that the knife had inflicted the wounds, just that it may have done. Lucas spoke of the difficulty in positively identifying Charlotte's body, which had decomposed rapidly in the hot weather. Although the clothing worn by the dead woman had been identified, Charlotte's body was only positively identified by an abnormality in her teeth, which the surgeon had extracted.

When Inspector Norris of Bath was called to give evidence, he told of finding Charlotte Pugsley's boxes at the prisoner's workplace in Daventry. Beale's only question to Norris was to ask what he intended to do with the money and the watch belonging to him, which had also been seized from Daventry.

Simeon Branscombe, the gardener and gamekeeper who worked at Badbey House, was also called. Beale challenged his evidence, first disputing having said that the luggage belonged to his dead sister, then discussing some bloodstains on the cuffs of a shirt belonging to him, found at Daventry. Branscombe eventually conceded that the blood could have come from a dead rabbit that he had seen Beale carrying shortly before the murder occurred, but refused to be swayed on Beale's explanation of the ownership of the luggage.

Having heard what he described as evidence that was indisputable, Morehouse remanded Beale in custody until the following Friday. He was taken to Taunton Gaol, being returned to Bourton for his next appearance before magistrates. This time, Mr E.M. Harris, a solicitor from Bath, defended Beale. Beale's father and sister (who was very much alive) attended the trial and were granted an interview with the prisoner before he was brought into court.

As soon as the magistrates reconvened, Morehouse announced that they were now satisfied that the blood on Beale's shirt cuffs did not originate from Charlotte Pugsley. Mr Harris then declined the opportunity to cross-examine any of the witnesses from the previous hearing.

Evidence was given regarding the luggage that had been left at the station and Louisa Ford, the housekeeper at Freshford and a great friend of Charlotte, testified to the fact that Charlotte had left with Beale on 9 September. Several witnesses spoke of seeing Beale in Bristol with a woman matching Charlotte's description and one, a Mr Jackson, spoke of seeing the couple walking together in Leigh Woods, he with his arm around her waist and she with her head on his shoulder. William Jones, who worked at the tailor's, told of seeing the small pistol in Beale's coat pocket. Beale said nothing in his own defence and was eventually committed for trial at the next assizes.

The trial was held at Taunton, opening on 22 December 1857 before Mr Justice Willes. Mr Stone and Mr Coleridge appeared for the prosecution, while Harris and T.M. Saunders defended the accused. After hearing much the same evidence as had been presented before the magistrates, the court was told that the case for the prosecution had been constructed so carefully that not a link in the chain of evidence was missing. Counsel for the defence argued that Beale might have been foolish in carrying a loaded pistol, but that foolishness did not make him a murderer. There was nothing to show that Charlotte had not been killed by someone other than Beale. Beale had no motive for killing Charlotte Pugsley and, even if she had met her death by his pistol, it was possible that her death had been accidental.

In summing up the case for the jury, the judge instructed them that Beale could be found either guilty or not guilty of murder – there was nothing in the case that warranted the charge being reduced to one of manslaughter. The jury found the accused man guilty and he was sentenced to hang at Somerset County Gaol.

In the days leading up to his execution, Beale was frequently visited by the prison chaplain and by Revd H.P. Liddon, of Christ Church College Oxford, who was also the vice-principal of the Theological College at Cuddesden. Liddon was the nephew of the prison surgeon and, by chance, knew the prisoner. Despite entreaties from both clergymen to confess and repent his sins, Beale remained tight-lipped to the end. He did make a statement to Liddon in which he intimated that he was not the actual murderer but merely an accessory. However, there was no evidence to support that version of events and since Beale refused to name the man he alleged had committed the killing, he went to the gallows without admitting any culpability in the death of Charlotte Pugsley.

Beale was visited by his wife, his mother and his sisters prior to his execution, which was carried out by William Calcraft on 12 January 1858. A crowd of around 10,000 people assembled at the prison, one fifth of which were women and children. At 9 a.m., the prison bell tolled, signalling that the condemned man had left the prison chapel. Escorted by two warders, Beale walked unhesitatingly to the scaffold where the rope was swiftly placed around his neck and the bolt withdrawn, causing the drop to fall. Beale's body hung for the customary hour before being cut down, later to be buried within the grounds of the gaol.

In May 1858, the reward of 100s offered for the capture of John Beale was divided among several people. Mrs Pickering and Mrs Styles, who had previously worked with Charlotte and had identified her clothing, each received 15s. Ten shillings went to Edwin Aplin, the tailor, and a further 10s to Thomas Jones. Both men had seen and conversed with Beale in Bristol around the time of the murder. The remaining 50s went to Mr Burt, the shoemaker who had recognised the boots that Charlotte wore. The dead woman had, at one time, lodged with Burt and his wife and it was he who had first approached the Bath police with a suggestion as to the identity of the dead woman. Mr Burt had died since the trial and his share of the reward went to his widow.

[Note: In various contemporary accounts, the gamekeeper who discovered Charlotte's body is also referred to as George Worts, George West or George Worth. The name of the house at Daventry is alternatively spelled Badbey and Badby. (Although the first spelling appears most frequently, it is thought that the latter is more likely to be correct since there is a village of Badby near Daventry.) Charlotte's employer is referred to as both Mr Bythsea and the Revd Bythsea, while Mr Burt the shoemaker is also called Mr Bart. Finally, there is some confusion as to the identity of Thomas Jones, who received a proportion of the reward money. It is probable that he is the member of staff at Aplin's the tailors who helped to measure Beale for his suit, although the tailor's assistant's first name is given as William.]

28
A POLICEMAN'S LOT

Yeovil, 1862

In the small hours of Sunday 12 January 1862, drinkers were returning noisily home after an evening at the Railway Inn at the bottom of Hendford Hill, Yeovil. Constable William Hubbard of the Yeovil Police was going on duty, walking towards the Quicksilver Mail nearby. As he passed the crowd, he wished them goodnight, and as he had expected, was greeted with catcalls and abusive language. One of the men, George Hansford, tried to jostle Hubbard, but he refused to react and walked on.

A few yards further on, Hubbard heard a clatter of heavy objects on the road, followed by cheering. He turned round to see Hansford picking up a stone to throw at him. Though Hubbard had no time to duck, the drunken Hansford's aim was so poor that the stone fortunately missed its target. Hansford tried again several times but eventually decided he was wasting his time, and Hubbard continued up Hendford Hill where a colleague, Constable William Penny, was waiting for him.

Aged forty-one, Penny was a conscientious police officer. His career was probably all he had, for his family life was tragic. His wife had been committed to a lunatic asylum for several years, and their two small children, whom he adored, lived with relatives in Wincanton as he was unable to look after them himself.

Penny had heard the noise and had roughly seen what had happened. The man responsible for throwing stones, he had decided, must be arrested. Hubbard pointed out Hansford to him, and Penny stepped forward and placed his hand on Hansford's shoulder, asking him his name. Hansford replied with the false name of Sandle, whereupon Hubbard charged him with throwing stones and ordered him to accompany them to the Yeovil police station. Hansford denied the accusation and actively resisted. As the navvies began shouting and swearing at the officers, Penny realised that the situation was about to get out of control. He walked away, calling Hubbard to join him, and suggested quietly that it was pointless trying to take Hansford into custody because they were in such a confrontational mood.

He suggested that they should return to the police station for help. They then hurried away, shouting at the men that they were going to Yeovil to get more men to take Hansford.

Sergeant Benjamin Keats, on duty in the town, had heard the noise and had already set out in that direction. As he began to climb the hill, he met the constables, and Penny asked for help to take Hansford into custody. The officers set off up the hill together to catch up with Hansford and his noisy companions. By the time they had caught up with the crowd, they had reached the Red House Inn at the Barwick and East Coker crossroads. Hubbard pointed out Hansford, and Keats ordered him to be taken into custody. Again Hansford resisted, but Penny drew out a pair of handcuffs and managed to snap one on the man's right wrist. Hansford shouted for help, but only George Chant and Charles Rogers came to help, as the rest ran away.

Chant and Rogers decided to go on the attack. Rogers produced a stick and struck Penny a savage blow on his head, knocking him over onto the road, and then struck Keats on the back of his head, also knocking him over. Rogers next struck Hubbard and turned to flee. Hubbard quickly recovered his balance, and though blood was pouring down his face, he ran after Rogers, and a running fight ensued, which ended in Rogers being felled by a furious blow from Hubbard. Rogers realised that further resistance was useless, and begged the officers not to strike him again as Hubbard picked him up by his collar and marched him towards the Red House Inn.

Sergeant Keats had been temporarily stunned. As he came round, he saw William Penny lying on the ground being savagely beaten by Hansford and Chant. He shouted to Penny to get up and as he moved to help the fallen officer, the navvies stopped attacking him and took to their heels. Now fully recovered and full of fury, Keats charged after them and dragged down Hansford, who no longer had the energy to put up a fight. Chant continued to run and managed to get away. Returning with his prisoner, the sergeant was horrified at the condition of Penny and called to Hubbard for help.

On hearing the call, Hubbard released Rogers, who quickly slipped away, and ran to help his sergeant. Both men carried the badly beaten Penny into the inn where Mrs Rendall, the landlady, made him comfortable in her parlour. Blood was pouring from wounds on the injured policeman's head and Hubbard was dispatched to Yeovil for medical assistance. When Dr Garland arrived, he found Penny close to collapse, but a drop of brandy and water helped to revive him. Garland's examination revealed three deep cuts in the skull, his left ear was nearly severed and his head was badly bruised. There did not seem to be any fractures, and though Penny was sick several times, he appeared lucid enough and asked if he could return to his home to West Coker. The doctor thought it advisable for him not to move, and suggested that he should be put to bed at the inn for a while. Meanwhile, George Hansford was in the town gaol and George Chant was arrested in bed in his lodgings at Stoford. Only Charles Rogers remained unaccounted for.

When Dr Garland came to see Penny again the next day, the latter insisted he was well enough to return home, but the doctor told him to stay at the Red House for a few more days until he was better. Nevertheless, Penny disregarded the doctor's

The grave of PC Penny, Church of St Martin, West Coker. (© Nicola Sly)

advice, and decided he would go home by cart that Monday afternoon. It was a decision he would not live long to regret. On 18 January, six days after the attack, he was dead.

On 21 January, an inquest was held in the New Inn at West Coker before the coroner, Dr Wybrants. After an account of the fight from the two surviving officers and medical evidence from Dr Garland, the jury returned a verdict of wilful murder against George Hansford, George Chant, and, in his absence, Charles Rogers who had been identified as the third assailant. On 24 January, Hansford and Chant were brought before the town magistrates and charged with the assault and wilful murder of Constable Penny. They pleaded not guilty and were remanded in custody for trial at the forthcoming Spring Assizes.

Charles Rogers was captured on the next morning, 25 January, hiding in the stables of the Greyhound Inn at Dorchester. When arrested by Superintendent Pouncey of the Dorset Constabulary, he said he had hit Constable Hubbard because he was afraid that if he had not acted in self-defence, he would have been killed. Brought before the Yeovil magistrates later that day, he was similarly charged with assaulting the police and the wilful murder of William Penny. He pleaded not guilty and was remanded in custody to stand trial with his two companions.

Proceedings began on 31 March 1862 before the Hon. Sir Colin Blackburn, a Justice of the Queen's Bench, with Mr Cole and Mr Hooper leading for the Crown and Mr Ffooks defending. Mr Cole opened the case for the prosecution and Sergeant Keats and Constable Hubbard recounted the events of 12 January. Under cross-examination, Dr Garland stated that the cause of death was a fractured skull. In his opinion, although the fracture resulted from a blow by a blunt instrument, he believed that a handcuff was more likely to have caused the major injury rather than a stick. He also admitted that he did not discover the fracture until the post-mortem as fractures were difficult to diagnose. However, he was quick to refute the theory that Penny had inadvertently hastened his own death by leaving the Red House Inn against medical advice, saying that in his opinion, death had been inevitable.

For the defence, Mr Ffooks suggested that the stone throwing had not been of a serious or malicious nature, and that Constable Hubbard had neither warned the accused nor taken any action against those involved. As the original offence had been of a very minor nature, he did not believe that the constable had reason to feel threatened or in any danger. In addition, the constable did not attempt to make an arrest outside the inn until three quarters of an hour after the stones were thrown. During that time, he continued, the police officers had not been engaged in continual pursuit of the alleged culprit or culprits, nor had there been a continual apprehension of danger. This being the case, the police officers had no right to arrest Hansford, and therefore, the accused were justified in resisting what, to all intents, was an illegal arrest and in using any force they considered necessary.

The prosecution argued that the pursuit had never been abandoned. When the stones were thrown, Mr Cole stated, Constable Hubbard realised he was heavily outnumbered by his attackers and went to seek assistance, and as soon as he had found Constable Penny, he renewed the pursuit. At this stage the trial was adjourned for the day.

When proceedings were resumed next morning, Mr Ffooks stated that one of the main points they would have to ask themselves before reaching a verdict was whether any assault was committed by the prisoners in the first place when the stones were thrown. If there was no assault, then the police were acting 'in exaggeration of their duty' in attempting to arrest Hansford for a minor misdemeanour and for which they had no such right. If they had no lawful right of arrest, he believed the men were not guilty of murder but of justifiable homicide. If there was no intention to commit an assault when the stones were thrown at the constable, Ffooks maintained, then no assault was committed. There was surely no intention on the part of the prisoners to assault the policeman and they were merely going home. For a person to be responsible for a criminal act, there had to be an intention. In this case, he submitted, there was no such intention to assault the police or to cause reasonable apprehension of danger. With regard to the question of continual pursuit, he suggested that it was reasonable to infer that Constable Hubbard had hastened to the top of the hill after the stones were thrown not to get help, but because it was his duty to be there at midnight and he was late.

He considered that the police were determined to secure a conviction, and had thus been 'guilty of a great exaggeration'. The result was an unlawful aggression by the policemen upon the liberty of the three men. Who, he claimed, possessing the proud name of Englishmen, would not be provoked to resist? These men would deserve the scorn of everyone if they had not resisted, and it would be impossible, even for the most benign of philosophers, not to do so under such circumstances. The men had acted with great forbearance, and had refrained from exercising any unnecessary violence in defending their liberty. (Since when, one might ask, did wilfully throwing stones at a person without regard for the consequences not constitute 'unnecessary violence'?)

Mr Ffooks also made much of the fact that Chant had tried to take the stick away from Rogers to prevent him from causing any unnecessary harm. There had been 'no preconceived design' to commit violence, and therefore, in this case, the law of common intent did not apply. If the jury found Chant guilty of this serious offence on the basis of the testimony produced, it would be a verdict which would not meet with the approval of anyone who had heard the trial. He believed, with confidence, that when the jury had considered all the evidence, they would not feel justified in bringing a guilty verdict against Chant. As for Hansford and Rogers, Mr Ffooks stated that they had no weapon which could be termed deadly. They had merely 'used those weapons which nature had given them' to resist unlawful arrest, and nobody could have foreseen that in defending themselves, an innocent man would have been killed. Moreover, he went on, the police had a duty to the public to operate their powers with proper moderation. Penny's tragic death had come about by the foolish conduct of the police, and he was confident that the jury would not find the prisoners guilty of wilful murder.

Did Ffooks bear some grudge against the police? His veiled attack on their conduct that January night, and what seems his over-earnest defence of a drunken crowd ready to throw stones at the merest provocation, suggests that his views were rather heavily weighted against the guardians of law and order.

Nevertheless, in his summing up, the judge appeared to take a similarly liberal stance as he explained to the jury that there were many distinctions with respect to an arrest. A policeman had a right to arrest on suspicion of a felony, but in the less serious case of a misdemeanour, he had no such power to arrest purely on the suspicion of a misdemeanour having been committed. In the latter case, it was his duty to go to the magistrates and obtain a warrant. A policeman could only arrest for a misdemeanour if the offence was committed in his sight, on the spot and in fresh pursuit. It was regrettable that Constable Hubbard did not wait until the next day and then go to Yeovil magistrates to obtain a warrant. Had he done so, the judge went on, Constable Penny would probably still be alive. Unless the jury found these questions in favour of the prosecution, the capital part of the charge failed. So if the defendants were not guilty of murder, did they face a charge of manslaughter? The judge saw nothing in the evidence which would reduce the charge below that. In that case, how many of the defendants were guilty? With these questions, the jury were sent to consider their verdict.

After a long absence, the jury found George Hansford guilty of manslaughter, but with a recommendation of mercy on account of the police having exceeded their duty. Chant and Rogers were acquitted of manslaughter, but found guilty of assaulting Sergeant Keats and Constable Hubbard in the execution of their duty. The judge stated that in view of the verdict on Hansford, he would order the acquittal of Chant and Rogers, as the jury considered that the police had been over-zealous in trying to maintain law and order. Hansford was sentenced to four years' penal servitude.

Constable Penny was buried in the churchyard at West Coker on 22 January, with six of his colleagues bearing his coffin to its final resting place. A headstone, 'erected by some inhabitants of this Parish as a mark of their deep regret at his untimely end and also as a testimony of their great respect for a faithful public servant', paid tribute to the memory of the police officer who had died a few days after 'receiving severe injuries in the execution of his duty.'

29

'OH DEAR, MY POOR CHILDREN'

Easton, 1900

After Edward Pembery left for work early on the morning of 4 May 1900, his wife, Mary Ann, took the chance to have a few moments' lie-in before starting her chores. As she lay comfortable in her bed, halfway between sleep and wakefulness, one can only imagine her mounting terror as she heard heavy footsteps slowly coming up her stairs, accompanied by soft groans and gurgling sounds.

Suddenly the bedroom door flew open and a pale figure dressed only in a nightdress burst through it. Mary Ann instantly recognised the ghostly presence as her sister-in-law, Ellen Milsted, who lived next door with her husband, Henry and their six children: Henry (Harry), Louisa, Sidney, Frank, Elizabeth (Fanny) and Rosie. Ellen was clutching her throat tightly with both hands and a horrified Mary Ann noticed blood flowing between Ellen's fingers. As Mary Ann jumped out of bed to help her sister-in-law, Ellen slowly sank to the ground in a swoon. She never got up again.

Mary Ann called for Mrs Elizabeth Grainger, who, with her husband, lodged in the back bedroom of the Pemberys' house at 193 Pennywell Road. Mrs Grainger rushed into the room and saw Ellen lying on the floor, bleeding heavily from her throat, her nightdress soaked in blood. She immediately ran downstairs to seek help and, as she came out of the front door of the house onto the pavement, she spotted Henry Milsted leaving the neighbouring house, carrying his hat and coat. 'You have killed your wife!' she shouted at him. Henry calmly concurred that he had and told her that he was on his way to turn himself in to the police.

A passer-by, Thomas Paisey, witnessed the exchange between Mrs Grainger and Henry Milsted and immediately ran into 193 Pennywell Road to see what he could

Pennywell Road, 2007.
(©N. Sly)

do to help. As soon as he entered the bedroom, he realised that Ellen was by now beyond any assistance, so he ran out again and set off up the road after Henry who was heading towards the city at a brisk pace. Paisey caught him up after about fifteen minutes and asked him, 'What have you done this for?' to which Milsted replied, 'I could not help it. I was bound to do it.'

The two men walked peacefully along together, chatting quietly, as if out for a morning stroll. Paisey soon learned that Milsted had six children. 'You haven't hurt them as well?' he asked. Milsted recoiled in horror, 'God forbid' he said, assuring Paisey that he 'wouldn't hurt a hair of their heads.'

As Paisey and Milsted neared the police station, Milsted expressed a desire to see his son, Harry. Thinking that he might spot a policeman on the way, Paisey agreed to this diversion and the two men made their way to Howe's hat factory in Newfoundland Road where Harry worked. At the factory gates they knocked for Harry and, when he appeared, Milsted calmly told him, 'Harry, I have been and killed your mother.'

As Harry ran homewards, his father and Paisey continued their leisurely journey towards the police station. After a while, Henry complained of being thirsty and Paisey managed to procure a glass of water for him from a newsagent's shop.

They finally reached the police station at Bridewell Road where Paisey told Sergeant Foley, the duty sergeant, that he had brought Milsted in for cutting his wife's throat. 'That's quite right' agreed Milsted, and he was promptly taken into custody.

Meanwhile, back at Pennywell Road, Elizabeth Grainger had managed to find a policeman, Sergeant John Bridge, who had been patrolling his beat nearby with PC Field. The two officers hastened to no. 193, where they found Ellen Milsted still lying on the bedroom floor, covered in blood. A doctor had been sent for, but had not yet arrived, so Bridge arranged for a stretcher to carry Ellen to hospital.

Sending PC Field in pursuit of Henry Milsted, Bridge then went next door to no. 191 where he met Sidney Milsted. Sidney took the officer to his parents' bedroom and picked up a shoemaker's knife from the floor near the bed, which he handed to Bridge. (The Milsteds' two youngest daughters were still fast asleep in that same bedroom, completely unaware of what had happened.) Bridge noted that the knife was stained with wet blood and that there were drops of blood on the bedclothes, as well as a distinct trail of blood leading from the bedroom at no. 191 to the bedroom at no. 193.

Ellen Milsted arrived at the Bristol Royal Infirmary just before eight o'clock and was pronounced dead on arrival. Edward Stack, a house surgeon, subsequently conducted a post-mortem examination, observed by police surgeon George Myles. The two doctors noted the presence of a wound in Ellen's neck, starting about 2in below the lobe of her right ear. Although the wound was 2½in long, it was scarcely deeper than a scratch at one end and the doctors described it as being more like a single stab wound than a cut. It was agreed by the doctors that the knife found in the Milsteds' bedroom was capable of causing the injury. Ellen's windpipe had been completely severed, as had her jugular vein and carotid artery. Apart from the injury to her neck, Ellen also had an ulcer on one leg and considerable fatty degeneration of her liver. Neither doctor

Bristol Royal Infirmary.
(Courtesy of Derek Fisher,
Bygone Bristol)

felt that these conditions were serious enough to cause her death and neither did they think that Ellen's wound was likely to be self-inflicted. They eventually recorded the cause of her death as haemorrhage from the wound to her throat.

An inquest was held into Ellen Milsted's death at the Crown and Dove Hotel, before Mr H.G. Doggett, the city coroner. The coroner first informed the court that he had received a letter from the governor at Bristol Gaol, telling him that Milsted was currently in the prison hospital receiving treatment for severe delirium tremens and that the prison medical officer had certified that Milsted would not be fit to attend the proceedings. In his absence, the coroner's jury returned a verdict of wilful murder against Milsted and thus it was not until the case was heard at the Magistrates' Court that the full story of the relationship between Henry and his wife and the events leading up to her death became known.

Henry John Milsted, then aged 44, was a hunchback who worked as an outworker for Mr Ballinger, a Montpelier shoemaker. About fourteen years prior to her murder, his wife had taken to drink. She had spent every penny that Henry managed to earn on alcohol. Their children wore rags and the house was so squalid and filthy that five of the police officers investigating the killing had actually vomited at the stench.

Henry had tried begging and pleading with his wife to mend her ways, but nothing he did or said had any effect on her debauched behaviour. Periodically, Ellen would take all the money from the house, pawn anything that might have a monetary value, however small, and go off on a drinking binge for weeks at a time. While she was away from her husband, she would invariably earn the money for drink by working as a prostitute or by stealing.

On one occasion, Henry was forced to pay a fine she had incurred for theft. After this, Ellen promised him faithfully that she would give up drinking and, for almost a week, she stuck to her vow. Then, she went off on another drunken binge, which culminated in her being arrested and placed in Horfield Prison. Henry got word of her arrest, went to the prison and bailed her out but, before long, she was arrested again for theft and this time he was not permitted to pay bail and secure her release. Instead, she was sentenced to four months' incarceration in prison, leaving Henry with six children to care for, one a mere babe in arms.

Released from prison, Ellen came straight back to Henry, weeping bitterly, begging his forgiveness and promising him faithfully that, this time, things would be different. True, Ellen stopped stealing after serving her sentence, but, if anything, the drunken binges increased in frequency and intensity. She regularly pawned all the family's clothes and squandered the rent money on drink, disappearing for weeks at a time only to return when her money had run out. On one occasion, when Henry finally hardened his heart and refused to let her into the house, she threw stones at the windows until they shattered.

In desperation, Henry suggested that they set up a fried fish shop together, thinking that a business might distract Ellen from her cravings for drink. Ellen was delighted with this scheme, so Henry went ahead and, for around a month, his idea seemed to be working. Then, one night, Ellen got so drunk that she was unable to fry fish. A few days later, she was standing outside the shop and, when Henry asked his son to call her back inside, she was nowhere to be found. She had taken every last penny from the shop and disappeared on yet another drunken binge. Henry was forced to let the fish shop go.

He had not seen her for a month, when he accidentally bumped into her on the Horsefair, in the company of another man. Henry and Ellen talked for a while and Ellen soon discovered that he had given up the fish shop and demanded to know how much money he had received. Foolishly, Henry told her £5, at which she insisted that it was her fish shop and demanded the money.

She followed Henry home, all the while begging him to buy her a drink. Eventually, he relented, treating her to two glasses of beer and drinking a pint himself. By the time they reached home, she had somehow managed to persuade Henry to take her back again. Together they examined the newspapers for advertisements for houses and found one in Bean Street that Ellen thought would be suitable, if only she could buy some things for it. Henry parted with £3, with which Ellen bought some curtains and blinds, predictably spending the rest of the money on drink. Henry was forced to use his remaining £2 to cover Ellen's outstanding debts.

The couple lived together in Bean Street for about three weeks before their previous landlord at Pennywell Road offered them the fish shop back. Henry made some improvements to the property, including increasing the size of the boiler, but once again Ellen was discontented. Now getting drunk every single day, she insisted that Pennywell Road was too confining. One morning, she went out and did not return.

Having spent six months living in a brothel, she returned to Henry just before Christmas, asking for money. Henry agreed to give her board and lodgings if she would promise to behave for three months, but she was only after the price of a drink. Dramatically, she said goodbye to all of the children, swearing that she was going to kill herself but Henry met her again by accident three days later, this time in Milk Street when, once more, she begged to come home.

As it was so near to Christmas, Henry agreed, on condition that the children had no objections. He led her into the house and told them, 'I've brought your mother home.' When the children looked far from happy to see her, Henry told them that it was Christmas time and that they should all forgive and forget.

Christmas was spent fairly agreeably, but because Henry was on holiday from work, there was no money coming into the house. Ellen flew into a rage. She pawned the small gifts Henry had managed to buy for the children, as well as his one and only suit and spent the money on alcohol.

Between Christmas and the day of the murder, the pattern of behaviour continued. Ellen would leave to drink herself senseless, then return to her husband when she ran out of money, swearing to mend her ways. Describing his life as 'a burden', Henry finally snapped on the morning of 4 May 1900. After a night of quarrelling with his wife, during which she had abused him, hitting him at least twice and calling him 'every name she could lay her tongue to', Henry had seemed despondent when he got up on the day of the murder.

All the Milsted children seemed to place the blame for Ellen's death squarely on her behaviour towards their father. Although they recognised that he too had a drink problem, their impressions were that their mother had, quite literally, driven their father to drink. Harry recalled his father asking him on 4 May if he was going to work and, when Harry replied that he was, his father said sadly that, 'It seems so miserable after you have gone.' Henry also asked his son if he would help him out of his trouble and Harry, assuming that he was referring to rent arrears, assured him that he would.

Sidney corroborated his brother's evidence, telling the court that his mother spent every penny that Henry managed to earn on drink and that his father did everything he could to try and make her stop. He added that his father had been ill since Christmas and had been unable to work and that, on 4 May, he was still recovering from a bad bout of influenza. He also informed the court that his father's brother had been confined in a lunatic asylum for many years.

Fanny, aged 10, told of her parents' quarrel on the eve of the murder and of seeing her mother get up and go downstairs on the following morning. She had assumed that her mother was ill, a common situation in view of her prolific drinking, and had simply turned over and gone back to sleep.

The magistrates formally committed Henry Milsted to stand trial for the wilful murder of his wife at the next assizes and his trial took place in July 1900. Mr Douglas Metcalfe and Mr G.A.S. Garland prosecuted, while Mr G.A. Hawke defended, in spite of the fact that the accused did not have the money to pay him.

The court heard a repeat of the evidence given in the Magistrates' Court, with the addition of testimony about Milsted's attack of delirium tremens, experienced shortly after his arrest. The Chief Warder of Horfield Prison, Charles Morrell, told the court that two days after being admitted to the gaol, Milsted had 'got excited' and caused some damage to his cell. He had complained to the warders because they would not fetch him a pint of beer and, for his own safety, had been moved to a padded cell. He had quickly recovered and had since caused no trouble.

Dr Stack informed the court that delirium tremens was one of the many manias arising from drinking and that it was possible that a sufferer might not be as mentally stable as a non-drinker and so less able to resist acting on impulse.

Mr Douglas Metcalfe summed up the case for the prosecution, pointing out that there was little doubt, in view of the accused man's confession, that it was the hand of Henry Milsted that caused the death of his wife. What the jury must consider was whether there had been any premeditation and whether or not there had been sufficient provocation to reduce the charge to manslaughter.

Mr Hawke, for the defence, acknowledged that the prosecution had treated the case with moderation and humanity. He pointed out that, but for Milsted's confession, there was little evidence to connect him to Ellen's murder. He then addressed the question of provocation, telling the jury that there were times in life when people must make inferences in the absence of proved facts. He asked the jury to consider carefully whether or not they thought Milsted was insane at the time of the murder and to try to gauge the degree of provocation he was under when he struck the fatal blow with his knife.

The jury retired for almost three-quarters of an hour before returning a verdict of guilty of wilful murder against the accused, albeit with a strong recommendation for mercy on the grounds of the extreme provocation that Milsted had received over so many years.

It was not the judge's place to consider such a recommendation, although he agreed to pass it on to the relevant authorities. All that he could do at the conclusion of the trial was to put on his black cap and pronounce sentence of death on Henry John Milsted. As he did so, Milsted broke down and sobbed bitterly, his noisy crying almost drowning out the judge's words. 'Oh dear, my poor children' Milsted cried, entreating, 'Lord have mercy upon them.'

The authorities obviously heeded the jury's recommendation for mercy, since there is no record of his execution. Instead, he appears as an inmate of Dorset's Portland Prison in the census taken on 31 March 1901. Thus, it seems reasonable to assume that his death sentence was commuted to transportation for life. There is no record of the fate of his 'poor children'.

30
'GO ON, PUT DOWN WHAT YOU LIKE'

West Hatch, 1933

West Hatch in 1933 was a sleepy little village with a small shop and a school with sixty pupils of mixed ages, local children entering as infants and then progressing to the segregated junior section. At the age of 11, they sat scholarship examinations, and those who passed went on to secondary school. Those who failed or did not sit the exam stayed on until they were 14, when they were expected to find jobs.

Childhood in the 1930s was a time of innocence, yet one pupil who attended the small school at West Hatch at the time had a secret. Twelve-year-old Doris Winifred Brewer was pregnant. She was one of six children and her mother suffered from ill health. For the last five and a half years, Doris had lived with her grandparents in Slough Green, a home she also shared with her uncles, Herbert, Harold and Frederick Morse. Frederick, 32 years old at the time, was almost certainly the father of the baby his niece was expecting.

On Thursday 23 February 1933, Doris and Frederick were seen walking arm in arm towards nearby Curry Mallet, Morse pushing a bicycle with his free hand. It was a walk from which only one of them would return. Several hours later, Morse was found alone, soaking wet and weeping, by his brother Harold. Of Doris, there was no trace. According to Morse, he had last seen Doris walking towards a shed in a field adjacent to the River Rag. He had left her there, with a packet of crisps that he had bought earlier, while he went to check on some rabbit traps. When he returned three-quarters of an hour later, Doris was gone. Morse had searched the riverbanks, at one point even falling into the river, but could see no signs of her. As it began to get dark, he decided to make his way home to summon help, and on his way there he met his brother.

Police were alerted and search parties were immediately organised to hunt for the missing girl. It was bitterly cold and dark and the ground was covered with snow, so it was hardly surprising that she was not found until the following day, when her body was spotted lying fully clothed in the River Rag, in the parish of Curry Mallet.

A post-mortem carried out by Dr Godfrey Carter at Taunton revealed that Doris had died by drowning. Apart from two faint bruises, one on each cheekbone, there was nothing abnormal noted about the body, except for the fact that she was 'in a certain condition'. Approximately 4oz of food were found in the dead girl's stomach, which were sent for further analysis.

On the day that the body was found, Fred Morse accompanied police voluntarily to Taunton police station, where he made a long statement and was subsequently released. In his first statement he said that on the morning of the murder, he had gone to work as normal. After breakfast, he had met Doris by prior arrangement at a nearby crossroads. He had tried to persuade his niece to go to school and had even escorted her there, but at the school gates, Doris had begun to cry and refused to either go inside or go home to her grandparents' house.

Morse had told her that he was intending to go to Curry Mallet to collect some wires and rabbit traps. Doris had wanted to go with him, so he put her on the back of his bicycle. They had called at the Bell Inn at about 10.40 a.m., where he had purchased beer, cigarettes, two packets of crisps and half a pint of rum, receiving one penny change from the 8s that he had given to Winifred Crossman, the daughter of the licensee.

Morse had left his bicycle on wasteland. He had directed the girl towards a galvanised iron shed in a field, telling her to wait there for him while he checked his traps. Then, having given Doris a bag of crisps and her attaché case and also his watch for safekeeping, he left her at the field gate. He had watched for a few moments as she walked across the field towards the shed, but did not see her go in.

When he returned about forty-five minutes later, the only signs he saw of Doris were her footprints in the snow and an empty crisp packet. He searched the area without finding her, falling into the river himself in the process, before deciding to return home and organise a search party. He passed witness Walter Woods at about 3.45 p.m., before meeting his brother shortly afterwards.

On the following Tuesday, Morse was escorted back to Taunton police station where he was detained overnight. At this point, he supposedly gave a second statement, contradicting his first. He later denied ever having made this second statement, claiming it was wholly fabricated by the police officers. The substance of the disputed second statement was that Morse had begun to have sexual relations with his niece some six months prior to her death. When he realised that she was pregnant, he and Doris had decided to commit suicide together by plunging into the river. The suicide pact had been largely Doris's idea, since she was frightened at the prospect of her mother's reaction to the news of her pregnancy. Accordingly, they had each drunk a quantity of rum before jumping together into the deep river backwash. However, once in the water, Morse had had second thoughts. He had managed to get Doris to the bank, but she had slipped and went underwater again. By this time he was feeling the effects of the extremely cold water and, having gone under twice himself, had barely managed to extricate himself from the river with the aid of an overhanging tree branch. He had been too weak to help his niece further, and was capable of little more than lying on the bank, coughing up water. By the time he had recovered, he was disorientated and unable to comprehend exactly what had happened.

After his second statement, he was charged by with the wilful murder of his niece by drowning her in a river at Curry Mallet, between 23 and 24 February. Morse had nothing to say in answer to the charge, referring Inspector Carter, who charged him, to the statement he had already made to Detective Inspector Bennett of Scotland Yard. He was remanded in custody at Exeter Prison.

The inquest for Doris was presided over by the coroner for West Somerset, Geoffrey Clarke. At the outset, Clarke asked if Morse was legally represented and was told that he was not. The coroner advised Morse to appoint legal representation for the forthcoming hearing, stating that it was beyond the power of a coroner's court to grant legal aid for this purpose. Although Morse was not called to give evidence, both of his statements were put to the court.

Several witnesses testified to having seen Morse walking arm in arm with the girl whom, they felt, seemed to want to go back in the opposite direction towards West Hatch. The couple stopped and talked several times as they walked through the village of Curry Mallett and, although the witnesses saw no signs of a struggle between them or any attempts by the girl to escape, the man seemed to be urging the reluctant girl to continue walking.

The coroner asked the jury to consider whether or not Morse was with his niece immediately prior to her death. How had she come to be in the river? Did she accidentally fall, or was she placed there, either by Morse or by another party? The jury decided that there was a case to answer, and Morse was remanded to appear before magistrates at Ilminster Police Court.

Much of the first session at the magistrates' court was taken up by ensuring adequate legal representation for the defendant. As he had not appointed counsel or a solicitor, due to lack of money, the magistrates granted him legal aid, the inquest being adjourned until 14 March, by which time a Taunton solicitor, Robert Young, had been retained to act for the defence. The second session concentrated largely on a review of the medical evidence, not just from Dr Carter, but also from the celebrated Home Office pathologist, Sir Bernard Spilsbury, who had carried out a second post-mortem examination on Doris's body on 1 March.

Carter testified that the body was that of an exceptionally well-developed girl who, physically, appeared much older than her actual twelve years. She had been fully dressed when found, wearing an outdoor coat and gum boots and, with the exception of one stocking, which was pulled down slightly below her knee, her clothing was undisturbed. He had found the girl to be in the advanced stages of pregnancy, actually in her eighth month. He had concluded that death was due to asphyxia as a result of drowning and had finished his examination by removing the contents of Doris's stomach, which he had sent for further analysis. The county analyst, Denys Wood, testified that the stomach contents smelled strongly of rum and were found to contain 4.3cc of 35 per cent alcohol.

Spilsbury then detailed the results of his own post-mortem examination. His findings corroborated those of Dr Carter and Denys Wood and he concluded that the analysis of the stomach contents suggested that Doris had drunk a 'fairly considerable quantity' of alcohol shortly before her death.

It fell to Mr Young, for the defence, to contest the evidence presented to the magistrates. He was quick to point out that his client vehemently denied engaging in sexual relations with his niece and fathering her child, and that there was absolutely no evidence to suggest that he had. He maintained that, had Morse pushed or pulled Doris into the river, there would have been some signs of a struggle on the riverbank, of which there were none. Finally, Young contested the validity of Morse's alleged second statement to the police.

Morse had always contended that the police had threatened and bullied him into signing the second statement, which they themselves had concocted. As part of their bullying, they had also invented a witness who had allegedly seen what had happened down by the river at Curry Mallet. Worn down by the constant pressure from the police, Morse had eventually told Detective Inspector Bennett, 'Go on, put down what you like', and then signed the statement just to get them to leave him alone. As Young pointed out, even though Morse was a poorly educated manual worker, his second statement was written without a single grammatical error. Naturally, Inspector Bennett denied all allegations of police misconduct relating to the second statement.

Young's eloquent defence of his client was in vain. The magistrates committed Frederick Morse to stand trial for the murder of his niece at the Somerset Assizes to be held in June. When formally charged, Morse responded, 'I plead not guilty. I have a complete defence and on my trial I will explain everything.'

The contentious second statement was the subject of lengthy argument at the opening of the trial, with Morse's counsel strongly questioning the admissibility of the so-called 'suicide pact' statement. Mr Caswell, now representing the accused, gained an admission from Inspector Bennett that he had been mistaken in stating that Morse had written the statement himself – he had simply signed it. Accusations were made that the police had bullied Morse, threatened him and lied to him. These accusations were denied by all the police officers concerned. As the presiding judge, Mr Justice Jeddard pointed out, if the allegations made against Inspector Bennett and Sergeant Salisbury, the officers from Scotland Yard, were true, then they were not fit to be members of the police force. It was suggested that the two officers had come from Scotland Yard to the country with the idea that the case must be cleared up quickly and that this had been accomplished without proper regard for the truth. The arguments continued back and forth, in the absence of the jury, before Jeddard finally ruled that he could see no reason to believe that the statement was not voluntary or that it had been obtained either by inducement or threat and it was thus presented as evidence to the jury.

The court heard from Doris's mother, Lily Brewer, who had been advised of her daughter's pregnancy less than a week before the murder. She had received a communication from local police officers, in which it had been suggested to her that she have her daughter medically examined. Less than three weeks before the murder, when Doris would have been in her seventh month of pregnancy, she had been taken to a local nurse, who had failed to discover her condition. On 17 February, a somewhat dissatisfied Mrs Brewer had taken her daughter to a doctor, this time obtaining the correct diagnosis.

Lily admitted that she had heard rumours about her daughter over the previous Christmas. She had questioned her brother, Fred, who had been most upset about her allegations. He had raised no objections to his niece being medically examined and had actually taken her to see the nurse himself.

Mrs Brewer was also questioned about her knowledge of the sleeping arrangements at her mother's home, denying that she was aware that Doris shared a room with her uncles, Herbert and Harold. She maintained that she had always believed that her daughter had had her own room.

On the second day of the trial, Morse himself entered the witness box. Having first described his various employments, he then went on to discuss Doris. She had lived with his parents since she was 7-years-old and he had often been responsible for plaiting her hair and preparing her school lunches. He again denied ever having a sexual relationship with his niece, claiming to have been shocked when he found out that she was pregnant. He also admitted that it had been he who had broken the news of her pregnancy to Doris on the night before she died. He initially stuck closely to the story he had related in his first statement and, when asked about the alcohol found in his niece's stomach, claimed that he had allowed her to take a sip of rum after she had complained of being thirsty. Far from the 'considerable quantity' of rum noted by Sir Bernard Spilsbury in the contents of the girl's stomach, he argued that Doris had drunk only about a tablespoonful.

Morse again contested the authenticity of his alleged second statement, which he still maintained had been a total fabrication by the police. He then dropped a bombshell by admitting that, while searching the riverbanks for Doris when she had first gone missing, he had actually found her body. Having searched for about two hours, he had found her lying on her back in the river. The water was just covering her face and she had drifted out of sight under some bushes. He had struggled to pick Doris up and onto the riverbank, but she had slipped from his arms. Eventually he had abandoned his efforts and dragged himself onto the bank, where he had consumed the remaining rum. Asked why he had not run to a nearby farm to get help, Morse stated that he had been too upset to think clearly. He had told no one about his grim discovery, as he had been too worried, particularly since his niece had been in his charge that day.

Under questioning from the counsel for the prosecution, Morse was unable to offer any explanation as to how his niece had ended up in the river. The jury chose to believe the evidence of the police officers over that of the accused and he was found guilty of the wilful murder of Doris Brewer and sentenced to death by hanging.

Morse appealed against his conviction, but it was dismissed. On 15 July, he petitioned the Home Secretary against his sentence but, having reviewed all the circumstances, the Secretary of State replied that he 'failed to find justification for asking His Majesty to interfere with the due course of the law'. With his last hope for clemency gone, Morse wrote to his mother from the condemned cell, asking that none of his relatives should visit him before he died.

Morse slept only fitfully on the eve of his execution at Horfield Prison, Bristol, but when told to dress himself, appeared outwardly calm. His only visitor, prison chaplain, the Revd Ivor Watson, chatted quietly to him as he waited to be escorted to the scaffold. At precisely 8 a.m. on 25 July 1933, Morse was handcuffed and led between two warders to the gallows, blindfolded and a few minutes later executed by Thomas Pierrepoint. His body was buried in a lime-lined grave within the prison grounds.

The day of his execution was a day of mixed emotions in the village of West Hatch. While the family of Frederick Morse grieved behind closed doors, the children from West Hatch School celebrated their annual charabanc outing to the seaside at Weston-super-Mare, leaving for their day out at almost exactly the same moment as Morse took his final walk to face the hangman's noose.

31

'I SHALL BE GLAD WHEN THE OLD BASTARD IS OUT OF THE WAY'

Bath, 1933

By 1932, Reginald Ivor Hinks had reached the age of 30 without having achieved much. He had been discharged from the army, dismissed from numerous jobs and had a history of petty crime. He moved from London to Bath, possibly with the idea of turning over a new leaf. For a while it seemed as though the move would be a good one for him. In 1933, he was offered employment by Hoover as a door-to-door vacuum cleaner salesman. While doing his rounds, he met Constance Ann Jeffries, a divorced woman and single mother, who was bringing up her 5-year-old daughter alone. He set out to woo Connie, they married after a whirlwind courtship, and he moved into the home that she and her daughter shared with her elderly father at Milton Avenue in Bath. He soon discovered that she was relatively well-off, having a £2,000 inheritance at her disposal. Her father, James Pullen, who was 81 years old and had senile dementia, was also wealthy and owned numerous properties, in Bath and in Dorking, Surrey.

Within a short time, Hinks had embezzled nearly £1,000 from his father-in-law, part of which he used to move the family into a new home in Englishcombe Lane, Bath. Pullen was becoming increasingly frail, and at the time of the move, probably had very little time left to live. However, Hinks was impatient to get his hands on the old man's money – far too impatient to wait for the unfortunate Pullen to die a natural death.

Having dismissed the nurse who looked after James Pullen, Hinks personally took over his care and began a dedicated campaign to speed up the old man's demise. He took Pullen for walks and abandoned him in the busy city centre, hoping he would either be run over or succumb to the cold weather. On another occasion, Pullen was found wandering down a country lane, closely followed by Hinks in his car. When these attempts to hasten Pullen's death failed to work, Hinks apparently decided on more direct action. On 30 November 1933, he called police and an ambulance to the house on Englishcombe Lane. He explained that he had been helping the old man take a bath and had left him for just a moment to fetch some clean clothes. When he returned to the bathroom, he had found Pullen lying seemingly lifeless under the water, his face black. By the time the police reached the house, Pullen was sitting up in the bath looking remarkably healthy for a 'lifeless' man.

On the following night, emergency services were again called to the house on Englishcombe Lane where they were told that Pullen had gassed himself. They arrived to find the old man lying dead on the kitchen floor, partially dressed, with his head about a foot from the gas stove. His skin had the characteristic bright pink colouring of someone who had died from carbon monoxide poisoning. Yet it was noted by the attending doctor that there was no residual smell of gas in the kitchen, apart from a very faint odour emanating from the mouth of the deceased. On examination of the body, a bruise was found on the back of Pullen's head. In addition, the shelves had been removed from the gas oven and two overcoats draped over it to prevent gas from escaping. Was it possible that a man like Pullen, who suffered from senile dementia, would have been capable of planning and carrying out his own suicide? His doctors were of the opinion that he would not.

A post-mortem determined that the bruise on his head was very recent. According to Dr J.W. Heathcote, who performed the examination, it was consistent with Pullen either falling backwards and banging his head, or being struck. It was thought that the blow that caused the bruise would have stunned the old man, and rendered him both incapable of placing himself in the gas oven and unable to struggle if he was placed there by somebody else.

The inquest lasted several weeks as the coroner tried to unravel the mystery surrounding his demise. At the opening of the proceedings, the coroner advised Hinks that he need not answer any questions unless he specifically wished to do so. Nevertheless Hinks assured the coroner that he wanted to make a voluntary statement. He testified that Mr Pullen frequently fell and, in the fortnight leading up to his death, had suffered three falls. He explained that four months earlier, he had given up work to become a full-time carer for his father-in-law, and that he usually washed him twice a day, shaved him twice a week and gave him a weekly bath.

Mr Pullen, he said, had had a regular daily routine. He would eat breakfast, and then, weather permitting, sit outside on the lawn and listen to the wireless. According to Hinks, Pullen had threatened to commit suicide numerous times, either by cutting his throat, throwing himself in front of a train, jumping out of a window or drowning himself in a millpond. He had often said that he was tired of life and believed that he was a nuisance to his daughter. On the night before his death, Hinks said he had bathed Mr Pullen, shaved him and cut his toenails, then briefly left him in the bath while he fetched clean clothes for him. When he returned to the bathroom after an absence of only three minutes or so, it was to find Pullen submerged beneath the bath-water. He had dragged his father-in-law into a sitting position and pulled out the bath plug to drain the water, then called for his wife who brought towels, with which she began to massage her unconscious father's heart. There was no doubt in his mind, said Hinks, that Pullen had tried to get out of the bath and slipped, banging his head on the porcelain and knocking himself out.

On the day of his death, Pullen had risen as usual and come downstairs for breakfast. Although he normally dressed himself, on this occasion, he had simply donned a clean nightshirt and had refused to allow Hinks to put on his pants, vest and shirt. Hinks described Pullen's mood that day as 'extremely strong willed' and stated that he was also 'extremely tottery'. After eating a substantial breakfast, Pullen remained in the dining room with Hinks's stepdaughter, while Hinks and his wife washed up the breakfast dishes in the scullery. Soon the little girl came running in to her parents to tell them that her grandfather had taken a banana from the bowl on the sideboard. Almost immediately, Hinks heard a loud thump. Rushing into the dining room, he found Pullen lying on the floor, complaining that he had bumped his head.

Obviously confused, Pullen then decided to set off to walk to Dorking. He managed about 2 miles before he was picked up by Hinks and returned home in the car. After eating his lunch, he fell asleep in his armchair. The whole family took a short walk to the Co-operative stores in the afternoon, after which they ate tea, and Pullen again fell asleep in his chair. Mrs Hinks then went alone to the cinema, leaving her husband in charge of both her daughter and her father. Pullen woke up shortly before 6 p.m., declaring that he wanted to go for a walk but was told that it was too late. Half an hour later, he made another attempt to leave, this time saying that he was going to see 'his people'. Hinks told him he did not have any people and managed to persuade him to sit down in front of the fire again. However, twenty minutes later, Pullen went out of the room once more, this time saying he was going to the lavatory.

Soon afterwards, Pullen's stepdaughter called downstairs from her bed to say that her night-light was smoking, her feet were cold and she wanted a drink of water. Hinks filled a hot water bottle from the kettle on the fire, and then went into the kitchen to get a cup of cold water for the child. It was there that he found Pullen lying on the floor with his head in the gas oven. He pulled the old gentleman out by his ankles and attempted artificial respiration, before summoning assistance when he was unable to resuscitate the old man.

At the inquest, Hinks was questioned by the coroner about a cheque made payable to Pullen, the proceeds of which had been used to buy the house on Englishcombe Lane. Hinks explained that Pullen had owned some property in Dorking, including a shop that had been condemned by the Dorking Council. On the advice of his solicitor, Pullen had sold the shop, eventually receiving a cheque for the sum of £900. Pullen had endorsed the cheque to his daughter, Connie, who subsequently turned it over to Hinks. The money had been used to buy 'Wallasey', the house on Englishcombe Lane, some furniture and a car. Hinks asked innocently, 'There is nothing dishonest suggested about the cheque, is there?' and was promptly admonished for asking questions.

It emerged that the sale of the Dorking property was directly against the advice of Pullen's solicitor, Dr J.S. Carpenter, whose firm had prepared a new will for Pullen after his wife's death, with Mrs Hinks being named as the main beneficiary. However, in due course, Carpenter had become concerned that Pullen's money was being dissipated by Hinks and had taken steps to protect the estate by appointing a Committee in Lunacy. Having consulted with Pullen's doctor, Carpenter felt that the old man was incapable of understanding any financial transactions and had thus explained to Hinks that no steps could be taken to dispose of any property owned by Pullen. Hinks had assured him that he understood. However, in selling the Dorking property, he had bypassed Carpenter, instructing a new firm of solicitors in Dorking itself to handle the sale.

A witness was called who testified to having heard Hinks say, 'I shall be glad when the old bastard is out of the way. He is a damned nuisance.' The witness, a Mr Hiscock, alleged that Hinks owed him money for a wireless set and had promised to settle the debt on 2 December, which, as it turned out, was the day following Pullen's death. Hinks had sent Hiscock a postcard on 2 December, informing him that Pullen had died and promising to pay him £7 immediately after the funeral.

Pullen's nurse, Elizabeth Smith, dismissed by Hinks when he had taken over the care of his father-in-law, was also called to give evidence. She too spoke of the frequent suicide threats made by Pullen, of his tendencies to wander away from home and of his tearfulness on numerous occasions. She denied ever having heard Hinks swearing at Pullen. She described Pullen's mental state, saying that he was puzzled by the gas fire and would try to burn paper on it and poke it with fire irons. Pullen was unaware of his wife's death and often confused the nurse with his daughter. In Smith's opinion, Pullen would have been physically capable of turning on the gas taps unaided, had he wished to, although she was unsure as to whether he would have the mental capacity to plan and actually commit suicide by that means.

PC Ford, the police officer called to Englishcombe Lane on the night of the alleged suicide, told of taking a statement from Hinks after Pullen's body had been removed from the house. Ford told the inquest that Hinks had attempted to explain away the presence of the bruise in advance, saying that, if a bruise was found, then it was caused by Pullen's head hitting the floor when he was pulled from the oven. Hinks assured the police officer that Pullen had still been alive when he had found him. He had pulled him away from the oven by the ankles, turned off the gas, and then attempted to revive him by putting the hot water bottle he had just prepared for his stepdaughter on his heart and massaging the old man's chest.

Mrs Hinks was also called to give evidence before the corner. She too testified that her father had exhibited suicidal tendencies for many years and that he was prone to wandering off if not constantly supervised. She spoke of her marriage, saying that her husband had always treated her father with kindness, tact and patience. The strain of giving evidence for two and a half hours took its toll on Mrs Hinks, who fainted no less than five times in the witness box.

Having heard all the evidence, the coroner's jury took only twenty-five minutes to return a verdict of wilful murder against Hinks, at which he simply exclaimed, 'Well. What a shame.' He was immediately arrested.

His first appearance before magistrates in Bath was brief. Handcuffed to a policeman, he wept silently in the dock, as magistrates quickly dealt with a drunkard whose charges were also being heard that day. The drunk, a vagrant, was ordered to pay a fine of 10s, but could not pay and was sentenced to seven days in prison. On hearing this, three journalists present in court offered to pay the fine for him and the vagrant was promptly released. Then magistrates turned their attention to Hinks and, in less than three minutes, remanded him in custody for one week to enable the police to consult with the director of public prosecutions and for his application for legal aid to be considered.

Englishcombe Lane, Bath.
(© Nicola Sly)

After considering the evidence against him, magistrates subsequently committed Hinks to stand trial at the Old Bailey in London on a charge of wilfully murdering his father-in-law. In reply to the formal charge, Hinks said firmly; 'I have nothing to say and nothing to fear. Nothing at all – except that it is absurd.'

The trial opened at the Old Bailey on 5 March 1934, and consisted mainly of a repeat hearing of the witnesses and evidence already presented at length before the coroner at the inquest. However, there were some dramatic developments. One of these was an assertion by a Dr Fraser of Bristol that the bruise on Pullen's head could have been caused by his head hitting the floor when he was pulled from the gas oven by his ankles. Dr Fraser demonstrated the experiments that he had carried out which had enabled him to reach this conclusion by dropping a 7lb weight, which fell with a resounding bang, startling everyone in the courtroom. Yet in spite of Fraser's efforts, he was outnumbered. The other medical witnesses still argued that the bruising had occurred immediately before his death, probably deliberately inflicted by Hinks in order to stun the old man so that he could be placed in the gas oven without a struggle.

Hinks himself gave evidence in court for almost three and a half hours, during which he emphatically denied any wrongdoing in what he called the 'plain, deliberate case of suicide' of his father-in-law. At one stage, while being questioned about his resuscitation attempts on Pullen, Hinks protested in a loud voice, 'I don't wish to repeat the ghastly features of this suicide. It is more than I can stand. I can't go through all the ghastly movements of suicide and I won't. Neither will my wife.'

Yet the trial continued in spite of his protests and concluded on 10 March. Having heard all the evidence, the jury chose to believe the results of the post-mortem examination – the bruise on Pullen's head had been inflicted shortly before he had inhaled the gas, and Hinks had dealt his father-in-law a blow in order to render him incapable of struggling as the so-called 'suicide' was carried out. They found Hinks guilty of murder and the presiding judge, Mister Justice Branson, passed the death sentence. He was executed at Bristol Prison by Thomas Pierrepoint on 3 May 1934.

32
'THE STRIFE IS O'ER, THE BATTLE WON'

Loxton, 1954

In 1954, two spinsters, Noreen O'Connor, aged 46, and Friederika Alwine Maria Buls, 77, were sharing a house in the village of Loxton, near Weston-super-Mare. Banker Mr Frank Tiarks, a former director of the Bank of England, had previously employed both women in a domestic capacity.

Miss Buls, known as Marie, had been in service to the Tiarks family for almost fifty years. Of German origin, she had come to England in 1899 to act as a ladies' maid to Frank's wife, Emmy Maria Franziska. When the Second World War began, Miss Buls, a German national, was not permitted to work in England and was interned for the duration of the hostilities. Noreen O'Connor, a state registered nurse, was engaged in her place to care for Mrs Tiarks, who was by now, an invalid. When she died in 1943, O'Connor stayed on to nurse Mr Tiarks, who was confined to a wheelchair after a hunting accident. By the time Miss Buls returned to Loxton after the war, O'Connor was acting as nurse, housekeeper, secretary, chauffeur and general companion to the elderly banker. They frequently attended horse shows and cricket matches together and Miss O'Connor even accompanied her employer on foreign holidays to Persia and South Africa.

When she was not busy working for Mr Tiarks, O'Connor immersed herself in village life, taking a keen interest in the school and helping to raise funds for an extension to the village hall. She was particularly fond of children and would always make homemade chicken broth for any child who fell ill. On the occasion of the wedding of Princess Elizabeth in 1947, she and Tiarks threw a party for the schoolchildren at their home, North Lodge in Loxton, and in June 1954, she assisted with a school trip to Weston-super-Mare.

In 1945, Tiarks had purchased 'Gardeen', an eight-roomed detached cottage in the village of Loxton and gifted it to Noreen O'Connor. He died in 1952, and when his will was read, he had made numerous other bequests to O'Connor, including a £20,000 trust fund, shares and cars. O'Connor moved into Gardeen after his death and asked the increasingly frail Miss Buls to join her. Buls had suffered at least two strokes and by 1954, had also broken her leg, an injury that kept her largely confined to her bedroom. O'Connor nursed her devotedly.

However, at around 7.20 a.m. on Wednesday 1 September 1954, Noreen O'Connor telephoned Peter Tiarks, the youngest son of her late employer. Rousing Peter from his bed, Noreen implored him to come at once as something terrible had happened to Marie and she was in the power of some evil. Tiarks immediately left his home in Bridport, Dorset to drive to Loxton. Less than an hour after the call, Mrs Eva Simmons, the daily help, arrived to begin work at Gardeen. Noticing that the curtains in Marie's bedroom were still closed, she too was told by O'Connor that something terrible had happened. Mrs Simmons assumed that Marie had had another stroke so she did not investigate further.

By the time Peter Tiarks arrived at Gardeen at 10 a.m., Noreen O'Connor was lying peacefully on the sofa in the sitting room, fully clothed. Tiarks asked her what had happened and O'Connor calmly explained that she had seen an evil look in Miss Buls's eyes. This evil look was a regular occurrence whenever Miss Buls looked into a certain corner of the room and, on the previous evening, the look had been so strong that she had plucked out Miss Buls' eyes. Tiarks asked if Marie was dead, to which O'Connor replied; 'I plucked out Marie's eyes but it is not Marie that is dead, it is the evil that was in her.' Horrified, he asked if she realised what she had done, but O'Connor just repeated her assertion that she had merely killed the evil in Miss Buls. Tiarks then sent for a doctor.

Dr Norman Cooper arrived from Winscombe and went upstairs to Miss Buls's bedroom. There he found the old lady lying fully dressed on the floor between her bed and the wall. Her eyeballs had collapsed into her eye sockets and her eyelids, upper lip and right nostril were torn. Cooper estimated that Miss Buls had been dead for between seven and ten hours, and that the cause of her death was shock following the injuries to her face.

Having satisfied himself that Miss Buls was beyond help, Cooper went back downstairs to the sitting room to talk to Noreen. She assured him that there had been a lot of evil things about on the previous evening. She claimed to have heard the sound of drawers being opened and closed and went upstairs to check on her elderly companion. There she formed the impression that Miss Buls did not look herself. As she approached Miss Buls, she had received an electric shock from the old lady's bedspread. She had sat with the woman, whom she felt was in some kind of grave danger, holding her hands and praying, at which point she had heard a strange, disembodied voice saying, 'This is my hate.' She then realised that it was Marie's eyes that were evil and that she had to get them out.

Cooper also asked Noreen if she realised what she had done, to which she maintained that she had simply got rid of evil. In those days, many telephone exchanges were manually operated and, fearful of an operator being able to listen in on his call, Dr Cooper did not pick up the telephone. Instead, he drove three kilometres to the nearest police station at Axbridge to report the crime.

Sergeant Woodriffe arrived and searched Miss Buls's bedroom where he found a tooth, some hair and a broken decorative comb of the kind that was often worn in the hair. He also took a sample of blood from the bedroom floor. In the bathroom he found numerous items of wet clothing, including a dress, an underskirt and a bra. Along with a bloodstained towel found in the bathroom and scrapings from beneath O'Connor's nails, these items were sent to the Forensic Science Laboratory at Bristol. Noreen O'Connor was detained in connection with the death of Miss Buls and taken to the police station at Weston-super-Mare.

There she remained quietly until that evening, when she began to shout, recite religious incantations and move furniture about so that she could kneel and pray. The police found it necessary to call a doctor to attend her. On the following morning, in the presence of her solicitor, Inspector Leslie Long formally charged Noreen O'Connor with the murder of her companion, Marie Buls. O'Connor took the news calmly, stating that she had no objection at all to telling what had happened and why. She was committed to appear before magistrates at Axbridge Magistrates Court. O'Connor was then transported to Exeter Prison, apparently showing more signs of mental illness on the journey.

Meanwhile, a post-mortem examination was performed on Miss Buls, at which consultant pathologist Dr A.T.F. Rowley found a large bruise on the back of the deceased's head. From this he concluded that it was highly possible that Miss Buls was unconscious at the time her atrocious injuries were received. One of her hands was bloodied and swollen and in it were clutched a few loose hairs.

When O'Connor was brought before the magistrates at Axbridge, the court heard that she and Buls had apparently lived together harmoniously, and O'Connor had been under no obligation under the terms of Mr Tiarks senior's will to allow the old lady to live with her. Neither did O'Connor benefit from Miss Buls's will, a fact that she was well aware of, having been a witness when the will was made. As far as anyone could conceive, O'Connor had no possible motive for wanting Miss Buls dead. Indeed, as Buls grew increasingly old and frail, she had been nursed by the accused with great devotion.

The court was made aware that O'Connor had recently been showing signs of mental illness. Peter Tiarks testified that, in speaking to Noreen on the morning of the gruesome discovery of Miss Buls's body, she had told him about a trip to Plymouth that she had taken on the previous weekend. She had confessed to feeling happy almost to the point of elation and to singing throughout her journey. She had then continued to describe a near-accident experienced on the outing – an accident she was convinced had been engineered by another passenger specifically to cause her death. When the party had taken lunch at Plymouth, it was suggested that they ate at a French restaurant. However, later they decided to take lunch at the Grand Hotel on Plymouth Hoe. Coincidentally, this had been a place at which she had last eaten with Mr Tiarks senior and, when she and her companion were directed to the very same table, she had taken it to mean that her employer was with her in spirit and had intervened to prevent her being taken to a French café. Her behaviour on the trip had been so bizarre that her companion had telephoned her a couple of days later to ask if she was alright.

Tiarks continued to describe O'Connor's account of a parish meeting on the Tuesday evening, stating that by this time. her conversation had become inconsequential and delusional. Questioned about the death of Miss Buls and her part in it, O'Connor did not seem to comprehend what she had done. Indeed, rather than killing her companion, she seemed to believe that she had simply killed something evil and that this was something to be happy about. In her mind, it was not Marie who was dead, but the evil within her.

The magistrates obviously recognised that O'Connor was suffering from some kind of mental illness, but had no other choice than to commit her for trial at the Somerset Assizes. O'Connor had pleaded 'Not Guilty' and, when it was announced that she should stand trial for the murder of Miss Buls, she bowed to the chairman of the bench, Mrs Greenhill, and said quietly, 'Thank you, madam.'

The trial opened at Wells on 18 October 1954, lasting just over two hours. Once again, the court heard evidence that O'Connor had been a kindly, very sympathetic and very efficient woman, a pillar of the Loxton community, until her behaviour had become increasingly strange in the period leading up to the murder. Mr Bailey, a former clerk to the Axbridge Rural Council had been one of the last people to see the accused before the events of the night of 31 August/1 September.

Noreen O'Connor had visited him at his office during the day and he had asked about her recent trip to Plymouth. She had related her experiences of escape from sudden death and told of eating at the Grand Hotel and her feelings that her late employer was guiding her. Bailey had formed the conclusion that O'Connor was 'mentally deranged'. She revisited his office later that same day and had babbled about several subjects which Bailey felt were nonsensical. At that visit, she had referred to a member of staff as a 'good man', stating that the goodness of his soul was reflected in his eyes. Noreen had asked Bailey if he felt that she had been behaving normally recently, saying, 'If I haven't it will be different now for the evil spirit is dead.' She had then begun to sing the first line of a well-known Easter hymn, 'The strife is o'er, the battle won.' Asked by Bailey if he would see her tomorrow, O'Connor replied that she did not know where she might be tomorrow. She felt so happy that she might go anywhere.

Noreen O'Connor was transferred to Holloway Prison on 25 September and Dr Thomas Christie, the chief medical officer of the prison was called to testify as to her medical condition. It was his opinion that the accused was suffering from an 'acute mania' which had caused defective reasoning. At the time of the murder, this defect of reason was so strong that he believed that she was incapable of knowing that what she was doing was wrong. Dr Desmond Curran, a psychiatrist based at St George's Hospital, London, backed his opinion. Curran also felt it highly improbable that O'Connor knew what she was doing when she murdered Miss Buls.

Norman Skelhorn, acting for the defence, summed up the situation for the jury. He stressed that there was no motive, financial or otherwise, for the murder of Marie Buls. He reiterated that it was unlikely that Miss Buls had suffered the terrible pain of her horrific injuries, since the medical opinion was that she was unconscious before they were inflicted, either as a result of a blow to the head, which was supported by the large bruise found at the post-mortem, or by having succumbed to a heart attack or another stroke. Inflicting the injuries was something that was completely foreign to the nature of the accused, who was known to be a kind, friendly person and a devoted and efficient nurse.

In his concluding remarks the presiding judge, Mr Justice Byrne, advised the jury that if they were satisfied with the evidence, they would have no doubt that Miss O'Connor was guilty of the murder of Miss Buls. However, he asked them to consider the second aspect of the case that according to medical opinion, the accused was unaware of what she was doing, or if she did know, then she did not know it was wrong. If they thought she was guilty then he advised them that the correct verdict would be 'Guilty but insane'.

The jury did not need to retire to consider the evidence further. In only a minute, they delivered their verdict, finding Noreen O'Connor guilty of the murder of Marie Buls, but insane, leaving Mr Justice Byrne, to direct that she be detained at Broadmoor Special Institution at Her Majesty's pleasure.

It is believed that Noreen O'Connor was eventually released from Broadmoor, spending the remainder of her life as an in-patient at St Andrew's Hospital, Northampton, a charitable organisation devoted to the care of patients with mental disorders, learning disabilities and acquired brain injuries, and she died there in 1983.

33
'THIS IS MURDER'

Stapleton, 1957

On Thursday 20 June 1957, Bristol was in the grip of a heat wave. As the weather gradually cooled in the late afternoon, 5-year-old Royston Sheasby, who lived in Brockworth Crescent in Stapleton, began to pester his older sister June to go for a walk. June, who was two years older, was not keen, but Royston was insistent – he wanted to visit a nearby field to see the horses there.

Having told their mother, Barbara, of their intentions, the two children set off hand in hand to the horse pasture. Barbara was engrossed in decorating and, when she next noticed the time, she was horrified to see that it was almost seven o'clock. Knowing that the two children should have been home by then, she immediately raised the alarm.

The disappearance of Royston and June Sheasby sparked one of the biggest searches ever known in England. Thousands of members of the public turned out to help the police comb the area. They painstakingly examined woodland, scrub and grassland around Stapleton, while firemen were called to lower the water in the 60ft-deep Duchess Pond so that divers could trawl its depths. Police dogs crisscrossed the countryside, streams and rivers were waded through, outbuildings were entered and searched, but there were no clues to the whereabouts of the missing children to be found.

Within days of the children's disappearance, a letter was sent to the editors of two Bristol evening papers saying that they were alive and well and demanding the sum of £200 for their safe return. The letter, signed 'West Indians', read:

> The children, June and Royston, are alive and well at the moment. It is useless for police to continue searching. We hope they enjoy their bath in the river. My brother and I took the children away Thursday night and they will be returned unhurt on payment of £200. This must be left at G.P.O. addressed to ——, to be called for on Wednesday afternoon. My brother will collect, but if he should be detained I shall kill the children after two hours from time he leaves here. If he is allowed to leave, children will be returned unhurt.

At a press conference, Chief Superintendent M. Phillips, the head of Bristol CID, dismissed the letters as 'a wicked and cruel hoax', stating that charges would be pressed should the writer be traced.

Meanwhile, the search for the missing children went on, hampered by the heavy rain that followed the breaking of the heat wave. Exhausted police officers ignored their days off and turned down overtime pay to continue scouring the countryside for the pair – sadly, the search wasn't to have a happy ending.

At about 9 p.m. on 1 July, PC Brough noticed a tiny hand protruding from the earth in dense undergrowth close to the river Frome as it flowed through Snuff Mills Park. It was Royston Sheasby's hand. Immediately, hundreds of police officers were deployed to the area to search for his sister by torchlight. However, when Royston's body was removed from its shallow grave, under the direction of Dr A.C. Hunt, the pathologist attached to the Home Office Forensic Science Laboratory at Bristol, it quickly became evident that June's body had also been concealed in the same place.

Royston's body was taken to a nearby mortuary, while that of his sister was left under police guard until first light. At a press conference held early on the morning of 2 July, Phillips announced: 'This is murder.' He added that Royston appeared to have injuries to his head, but that no investigation had yet been conducted on June's body. He appealed for information from the public about anyone seen to be acting suspiciously in the area on 20 June.

A later post-mortem examination of the two bodies showed that both children had suffered severe head injuries, probably inflicted with a blunt instrument, which had caused skull fractures. There was no evidence of any sexual assault on either child and no immediately apparent motive for their murders.

Police once again appealed for witnesses, asking specifically for information about a man in a blue striped suit who had been spotted sitting on a log near to the burial site at around the time when the children disappeared.

Exhaustive enquiries were made at four mental hospitals in the immediate vicinity. One patient had failed to return after parole to the nearby Bristol Mental Hospital, but since he had no record of violence and had failed to return from leave on previous occasions, he wasn't considered a particularly high priority for the investigating team.

The police then issued a detailed description of George Weston, a patient who had escaped from Purdown Mental Institution. He was quickly traced and eliminated from their enquiries, but they renewed their appeal in the press for the identity of the man in the blue suit. They also asked for help in tracing a girl, aged about 13, who had been seen with two children at about 7 p.m. on 20 June and two boys who had been fishing on the river bank between about 6 p.m. and 9.30 p.m.

Meanwhile, a number of items of the children's clothing were submitted to the Forensic Science Laboratory for testing and, on 5 July, the police announced enigmatically that not all of the tests had proved negative.

Two days later, it was announced that officers were focusing their attention on the patients of one mental hospital and also on those local residents who had previously been convicted of offences against children. The proximity of so many mental hospitals caused problems for the investigating team as they had received numerous false confessions from patients – it was essential that they eliminated every one of these before continuing with their enquiries. They had still been unsuccessful in tracing 'blue suit'.

The case took a promising turn during the weekend of 6–7 July. Firstly, the police received an anonymous letter. Handwritten on pale blue notepaper and placed in a white envelope, the letter numbered less than twenty words in total, but was said by police to contain vital information. The writer had apparently seen something that confirmed a suspicion already held by the police. Then, a blue suit was recovered from a storeroom at the Bristol Mental Hospital. It was sent for forensic testing, while the police concentrated on the 146 patients at the hospital who were normally subject to parole. One patient in particular was of great interest and was interviewed several times. His parole was cancelled and he was confined to a special ward under the 24-hour guard of male nurses.

By 11 July, police announced that the writer of the letter, a woman, had come forward. They revealed that the information she had given them was 'useful' and, as a result, they expected to interview a man who had since left Bristol. They also issued a description of a 67-year-old man from Newport, Monmouthshire, who they urgently

Brockworth Crescent, Stapleton. (© N. Sly)

Duchess Pond, Stapleton. (Courtesy of Derek Fisher, Bygone Bristol)

Snuff Mills – where the bodies of Royston and June Sheasby were discovered. (Author's collection)

Bristol and County Asylum, 1906. (Author's collection)

wanted to trace, as he had been missing from home since the night on which the children's bodies were discovered. Both men were later eliminated from enquiries.

Despite exhaustive police efforts, during which they interviewed more than 25,000 people and took over 2,000 statements, the killer was not apprehended. Although the police continued with their investigation, as time went by, it seemed that they were no nearer to finding the perpetrator of the double murder and the case of the 'babes in the wood', while remaining open, grew cold.

Then, in 1964, there was a sensational new development. Dr A. Hyatt Williams, a consultant psychiatrist, claimed at the International Congress of Psychotherapy in London that a prison inmate who had recently 'died of conscience' had confessed to him that he had killed a young boy and a girl. The inmate, imprisoned for a minor offence, had spoken to the doctor in his capacity as a visiting prison psychiatrist.

The doctor had battled with his own conscience before deciding to reveal the information, although he refused to name the individual concerned, likening himself to a priest who had received confidential evidence in the confessional.

The police went straight to the Home Office who distanced themselves from the controversy, stating that a visiting psychiatrist's confidential notes did not form part of Prison Department records. The confession was not a matter of public safety, since the prisoner was now deceased. It was therefore regarded as subject to professional confidence and the police were advised to contact the doctor directly.

Although it was not even certain that the two killings allegedly spoken about by the prisoner were the 'babes in the wood' murders, there were no other known cases in the relevant timeframe involving both a boy and girl as victims. And, since the inmate was now dead, there was now no way of establishing conclusively whether or not the confession was genuine, rather than another false confession such as those already encountered by the police in their investigations of the patients of Bristol mental hospitals. Mr Alan Hopkins, the then MP for Bristol, made his own enquiries of the Home Office and questions were asked in parliament, but the doctor remained steadfast – he would not reveal any more information and could not legally be forced to do so.

So officially, fifty years on, the tragic murders of Royston and June Sheasby remain unsolved and the case remains open to this day.

BIBLIOGRAPHY & REFERENCES

BOOKS

Anon, *St Petrock's Church, South Brent*, A.C. Brown, 1951

Bird, Sheila, *Cornish Tales of Mystery and Murder*, Countryside, 2002

Byford, Enid, *Somerset Murders*, Dovecote, 1990

Casswell, J.D. QC, *A Lance for Liberty*, George Harrap, 1961

Chard, Judy, *Devon Tales of Mystery and Murder*, Countryside, 2001

Dell, Simon, *The Beat on Western Dartmoor: A celebration of 150 years of the policing of Tavistock*, Forest, 1997

Eddleston, John J., *The Encyclopedia of Executions*, John Blake, 2004

Evans, Roger, *Somerset Tales of Mystery and Murder*, Countryside, 2004

Evans, Stewart P., *Executioner: The chronicles of a Victorian hangman*, Sutton, 2004

Fielding, Steve, *The Hangman's Record, Vol. 1, 1868-1899; Vol. 2, 1900-1929; Vol. 3, 1930-1964*, CBD, 1994-2005

Harrison, Paul, *Devon Murders*, Countryside, 1992

Hocking, Dr Denis, *Bodies and Crimes: A Pathologist's Casebook*, Book Guild, 1992

Holgate, Mike, and Waugh, Ian, *The Man They Could Not Hang: The true story of John Lee*, Sutton, 2005

Hurley, Jack, *Murder and Mystery on Exmoor*, Exmoor Press, 1982

James, Ann, *Murders and Mysteries in Devon*, Obelisk, 1996

Johnson, Bill, *History of Bodmin Gaol*, Bodmin Town Museum, 2006

Penhaligon, Annette, *Penhaligon*, Bloomsbury, 1989

Simpson, Keith, *Forty years of murder*, Granada, 1978

Smith, Veronica, *Twenty Bristol Murders*, Redcliffe, 1992

-- *Murder and Mayhem in the West*, Redcliffe, 1993

-- *Foul Deeds and Suspicious Deaths in or around Bristol*, Wharncliffe, 2006

Sweet, Jack, *Shocking Somerset Murders*, Somerset Books, 2000

Wilson, Colin, introduced by, *Murder in the westcountry*, Bossiney, 1975

Worthy, David, *A Quantock Tragedy: The Walford Murder of 1789*, Friam, 1998

Wynn, Douglas, *On Trial for Murder*, Pan, 2003

JOURNALS

Bath Weekly Chronicle

Bristol Evening Post

Bristol Mercury

Bristol Times and Mirror

Cornish and Devon Post

News of the World

Sherborne Mercury

Somerset County Gazette

Taunton Courier

The Times

True Detective

Wells Journal and West of England Advertiser

West Briton

Western Flying Post

Western Gazette

Western Morning News

Western Evening Herald

INDEX